MacDonald versus Henderson

THE FOREIGN POLICY OF THE SECOND LABOUR GOVERNMENT

David Carlton

Macmillan

First published 1970 by
MACMILLAN AND CO LTD
Little Essex Street London WC2
and also at Bombay Calcutta and Madras
Macmillan South Africa (publishers) Pty Ltd Johannesburg
The Macmillan Company of Australia Pty Ltd Melbourne
The Macmillan Company of Canada Ltd Toronto
Gill and Macmillan Ltd Dublin

Printed in Great Britain by
R. & R. CLARK LTD
Edinburgh

TO ANN

Contents

List of Illustrations

A 2

Author's Note

An earlier version of this work was submitted in 1966 to the University of London as a Ph.D. thesis. It has since been revised to take account of the official material made available to researchers at the beginning of 1968 under the new 'Thirty-Year Rule' covering governmental archives.

It is a pleasure to acknowledge my indebtedness to a number of people who have helped me at various stages in the preparation of this work. First, I wish to thank the staffs of the British Museum, the Public Record Office, the Royal Archives at Windsor, the British Library of Political and Economic Science, the Labour Party Library, the Library of Churchill College, Cambridge, and the University of Birmingham Library. Secondly, I must record my gratitude to the following who have variously guided me on matters of fact, interpretation and presentation: Dr Douglas Dakin, Mr W. N. Ewer, Lord Henderson, the Hon. Margaret Lambert, the late Sir Harold Nicolson, Mr Peter Richards and the late Lord Rowley. Finally, I am especially grateful to Professor W. N. Medlicott, who first suggested this subject to me and who supervised the preparation of my thesis. Needless to say, I remain solely responsible for all eccentricities of interpretation and for errors of fact.

Extracts from the papers of King George V are reproduced by gracious permission of Her Majesty the Queen. Extracts from Crown Copyright records in the Public Record Office appear by permission of the Controller of H.M. Stationery Office. The following are also thanked for consenting to my use of copyright material: Mr Francis Noel-Baker, the Hon. Anne Crawshay, Sir Patrick Duff, Lady Beatrix Evison, Mr Martin Gilbert, Mrs Katharine Gordon, Lord Hankey, Lord Henderson, Lord Howard of Penrith, Professor Ann Lambton, Lord Lloyd, Mr Malcolm MacDonald, Lady Rugby, Sir Anthony Rumbold, Lady Selby, Mr H. B. Usher, Lady Vansittart, the Librarians of the University of Birmingham and of the British Library of Political and Economic Science.

DAVID CARLTON

Abbreviations

B.D.   *Documents on British Foreign Policy, 1919–1939*, 2nd series, ed. E. L. Woodward and Rohan Butler

Cabinet
Minutes   Conclusions of Meetings of the Cabinet, deposited at the Public Record Office (P.R.O.), London

C.A.H.C.   Records of Cabinet Ad Hoc Committees, P.R.O.

C.P.   Cabinet Papers and Memoranda, P.R.O.

C.R.F.   Cabinet: Registered Files, P.R.O.

F.O.   Foreign Office Confidential Prints and General Correspondence, P.R.O.

F.R.   *Papers Relating to the Foreign Relations of the United States*

G.F.M.R.   German Foreign Ministry Records, deposited at the Foreign and Commonwealth Office Library and the P.R.O.

H.C. Deb.   *House of Commons Debates (Hansard)*, 5th series

H.L. Deb.   *House of Lords Debates*

I.C.   Records of International Conferences, P.R.O.

Premier   Records of the Prime Minister's Office, P.R.O.

R.A. GV   The Papers of King George V, deposited at the Royal Archives, Windsor

CHAPTER ONE *The Setting*

AT the British General Election of 30 May 1929 the Labour Party, for the first time in its history, became the largest grouping in the House of Commons; but it came 21 seats short of an overall majority.[1] On 4 June Stanley Baldwin resigned as Prime Minister and advised King George V to send for Ramsay MacDonald. Despite the unhappy experience of minority rule in 1924, the Labour leader again decided to accept office without unfettered power.

It thus fell to a Labour Cabinet to preside over the remarkable domestic happenings of the ensuing twenty-seven months, which saw the growth of unemployment to unparalleled proportions and culminated in the creation of the so-called National Government in the middle of the spectacular financial crisis of August 1931. These unusual developments have deservedly attracted considerable attention from students of economics, constitutional history and Socialism. By contrast, the less dramatic and less seminal aspects of the Labour administration's record have so far been the subject of only cursory analyses. In particular, little has yet been written on foreign policy, although this represented the least unsuccessful feature of the history of the second Labour Government. In the following pages an attempt is made to correct this omission.

When it became clear that MacDonald was about to form his second Cabinet, a series of struggles for various coveted offices ensued among his lieutenants. Perhaps the sharpest contest was that between Arthur Henderson and J. H. Thomas for the Foreign Office. The Prime Minister with marked reluctance chose Henderson only after the latter had indicated that he would accept no other post.[2] The Foreign Secretary

[1] The actual figures were: Labour, 287; Conservatives, 260; Liberals, 59; Independents, 9. One Liberal and one Independent subsequently indicated that they intended to support the Labour Government: *The Times*, 15 June 1929. For a detailed account of this election, see E. A. Rowe, 'The British General Election of 1929', unpublished Oxford University B.Litt. thesis, 1960.

[2] For details of the struggle between Henderson and Thomas, see Reginald

therefore began his duties in the knowledge that his Prime Minister lacked full confidence in him and that he could not expect unquestioning support if he ran into difficulties. Sir Austen Chamberlain, the Opposition spokesman on foreign affairs and outgoing Foreign Secretary, also doubted Henderson's suitability. He wrote to his sisters:

> I am only sorry that J. H. Thomas is not apparently to be my successor, but Henderson is to follow me. I hear that there has been a battle royal between them for the post. I should have preferred Thomas because he is by far the abler man and is sound in essentials. Henderson I have always thought very stupid and rather afraid of responsibility.[1]

In the event Henderson confounded his critics, having been generally acknowledged as one of the successes of the second Labour Government.

There can be no doubt that he was well qualified by his previous experience for the post of Foreign Secretary despite his lack of formal education and his inability to speak foreign languages. He had served in the coalition War Cabinets and had undertaken a difficult mission to Russia; he had had much experience on the Socialist International; and in 1924 he had accompanied Lord Parmoor to the League of Nations Assembly where they had jointly negotiated the Geneva Protocol. He was, moreover, an able administrator, having been General Secretary of the Labour Party continuously from 1911 and Chairman of the Parliamentary Labour Party from 1908 to 1911 and again from 1914 to 1915. He was essentially in the broad tradition of British Utopian Socialism, his beliefs owing nothing to Karl Marx, little to the Independent Labour Party and much to Nonconformist Christianity. Although an idealistic visionary, he was at the same time a skilful tactician in day-to-

---

Bassett, *Nineteen Thirty-One: Political Crisis* (London, 1958) pp. 27–8 and Gregory Blaxland, *J. H. Thomas: A Life for Unity* (London, 1964) pp. 220–1. For an unsupported claim that Oswald Mosley was considered for the post, see the summary of a letter by Harold Laski in Kingsley Martin, *Harold Laski (1893–1950): A Biographical Memoir* (London, 1953) p. 76. Lord Stamfordham, the monarch's Private Secretary, recorded that MacDonald told the King that he had vainly offered to give up the Premiership and to take the Foreign Secretaryship instead in order to restore harmony in his party's leadership: Sir Harold Nicolson, *King George the Fifth: His Life and Reign* (London, 1952) p. 435. The present writer knows of no evidence to confirm that MacDonald made any such offer to his colleagues.

[1] Sir Austen Chamberlain to Ida and Hilda Chamberlain, 6 June 1929, Austen Chamberlain Papers deposited at the University of Birmingham Library.

day matters, rarely straying beyond the limits of what was generally believed to be practicable. Within the Labour Party he was identified with neither the far Right nor the far Left, but consistently sought to promote unity in the ranks of an organisation which has always been an uneasy coalition. G. D. H. Cole wrote of him: 'Belonging to the right, he saw the need to carry the left along with it in a united Party, if that could possibly be done consistently with his belief in Parliamentarism at home and the League of Nations and collective security in the world as a whole.'[1] Henderson, then, was well prepared not only to deal with foreign affairs but also to act as a senior Cabinet Minister.[2]

The same cannot be said of two other Cabinet Ministers, Albert Alexander and Thomas Shaw, whose respective duties as First Lord of the Admiralty and Secretary of State for War involved them in certain aspects of foreign policy. While Lord Thomson's private judgement that Alexander 'has been a mere agent of the admirals' may be rather harsh, there is no evidence that he played any decisive part in the negotiations for naval disarmament or the handling of any other international issues.[3] Even more unsatisfactory was the performance of Shaw at the War Office. His appointment was undoubtedly a major blunder on the part of MacDonald, as is shown by the following recollections of a permanent official:

> On a Saturday afternoon in August, 1929, I was summoned from the cricket field where I was playing for my local Club to the telephone in the nearest public house, where I was told that the War Office wanted to speak to me. . . . I was *de facto* Chief of Staff in an emergency. I

[1] G. D. H. Cole, *A History of the Labour Party from 1914* (London, 1948) p. 305.

[2] Two biographies of Henderson are Mary Agnes Hamilton, *Arthur Henderson: A Biography* (London, 1938), and Edwin Alfred Jenkins, *From Foundry to Foreign Office: The Romantic Life Story of the Rt. Hon. Arthur Henderson, M.P.* (London, 1933). See also Henry R. Winkler, 'Arthur Henderson', in G. A. Craig and Felix Gilbert, *The Diplomats, 1919–1939* (Princeton, N.J., 1953) pp. 311–43.

[3] Beatrice Webb Diary deposited at the British Library of Political and Economic Science, entry for 23 Mar 1930. Lord Thomson himself was in the Cabinet as Secretary of State for Air. His death in October 1930 in an air crash was a sad blow for his friend MacDonald, perhaps also for the Labour Government. In his short tenure of the Air Ministry he made a good impression on at least one highly qualified judge. See Basil H. Liddell Hart, *Memoirs*, 2 vols (London, 1965; in progress) I 148–52. Lord Amulree, Thomson's successor, was no more than mediocre.

learnt on the telephone that riots had broken out in Palestine and the
Acting High Commissioner had wired both to Egypt and to the War
Office for immediate military assistance. I jumped into a car and went
to the War Office immediately. After consultations there I arranged
for the despatch of one battalion from Egypt by troop-carrying aeroplanes and another from Malta to be taken by the Navy, who undertook to place cruisers at our disposal. When this had been done I
thought of the Secretary of State, as the movements of troops was a
grave question of policy, which he ought to endorse. His private
secretary managed to get him on the telephone and the only answer I
got was, 'Mr Tom Shaw says that he is a pacifist and does not wish to
have anything to do with war or military operations. All he wants
General Temperley to do is to put down on a piece of paper the
number of troops that are being moved so that he will be in a position
to tell the Cabinet what has taken place.'

There was an attractive candour about his point of view, even if it
was not particularly helpful as political head of the department.[1]

Three political appointments below Cabinet level turned out rather
better. Hugh Dalton became Parliamentary Under-Secretary and made
an extremely useful and energetic contribution to the formulation of
Henderson's policies. Philip Noel-Baker, who was appointed Parliamentary Private Secretary to the Secretary of State, was in some respects
a rather less experienced figure than Dalton, but he enlivened the
Foreign Office with his idealism and enthusiasm. Finally, Viscount Cecil
of Chelwood (formerly Lord Robert Cecil) was persuaded to become an
adviser on questions relating to the League of Nations. He had held a
similar position in the two previous Conservative Governments but had
resigned in 1927 because of a difference of view on naval disarmament
policy. Although not a Cabinet Minister under MacDonald as he had
been under Baldwin, he had possibly more influence than hitherto in
formulating policy after Henderson, despite opposition from the permanent officials, had insisted that he should be given a room in the
Foreign Office.[2] The acknowledged leader of the British League of

[1] A. C. Temperley, *The Whispering Gallery of Europe* (London, 1938)
pp. 118–19. As Liddell Hart wrote, 'Tom Shaw, a trade union secretary who
had been put into the War Office, soon became a joke there as being merely
"a rubber stamp" for decisions taken by his official advisers': Hart, *Memoirs*,
1 148.

[2] Both Lord Curzon and Austen Chamberlain had resisted Cecil's repeated
requests for a room in the Foreign Office. In addition, his interventions in
Baldwin's Cabinets had rarely had much influence on his colleagues. See David

Nations Union, he declined to become a formal member of the Labour Party but his sympathies in international affairs clearly lay with the Left rather than the Right. For example, after hearing the 1929 General Election results, he had written to MacDonald: 'The task is tremendous, and the opportunity unequalled, and it is my profound conviction that your tenure of office will be of the highest historical importance. I cannot tell you what a relief it is to me to think that a genuine and whole-hearted Peace Ministry is installed in office at this critical time.'[1]

Not all Socialists, however, approved of Cecil. Philip Snowden, in particular, sought to influence MacDonald against him:

> I cannot for the life of me understand [he wrote] why he is allowed to represent our Government. His position in the League of Nations Union – which under his influence is a most harmful organisation – ought of itself to debar him from an official position in the Government. He is on the official staff of the Foreign Office as you know. Philip Baker has been his colleague for years and the two together ought not to have the influence they have. Cecil is just a Tory Jesuit.[2]

Even MacDonald himself had turned sufficiently against Cecil by 1931 to suggest to Henderson that Jan Christiaan Smuts should be invited to supersede him as Great Britain's principal day-to-day planner and spokesman in the Geneva disarmament negotiations. 'Whatever we may think of Cecil,' wrote MacDonald, 'there is no use shutting our eyes to the fact that, in spite of all his hard work and his great mental resources, he is not a powerful figure at Geneva.'[3] To this suggestion Henderson sent a tart reply:

> So far as General Smuts is concerned, he unquestionably possesses many eminent qualifications for the task you have in view. But to appoint him at this stage of the proceedings would raise a very serious difficulty, as it would involve a supersession of Cecil, who has

Carlton, 'Disarmament with Guarantees: Lord Cecil, 1922–1927', *Disarmament and Arms Control*, III (1965) 143–64. Henderson's forthright way of overruling his advisers on the issue of a room for Cecil in 1929 is described in Hugh Dalton, *Call Back Yesterday: Memoirs, 1887–1931* (London, 1953) p. 222.

[1] Cecil to MacDonald, 21 June 1929, Cecil Papers deposited at the British Museum, Add. 51081.

[2] Snowden to MacDonald, 27 Sep 1930, MacDonald Papers deposited at the Public Record Office.

[3] MacDonald to Henderson, 5 May 1931, Henderson Papers, 1929–31, deposited at the Public Record Office, F.O. 800/283.

been in charge of disarmament work at Geneva on our behalf since we came into office, and has discharged his task with great energy and efficiency. To supersede him at this moment would, in my opinion, be an unmerited slight upon him. . . .

I confess to some little surprise as to your estimate of Cecil's influence at Geneva. While I might agree that he arouses misgivings in certain circles at home, I should have said that the prestige he enjoys at Geneva was exceptional and that, on that account, we need have no hesitation in choosing him as our representative.[1]

It is hardly surprising that MacDonald, in the face of such uncompromising resistance, quietly abandoned his campaign for Cecil's demotion.

Although Cecil, Dalton and Noel-Baker did not hold positions of great nominal importance, their influence on Henderson was indeed considerable, since they were an *avant-garde*, much more sympathetic to the Labour Party's distinctive foreign policies than were the permanent staff in the Foreign Office or the British envoys abroad. Most of these officials were closer to the Conservatives than to the Labour Party in their general outlook, and this was usually reflected in the advice they gave to the Labour Government. It is extremely unlikely, however, that the majority was as consciously biased as Lord Tyrrell, British ambassador in Paris, who, on hearing the 1929 General Election results, wrote to Chamberlain, his late chief: 'I cannot tell you how happy I was to see your return but also how depressed I am at the general result. . . . I am glad you have got in, but what a comment on democracy that the majority should hate B. [Baldwin].'[2] Whatever its more suspicious and class-conscious followers may have imagined, the Labour Government was rarely up against conscious prejudice of this order, still less outright sabotage on the part of officials. Nearer the mark were those who argued that Labour's policies were unlikely to be interpreted sympathetically by officials whose background and training had encouraged them to place great stress in foreign affairs on prudence, continuity and, above all, the defence of the national interest.[3] Rightly or wrongly, most members of the Labour Party between the wars believed in different priorities,

[1] Henderson to MacDonald, 6 May 1931, ibid.
[2] Tyrrell to Austen Chamberlain, 31 May 1929, Austen Chamberlain Papers.
[3] Of the officials in the Foreign Office at this period Cecil later wrote that 'they were all very competent and some of them helpful': Viscount Cecil of Chelwood, *A Great Experiment* (London, 1941) p. 201.

deriving inspiration from the internationalist teachings of President Woodrow Wilson and the Union of Democratic Control.

Faced with examples of this divergence of outlook, Henderson, in his dealings with the permanent officials, did not hesitate to assert his authority. In his first encounter with the Permanent Under-Secretary, Sir Ronald Lindsay, he refused, according to Dalton, to be rushed into approving despatches thrust before him and went on to declare that there could be 'too much continuity in foreign policy'.[1] Thereafter Henderson quickly won the respect though not always the admiration of his officials, and he in turn treated them with scrupulous fairness. He was particularly well served by Sir Walford Selby, his Private Secretary, who developed a keen appreciation of the general principles for which his chief was working. Even Sir Robert Vansittart, who succeeded Lindsay early in 1930, was able to co-operate affably enough with Henderson notwithstanding the immense philosophical gulf between them.[2]

With his principal envoys the Foreign Secretary maintained normal if not very warm relations, except in the case of Lord Lloyd, whom he recalled from Cairo in a somewhat precipitous fashion. Those then serving were competent rather than brilliant. Tyrrell, a former Permanent Under-Secretary, was probably the most able among them and, despite his preference for Baldwin and Austen Chamberlain, his opinions on the European situation came closer to those of his chief than those of other principal envoys. Sir Horace Rumbold in Berlin was a diplomatist of the traditional type. Although he had no sympathy for German nationalism, he did not at this period perceive with any great clarity the threat which Adolf Hitler already represented.[3] The British ambassadors in Washington were first Sir Esmé Howard and later Lindsay,

[1] Dalton, *Call Back Yesterday*, pp. 218–19. Later, Henderson authorised Dalton to circulate copies of *Labour and the Nation* around the Foreign Office, following dissatisfaction with certain draft answers to Parliamentary Questions: ibid., p. 223.

[2] Lord Vansittart, *The Mist Procession* (London, 1958) pp. 397–8. A recent study of this colourful official is Ian G. Colvin, *Vansittart in Office: an Historical Survey of the Origins of the Second World War Based on the Papers of Sir Robert Vansittart* (London, 1965).

[3] On Rumbold, see Franklin L. Ford, 'Three Observers in Berlin: Rumbold, Dodd and François-Poncet', in Craig and Gilbert, *The Diplomats*, pp. 438–47. Vansittart, unlike Rumbold, was acutely conscious of the National Socialist menace as early as 1930, when he described Hitler as 'the half-mad and ridiculously dangerous demagogue': Colvin, *Vansittart*, p. 19. For a study of the

who had previously served as Permanent Under-Secretary. Neither appears to have been greatly valued at this time in either Washington or London, and they played no decisive part in the naval disarmament discussion which dominated Anglo-American relations during the first year of the Labour Government's tenure of office. The contrast with the American ambassador in London, General Charles Gate Dawes, was striking.

Although Henderson was no pliable figure in the hands of his officials, there are unmistakable signs that he gave less time to his day-to-day duties than was appropriate for a modern Foreign Secretary. As Austen Chamberlain put it:

> the Government use him so much for Party and Home politics that he has not time for foreign affairs. 'I don't see how he can do his work', I said to Craigie who answered 'He doesn't do it.' They would be glad to have a minister again who would give himself to his office.[1]

As a leading figure in a Cabinet distracted not only by Imperial troubles, particularly in India and in Palestine, but also by a severe economic crisis, Henderson's neglect of detail in foreign affairs was to some extent inevitable. But he made matters worse by remaining General Secretary of the Labour Party, in which capacity he habitually spent at least one hour of his normal working day.[2] In order to save time he insisted on dealing with most matters on an oral basis in collaboration with his senior officials, refusing generally to be submerged under a mass of Foreign Office papers. Indeed, Sir Ivone Kirkpatrick stated with pardonable exaggeration that he 'never wrote a minute'.[3] Yet however weak

---

reaction of British quality newspapers to the rise of the National Socialists, see Brigitte Granzow, *A Mirror of Nazism: British Opinion and the Emergence of Hitler, 1929–1933* (London, 1964).

[1] Austen Chamberlain to Ida Chamberlain, 25 Apr 1931, Austen Chamberlain Papers. R. L. Craigie was a Counsellor in the Foreign Office.

[2] Jenkins, *From Foundry to Foreign Office*, pp. 168–9.

[3] Sir Ivone Kirkpatrick, *The Inner Circle: Memoirs* (London, 1959) p. 43. While Henderson's lack of attention to detail must be judged a serious weakness, it may also paradoxically have been a source of strength in that his mind was free to concentrate on matters of broad principle. In this connection an extract from Dalton's diary for 17 July 1929 is relevant: 'I told Cecil that Uncle [Henderson] was rather too immersed in detail. He said "Yes, the Office will try to drown him in detail so that he shan't have time to do any mischief"': Dalton, *Call Back Yesterday*, p. 223.

on detail, Henderson maintained an unchallenged mastery over the Foreign Office on questions of broad principle and, with an energy remarkable in a man verging on seventy, made numerous visits to foreign capitals and to Geneva, carrying personal diplomacy to even greater lengths than did Austen Chamberlain.

Although clearly master of his own department, Henderson did not similarly dominate his Cabinet colleagues when foreign affairs were under consideration. The Service Ministers, for example, made a practice of resisting Henderson's policies in the spheres of disarmament and arbitration; and the Foreign Secretary, according to Cecil, was often disinclined to stand up to determined opposition, preferring instead to adopt waiting tactics.[1] Still more important in curbing Henderson's powers was the Treasury, whose Permanent Secretary, Sir Warren Fisher, succeeded in resurrecting the famous Minute of 1919 which placed at his disposal all Foreign Office appointments. The decisive point came when MacDonald, acting on the advice of Fisher rather than on that of Henderson, appointed Vansittart as Permanent Under-Secretary for Foreign Affairs.[2] The Treasury was moreover extremely meddlesome in the broad conduct of foreign policy. This was especially marked in 1931, when both the Chancellor of the Exchequer, Philip Snowden, and the Governor of the Bank of England, Montagu Norman, pursued an international financial policy which was independent of and to some extent in conflict with that of the Foreign Office. By way of justification it might be argued that economic and financial questions were particularly important at this time. On the other hand, Fisher's refusal to support the Foreign Office's request for the creation of its own economic section shows that there was a distinct rivalry between the two departments.

As well as facing inter-departmental difficulties, the Foreign Secretary was plagued with an assertive and often hostile Prime Minister. Unlike

[1] See, for example, Cecil to Noel-Baker, 1 Aug 1929, Cecil Papers, Add. 51107.

[2] Sir Walford Selby, *Diplomatic Twilight, 1930–1940* (London, 1953) pp. 4–5. For earlier developments, see G. A. Craig, 'The British Foreign Office from Grey to Austen Chamberlain' in Craig and Gilbert, *The Diplomats*, pp. 15–48. Vansittart was probably sent to the Foreign Office to keep a critical eye on Henderson on behalf of the Prime Minister, whose Private Secretary he had previously been. There may therefore have been an element of poetic justice in the treatment Vansittart later received at the hands of Neville Chamberlain.

Baldwin, MacDonald took a lively interest in foreign affairs, having acted as his own Foreign Secretary in 1924. Although he did not feel able in 1929 to undertake this heavy burden for a second time, he made it clear to his colleagues and to the King that he intended to keep the direction of Anglo-American relations under his own control.[1] Not content with this arrangement, he constantly interfered in other questions and made little secret of his lack of confidence in Henderson. Even Lord Thomson, a close friend of MacDonald, was reported by Beatrice Webb as saying that 'Arthur Henderson has been abominably treated by the P.M.'[2] Emanuel Shinwell recorded an episode which, if authentic, supplies a good example of MacDonald's disloyalty:

> . . . Henderson became deeply disturbed by hostile articles in the Press about his negotiations on the Egyptian question. They had reached a critical stage and Henderson believed that the Press criticism might be misunderstood abroad. He invited the editor of the paper carrying the most vitriolic attacks to send a reporter so that the official Foreign Office attitude could be explained.
>
> Henderson was told by the reporter that he thought the Foreign Secretary should know that the article had been written at the request of the Prime Minister.[3]

Another example of the Prime Minister's attitude arose when Henderson, seeking the establishment of an economic section in the Foreign Office, wrote:

> Broadly speaking it is I think correct to say that economic considerations are becoming, if they have not actually become the dominant factor in the relations as between foreign countries and ourselves, and that unless our foreign policy is so equipped as to take the fullest account of the movements in the economic sphere we cannot expect to derive all the advantage to which the country is entitled from the activities of its foreign service.
>
> The question has been under examination here [the Foreign Office] by a small departmental committee under my direction. . . .
>
> My proposal is to set up forthwith in the Foreign Office a small politico-economic department with a staff of four, one of whom would be an economic adviser brought in from outside. . . .
>
> I propose also that economics be made a compulsory subject in the examination for the Foreign Office and the Diplomatic Service. . . .

[1] Nicolson, *King George the Fifth*, p. 435.
[2] Beatrice Webb Diary, entry for 23 Mar 1930.
[3] Emanuel Shinwell, *The Labour Story* (London, 1963) pp. 135–6.

My object in writing is to express the hope that the reorganisation I propose will meet with your approval and support. I believe that you have already shown some interest in the question and attach importance to it, so that I am sanguine enough to hope that you will be sympathetic with the object I have in view.[1]

But according to Vansittart, MacDonald gave Henderson no support 'and the idea was dropped'.[2]

The differences between MacDonald and Henderson were both personal and political. Although they were the two most important architects of the modern Labour Party, they were never able to achieve a warm relationship. There were no doubt contributory faults on both sides, but of the two men Henderson was the more conciliatory. As leader of the Labour Party during the First World War, he had shown great magnanimity towards MacDonald in refusing to allow him to be driven off the party's National Executive Committee; and in the 1920s, when the party leadership was restored to MacDonald, he proved a loyal – perhaps too loyal – follower. In the post-1924 inquest, for example, Henderson refused to be drafted as a rival for the leadership, even though his chances of winning were by no means negligible. Even after MacDonald had formed his National Government in 1931, Henderson, possibly with tongue in cheek, surprisingly told Patrick Duff, one of the Prime Minister's secretaries, that 'we must not take this too seriously'. 'At the time of the war, when Mr MacDonald left the Party [sic],' Duff's account continued, 'he [Henderson] had kept it together and it was ready to receive Mr MacDonald back again. He was parting with the Prime Minister now in no spirit of anger or resentment.'[3]

In their political relationship, the first serious divergence arose in August 1914 when MacDonald, without being an out-and-out pacifist, refused to endorse the British decision to go to war. He felt obliged to

[1] Henderson to MacDonald, 13 Mar 1931, MacDonald Papers. Henderson also sent to MacDonald a supporting memorandum by Sir Victor Wellesley of the Foreign Office. Wellesley later wrote a partisan account of the ill-treatment of the Foreign Office during the inter-war period. See *Diplomacy in Fetters* (London, n.d., 1947?). A more balanced picture emerges from Donald G. Bishop, *The Administration of British Foreign Relations* (Syracuse, N.Y., 1961).

[2] Vansittart to MacDonald, 14 Mar 1932, MacDonald Papers.

[3] Memorandum by Duff, 25 Aug 1931, Rose Rosenberg Papers deposited at the Public Record Office. Rose Rosenberg was MacDonald's personal private secretary. Duff had been instructed by MacDonald to offer Henderson a peerage. This Henderson refused.

resign the chairmanship of the Parliamentary Labour Party and went into the political wilderness, from which he did not return until 1922.[1] Henderson, always more willing than MacDonald to recognise the importance of military force in international relations, found himself in sympathy with the view that Belgian independence had to be defended by more than words. He accordingly accepted the Parliamentary leadership vacated by MacDonald and subsequently represented the Labour Party in the Asquith and Lloyd George coalition administrations. The two drew together for a short time during the controversy which developed over the peace terms to be imposed on Germany, but later new disagreements arose between them over the basic question of the importance of military power when, during the period 1923–5, a prolonged international debate took place regarding the desirability of multilateral security arrangements as a preliminary to a disarmament agreement.

The first security arrangement recommended by the Temporary Mixed Commission of the League of Nations was the Draft Treaty of Mutual Assistance. It fell to the first Labour Government to declare the British verdict on this scheme. MacDonald, to the disappointment of most Europeans, chose rejection. At the Labour Party Annual Conference he called the proposal 'a great menace to the League of Nations and essentially a war preparation document'.[2] By contrast, Henderson's verdict was that 'there was much to be said for this scheme in default of a better plan'.[3]

The next effort in the direction of security guarantees came at the 1924

[1] There is at present no first-class biography of MacDonald. The following studies, however, throw some light on his complicated character: Lord Elton, *The Life of James Ramsay MacDonald (1886–1919)* (London, 1939); L. MacNeill Weir, *The Tragedy of Ramsay MacDonald: A Political Biography* (London, n.d., 1938?); Benjamin Sacks, *J. Ramsay MacDonald in Thought and Action* (Albuquerque, N. Mex., 1952). See also the sketch in Francis Williams, *A Pattern of Rulers* (London, 1965) pp. 61–134.

[2] *Labour Party Annual Conference Report, 1924*, p. 108. The official Conservative Opposition endorsed MacDonald's rejection of the Draft Treaty. With good cause MacDonald had written privately as early as June 1923 of Baldwin that 'on foreign politics his own personal views are, as near as no matter, the same as mine': M. S. Venkataramani, 'Ramsay MacDonald and Britain's Domestic Politics and Foreign Relations, 1919–1931: A Study based on MacDonald's Letters to an American Friend', *Political Studies*, VIII (1960) p. 238.

[3] Arthur Henderson, *The New Peace Plan: Labour's Work at the League of Nations Assembly* (London, 1924) p. 6. This pamphlet was the text of a speech delivered by Henderson on 12 Oct 1924 at Burnley.

League General Assembly where Henderson and Lord Parmoor, the Lord President of the Council, negotiated the so-called Geneva Protocol which provided for a systematic advance towards compulsory arbitration, automatic sanctions against aggressors and an all-round reduction of armaments.[1] The security provisions were, as Henderson saw, an essential prerequisite for French participation in any general scheme for the reduction of armaments. MacDonald, however, like most British statesmen between the wars, was unwilling to pay this necessary price. He was even reluctant to acknowledge the importance of the obligations contained in the League Covenant. Of the provisions for sanctions against aggression he wrote in 1925: 'I never have regarded these powers as being of any importance except in so far as their presence on paper is a harmless drug to soothe the nerves.'[2] It is extremely doubtful whether MacDonald would have consented to the ratification of the Protocol if the Labour Cabinet had remained in office. Wishing, however, to maintain the unity of his party following defeat in the House of Commons and at the polls, his attitude in the subsequent debate with the new Conservative administration, which decided to reject the Protocol, was ambiguous and imprecise; but in private he told Austen Chamberlain that he would never have signed it in its existing form.[3] Henderson by contrast made a vigorous public defence of the Protocol both in the General Election and in a subsequent House of Commons debate; and he made no attempt to play down its coercive element.[4] In October 1924 he even claimed that 'the frustration of our efforts, from whatever cause, will be a disaster which unborn generations may have bitter reason to deplore'.[5]

[1] For further details on the provisions of the Geneva Protocol, see Philip J. Noel-Baker, *The Geneva Protocol for the Pacific Settlement of Disputes* (London, 1925), and David Hunter Miller, *The Geneva Protocol* (New York, 1925).

[2] James Ramsay MacDonald, 'Protocol and Pact', *Labour Magazine*, III (1925) 533.

[3] Austen Chamberlain to Cecil, 19 June 1925, Cecil Papers, Add. 51078. Little reliance can be placed upon the recollection of one contemporary, writing thirty years later, that MacDonald had been an eager supporter of the Protocol: Vansittart, *The Mist Procession*, p. 332.

[4] One historian has commented that this was 'the most striking element in his position': Winkler, in Craig and Gilbert, *The Diplomats*, p. 316.

[5] Henderson, *The New Peace Plan*, p. 5. For his speech in Parliament see *House of Commons Debates*, 5th series (hereafter abbreviated to *H.C. Deb.*), clxxxii, cols 291–307, 24 Mar 1925. It is reprinted as *Labour and the Geneva Protocol* (London, 1925).

The conflict between Henderson and MacDonald on international security continued throughout the period of the second Labour Government and was particularly intense during the London Naval Conference of 1930, when the Prime Minister defeated the Foreign Secretary's efforts to satisfy French demands for guarantees of military assistance.[1] Throughout this period MacDonald was much impressed by the advice of Sir Maurice Hankey, who was Secretary to both the Cabinet and the Committee of Imperial Defence. Hankey was a bitter opponent of Henderson's attitude towards international security and arbitration, as is evident from these lines written to MacDonald:

> I am a profound believer in the League's capacity for conciliation and gaining time for averting war. I am an equally profound disbeliever in its capacity to advise action. It will fail in that respect as the Holy Roman Empire failed and for the same reasons. Nevertheless sanctions have a certain value. They are like a big stick believed to be in the cupboard; and as long as the boys do not realise that it is made of paper it is a deterrent. But if you bring the stick out into the light of day I fear its true character will be exposed.[2]

Cecil was even driven to the conclusion that, under Hankey's influence, MacDonald had become an enemy of the League of Nations. Referring to a German plan for a treaty of mutual assistance, he wrote to Noel-Baker:

> Temperley tells Cadogan that when it [the treaty] came to be considered by the Committee [of Imperial Defence], the Prime Minister declared himself to be opposed to the whole Treaty, and only accepted my formula because he was confident that it would destroy the treaty. Temperley says, in so many words, that he shewed himself more hostile to the treaty than the Chiefs of Staff. Cadogan agrees with me that this is surely due to Hankey, who, in his view, has always been opposed to the League of Nations since he refused the position of Secretary General. Whatever the reason the situation really is extremely serious. It does definitely mean that the Prime Minister is, as

[1] At the end of the London Naval Conference MacDonald explained his policy to the King in unambiguous terms: '. . . one rule must be firmly observed. Great Britain must not take on further responsibilities and must not be put in the position of having to act mechanically and without freedom of judgment should trouble arise in Europe. France is trying hard to get us into that position': MacDonald to King George V, 12 Apr 1930, King George V Papers deposited in the Royal Archives at Windsor (hereafter abbreviated to R.A. GV), G 2258/18.

[2] Hankey to MacDonald, 10 Apr 1930, MacDonald Papers.

the French with their usual acuteness perceived, opposed to the League.[1]

But if MacDonald and Hankey were opponents of the League, it was the League which the French and certain British politicians, in particular Henderson and Cecil, wished to create, and not the League which in fact existed between the wars. While MacDonald thought that the League was and should remain no more than a world forum, Henderson and Cecil regarded it as an embryonic super-state and resented his attempts to prevent it evolving along the lines they considered essential to its success. Inevitably this lack of basic agreement between MacDonald and Henderson was reflected in much of the external conduct of the second Labour Government, and it goes far to justify the claim of one historian that 'in a sense, Great Britain had two foreign policies from 1929 to 1931'.[2]

The foreign policy makers of the second Labour Government appear not to have been greatly influenced by manifestations of public opinion. Protagonists of conflicting views had no difficulty in persuading themselves that they were in complete harmony with the mood of the people. For example, when the possibility of providing France with additional security guarantees was mooted, J. L. Garvin of *The Observer* wrote:

> ... I don't believe that we can get any good whatever by countenancing the arguments of the French or by giving into them just now in any way.... I think I may fairly claim to be as experienced a specialist on public opinion as there is in this country, and what I do know is that there is a tense possibility here of an explosion of public opinion against France such as I mean to do my best to prevent.[3]

[1] Cecil to Noel-Baker, 9 May 1930, Cecil Papers, Add. 51107. A. C. Temperley and Alexander Cadogan were officials in the War Office and the Foreign Office respectively. Cecil added: 'It is impossible I think to get rid of the Prime Minister but in my view it becomes essential to get rid of Hankey. As soon as you [Noel-Baker] get back to England I should like to have a serious talk with you as to what steps if any can be taken with regard to that object.' Cecil's design for Hankey's future came to nothing; he continued to retain MacDonald's confidence throughout the period of the second Labour Government and beyond.

[2] Winkler, in Craig and Gilbert, *The Diplomats*, p. 321.

[3] Garvin to Cecil, 8 Apr 1930, Cecil Papers, Add. 51167. Not surprisingly Garvin himself personally favoured the views, which he claimed were representative of public opinion. In the same letter to Cecil he wrote: 'I don't think

But Henderson, in the Burge Memorial Lecture of 1931, spoke in a rather different vein:

in respect of every forward policy in the last twelve years, the public opinion of the nations has always been ahead of what the Governments were prepared to do. Consider the Optional Clause and the General Act. When they faced the question of the acceptance of these great instruments, there were many Governments who were assailed by doubts and hesitations. But the nations for whom they acted had none. Hardly a voice was raised in opposition.[1]

In reality, public opinion, distracted by the magnitude of the unemployment problem at home, was seldom vocal on foreign affairs during this period of relative calm on the international scene.

Although the Labour Cabinet in formulating its external policies had little need to worry about the attitude of the general public, it was by no means assured of a totally free hand. In particular, close attention had to be given, because of the minority status of the ministry in the House of Commons, to the views of the Liberal Party. Generally, however, the Liberals concentrated on domestic questions and appear to have worked on the assumption that no foreign policy issue was likely to arouse public feeling to a level where they would be justified in – or would benefit from – defeating the Government and precipitating a General Election.

The interrelationship between the domestic and foreign policies of the second Labour Government was weaker than it might have been, considering that the mounting unemployment problem, which overshadowed all else at this period, was thought to be as much international as national in character. The Foreign Secretary, however, was no more able to prescribe a cure than Snowden or Thomas, and shrewdly made fewer attempts to do so.

The number of workless grew remorselessly. Unemployment, which in June 1929 stood at just over a million, rose by the end of June 1930 to

---

there is going to be any real hope of peace until we stop thinking and talking everlastingly of precautions against war.' For an elaboration of Garvin's view, see 'Britain's "No": The End of Entanglements', *The Observer*, 30 Mar 1930.

[1] Arthur Henderson, *Consolidating World Peace* (London, 1931) p. 29. Not surprisingly Henderson himself personally favoured the views, which he claimed were representative of public opinion.

over two million. By the end of that year it was more than $2\frac{1}{2}$ million, and continued above that level until 1933. Ideally the problem should have been tackled by the application of what are now called Keynesian methods, and in particular by the acceptance of deficit financing and the inauguration of a vast programme of public works. But although such a panacea had been propounded by the Liberal Party in the 1929 General Election, experts, especially in the Treasury, were outraged by this 'advanced' thinking, which seemed to many fundamentally mistaken and to a few tantamount to national dishonesty.[1]

That the Labour Party found itself on the side of orthodoxy was in large measure due to the rigid and doctrinaire approach of Snowden, who was Chancellor of the Exchequer in the first two Labour Governments and who acted as 'Shadow Chancellor' in the intervening period of Conservative rule.[2] There was certainly no absence of opposition within the Labour Party to Snowden's policies, but he was too strongly entrenched in his position to be seriously deflected. The standard of revolt against him was first raised in 1925 when the Independent Labour Party produced its famous programme known as 'Socialism in Our Time', a more moderate series of proposals than the title suggested. It was to a large degree based on 'the under-consumptionist economics of J. A. Hobson'.[3] Apart from the demand for the socialisation of banking and the institution of a national minimum wage, the I.L.P. programme was not markedly to the Left of that which the Liberal Party advanced in the 1929 General Election. It proved nevertheless to be quite unacceptable to MacDonald and Snowden.[4]

The next Labour grouping in opposition to economic orthodoxy emerged only in 1930, after the second Labour Government's failure to

[1] The Liberal policy was embodied in *We Can Conquer Unemployment* (London, 1929). For a critique of the Liberals' campaign in 1929, see S. Maccoby, *English Radicalism: The End?* (London, 1961) pp. 491–4.

[2] On Snowden see Colin Cross, *Philip Snowden* (London, 1966); Philip, Viscount Snowden, *An Autobiography*, 2 vols (London, 1934); A. Andréadès, *Philip Snowden: The Man and his Financial Policy* (London, 1930); and P. J. Grigg, *Prejudice and Judgment* (London, 1948).

[3] Robert E. Dowse, 'The Left-Wing Opposition during the First Two Labour Governments', *Parliamentary Affairs*, XIV (1960–1) 89.

[4] For details see ibid., pp. 90–1. See also Robert Keith Middlemass, *The Clydesiders: A Left-Wing Struggle for Parliamentary Power* (London, 1965) pp. 182–5. This work emphasises and possibly exaggerates the role of John Wheatley.

cure unemployment had become manifest. The focal point of the content on this occasion was the person of Oswald Mosley. In January 1930 Mosley, at that time Chancellor of the Duchy of Lancaster with subordinate responsibility for unemployment policy under the general direction of Thomas, submitted to the Cabinet a memorandum, which advocated a number of measures borrowed from Keynes and from 'Socialism in Our Time'.[1] These were vigorously resisted by Snowden, who easily secured Cabinet backing. On 20 May Mosley resigned from the administration and carried on the struggle first at a meeting of the Parliamentary Labour Party and later at the party's annual conference at Llandudno. On both occasions his tone and demeanour cost him support. He then decided to abandon the Labour Party and establish a rival electoral organisation. Thereafter Snowden's policies were never seriously challenged until the onset of the 1931 crisis which led to the fall of the Labour Government.[2]

Although unemployment was considered to be an international malaise, Henderson was a largely passive observer in the struggle between Mosley and Snowden. In the final crisis, it is true, the Foreign Secretary came out against the Chancellor in the Cabinet, but in so doing he acted primarily as a class-conscious trade unionist and not as an advocate of 'advanced' economics, a subject at which he did not excel. It is clear also that his opposition to the Treasury's proposed cuts in unemployment relief was in no sense a reflection of the views of his department, which, lacking an economic section, had no specific advice to offer and merely concentrated on its traditional duties. Any account of the work of the Foreign Office under the second Labour Government must therefore inevitably reflect its essential isolation from the more dramatic domestic developments of the period.

[1] For details see Robert Skidelsky, *Politicians and the Slump: The Labour Government of 1929-1931* (London, 1967) chap. 8.

[2] For further information on the extremely abnormal domestic scene under the second Labour Government, see Skidelsky, *Politicians and the Slump*; A. J. P. Taylor, *English History, 1914-1945* (London, 1965) chap. 8; and Charles Loch Mowat, *Britain between the Wars, 1918-1940* (London, 1955) chap. 7. For a strongly pro-MacDonald account of the last months of the Labour administration, see Bassett, *Nineteen Thirty-One*.

CHAPTER TWO *The German Problem to the End of the First Hague Conference*, 1929

HOWEVER divided British statesmen were on the issue of the League of Nations and collective security, they were almost unanimous in their desire to pacify and conciliate pre-Hitler Germany. Certainly all members of the second Labour Government earnestly believed that solutions to the outstanding questions relating to Germany, especially those concerning reparations and the early evacuation of occupation forces from the Rhineland, were both desirable and attainable; and in this respect at least they also had the support of most of the outgoing Conservative Ministers. But if there was no divergence of aim between the two administrations, there was undoubtedly a contrast in the methods employed, for whereas Austen Chamberlain and his colleagues had sought European pacification in close co-operation with Paris, most of the new Labour Ministers preferred the tactic of pushing rather than cajoling the French into making concessions to Germany.

The Labour Party came into office with a long tradition of Francophobia dating back to the war and even beyond.[1] Snowden, in particular, was thought of as the personification of this attitude. Henderson was exceptional in having a reputation for being well disposed towards Paris.[2]

[1] This was so well known in Paris that, according to Tyrrell, 'the French Government always cherished the hope that the Baldwin Government would be again returned to power' in 1929. Tyrrell 'had told them they were unduly optimistic but added that if they wished the Conservatives to remain in office they ought to help Baldwin before the Elections by agreeing to the evacuation of the Rhine; and settling the Reparations question; but they refused to do anything though dreading the possibility of a Labour Government': Stamfordham memorandum of a conversation with Tyrrell, 9 Sep 1929, R.A. GV, M 2232/1.
[2] Tyrrell wrote of Henderson: 'I think he has thoroughly realised that you can do a great deal with the French by coaxing and humouring, but very little by bullying': Tyrrell to Selby, 26 Jan 1931, Henderson Papers, F.O. 800/283. Henderson's Parliamentary Under-Secretary, Dalton, was even less in sympathy with the views of France held by the majority in the Cabinet. Ironically another

B

In addition to Francophobia, the Labour Party also had a somewhat milder tradition of sympathy for post-Versailles Germany, deriving from a characteristic concern for the underdog and from a rejection of the 'war guilt' thesis embodied in Article 231 of the Treaty. Demands for the outright repudiation of reparations were passed at party conferences in the early 1920's, and although the first Labour Government endorsed the Dawes Plan, this action was widely regarded as a step towards the ending of reparations rather than a deliberate defiance by the Parliamentary Labour Party of conference decisions.[1]

Yet whatever ideals the Labour leaders may have had regarding the conciliation of Germany, their practical policy on reparations, like that of the Conservatives, was based on the famous Balfour Note of 1922;[2] neither front bench was prepared to take a unilateral initiative or even to accept any unfavourable redistribution of German payments prior to a multilateral liquidation of the whole problem. The principal reason for this was that, in the minds of British Ministers, both Conservative and Labour, the question of reparations was inextricably bound up with that of inter-allied war debts. Great Britain, whose major debt was to the United States, was the only power in the 1920's making a sustained effort to meet its obligations. The British Ministers accordingly felt a double sense of grievance when, in 1929, the Latin powers sought to secure a redistribution of German payments without attempting to meet their debts to Great Britain. During the first months of the second Labour Government, therefore, Great Britain's efforts to liberate Germany from the shackles of the Versailles Treaty took second place to efforts to secure fair play for herself.

The earlier history of the reparations question cannot be dealt with here except in briefest outline.[3] The powers at Versailles had found

---

Francophil was appointed to the Foreign Office in 1930 when Vansittart became Permanent Under-Secretary.

[1] See W. R. Tucker, *The Attitude of the British Labour Party towards European and Collective Security Problems, 1920–1939* (Geneva, 1950) pp. 85–93, for a detailed examination of the issues involved.

[2] The Balfour Note was published as Cmd. 1737 of 1922. Great Britain, it declared, 'would be prepared . . . to abandon all further rights to German reparation and all claims to repayment by Allies, provided that this renunciation formed part of a general plan by which this great problem could be dealt with as a whole and find a satisfactory solution'.

[3] More detailed accounts are to be found in W. M. Jordan, *Great Britain, France and the German Problem, 1918–1939* (London, 1943) pp. 102–29;

Germany and her allies guilty of causing the world war and ordered her to make good the damage she had brought about without, however, immediately naming a specific sum. In 1921, in a vain attempt to encourage the Germans to face up to their task with the same enthusiasm as the French had shown in 1871, the allies, after protracted negotiations, had finally fixed Germany's obligations at 132 billion gold marks. After a phase of German payment default and passive resistance, and the resultant Franco-Belgian occupation of the Ruhr, a new start had been made in 1924 with the famous Dawes Plan – 'the first departure from the atmosphere of *Diktats*, ultimatums and sanctions'.[1] In spite of German acquiescence and the adoption of a policy of fulfilment by Stresemann, this arrangement had never been regarded as of more than a temporary character. It was therefore only a matter of time before a new initiative occurred.

It fell to Parker Gilbert, the Agent-General for Reparations, to make the first important move towards a further revision in the amount of Germany's liabilities when, in his report on the working of the Dawes Plan, issued in December 1927, he called for the renewal of negotiations. The question was duly raised in the League of Nations Assembly in September 1928, and it was provisionally agreed to hold an international conference to consider both reparations and the evacuation of the Rhineland, even though the two issues were theoretically separate. It was further agreed that a Committee of Experts should be appointed to draw up proposals for a new scale of reparation payments. Thus it was that in the early part of 1929 at Paris, Owen Young and ten other representatives began the acrimonious deliberations which eventually culminated in the issuing of the Young Plan in May 1929. The surprising thing was that the experts were able to reach unanimity at all. This owed much to the desperate entreaties of the chairman and more to the weakness of the British representatives. One of these, Sir Josiah Stamp, must bear the main responsibility for sacrificing British interests, since his colleague,

---

Andrew McFadyean, *Reparation Reviewed* (London, 1930); Hans Ronde, *Von Versailles bis Lausanne: Der Verlauf der Reparationsverhandlungen nach dem ersten Weltkrieg* (Stuttgart and Cologne, 1950); Arnold J. Toynbee, *Survey of International Affairs, 1924* (London, 1926) pp. 323–99; and Arnold J. Toynbee et al., *Survey of International Affairs, 1929* (London, 1930) pp. 111–66.
    [1] Julius Curtius, *Der Young-Plan: Entstellung und Wahrheit* (Stuttgart, 1950) p. 13.

Lord Revelstoke, died half-way through the proceedings and had to be replaced by a stand-in, Sir Charles Addis. Stamp was not technically a delegate of the British Government, but he was fully aware of its views and even appears to have shared them.[1] None of the other experts – two each from France, Italy, Belgium and Germany – showed any inclination to adopt a non-partisan attitude and hence it is all the more surprising that Stamp should have capitulated to the demands of the Latin majority for a redistribution in the percentages of the German payments which had applied continuously since the Spa Agreement of 1920.

The main proposals of the Young Report, as they affected Germany, tended to be lost sight of in the controversy over the Spa percentages. Nevertheless, they were of much greater potential significance. German payments were now firmly fixed within a fifty-nine-year plan and not left unsettled as in the Dawes Plan, while the total amount to be paid was reduced by some 20 per cent. Whether these changes brought much comfort to Germany may be doubted, since, as one writer has put it, 'it might appear that an unpleasant certainty was little preferable to an unpleasant uncertainty'.[2] Perhaps more important were the proposals that involved the abolition of foreign controls within Germany and the institution of new methods of payment. In this connection it was suggested that a Bank for International Settlements should be established to take the place of the Agent-General. In addition, it was proposed that a part of the reparations debts should take the form of bonds for sale to private investors.[3] This change in the system of payments, however, was

[1] That Stamp was not a delegate of the British Government was made clear by Winston Churchill while the Committee of Experts was still in session. See *H.C. Deb.*, ccxxvii, col. 2310, 9 May 1929. On the other hand, in a controversial speech at The Hague, Henri Chéron, the French Minister of Finance, implied that the British experts had acted on the advice of the Treasury. For the text of this speech, see German Foreign Ministry Records (photostatic copies held in London at either the Public Record Office or in the Foreign Office Library – hereafter abbreviated to G.F.M.R.), 4498/E 107532–40. Stamp's part on the Young Committee is inadequately dealt with in his official biography; see J. Harry Jones, *Josiah Stamp, Public Servant: The Life of the First Baron Stamp of Shortlands* (London, 1964).

[2] E. N. Peterson, *Hjalmar Schacht: For and Against Hitler: A Political-Economic Study of Germany, 1923–1945 (Boston, 1954)* p. 83.

[3] The Young Report was published in Great Britain as Cmd. 3343 of 1929–30. For a useful short summary of the implications of the Plan, see Thomas W. Lamont, 'The Final Reparations Settlement', *Foreign Affairs* (New York), VIII (1929–30) 336–63.

only superficially an improvement for Germany, since there would now be far less flexibility in the event of a severe recession.

While none of these main proposals was unacceptable to Great Britain, the recommended changes in distribution and in provisions for deliveries in kind met with strong resistance from the outset in London. Indeed, once the details of the Young Plan became widely known, an international crisis on these questions was unavoidable, for if the British were opposed to the proposed redistribution, the French, Italians and Belgians were equally disposed to insist upon it. The British were initially in the weaker bargaining position, since it was apparent that they were most eager to conciliate Germany and to bring about a reduction of her reparations burden as well as the evacuation of the Rhineland; while in the Latin countries, by contrast, many elements were secretly or even overtly unenthusiastic about the whole project. Nor was the British position made easier by the change of Government in June, for the Labour Ministers were reputedly hostile to the whole idea of reparations and might therefore have been expected to weaken on the issue of the Spa percentages in order to help Germany. On the other hand, the new British Government knew that Churchill, just prior to the General Election, had openly repudiated Stamp and that David Lloyd George was also opposed to capitulation.[1] The prospects were therefore far from auspicious. That the Government in the event managed to obtain an agreement with the continental powers and at the same time to win domestic approval owed much to the felicitous combination of the inflexibility of Snowden and the personal diplomacy of Henderson. It is sometimes said that international conflicts are made over the heads of the peoples by the secret machinations of diplomats and statesmen. In 1929, at the first Hague Conference, summoned to consider the Young Report, the reverse occurred: agreement was miraculously arrived at by the politicians in defiance of the irreconcilable forces of public opinion in the principal countries concerned.

The British delegation to the conference, which opened in the Binnenhof at The Hague on 6 August 1929, consisted of Snowden, Henderson, Hankey, Noel-Baker, William Graham, the President of the Board of Trade, and Sir Eric Phipps, the British minister in Vienna. The fact that Snowden and not Henderson was chief delegate has occasioned some

---

[1] For Churchill's views, see *H.C. Deb.*, ccxxvii, col. 2311, 9 May 1929. For the attitude of Lloyd George, see *H.C. Deb.*, ccxxx, cols 1667–76, 26 July 1929.

criticism.[1] It has been seen, for example, as symptomatic of undue Treasury influence vis-à-vis the Foreign Office.[2] But a report to Berlin from the German ambassador in London, Friedrich Sthamer, provides the most convincing explanation for Henderson's 'demotion'. In it the ambassador claimed that at a meeting of the Cabinet Henderson had indicated a willingness to accept the Young Plan 'in principle' and to work only for 'certain modifications'. Thereupon, Snowden had opposed Henderson and had 'secured the support of the remaining Cabinet Ministers'.[3]

Snowden did not, however, receive a completely free hand. According to the Cabinet Minutes, the Chancellor was told to do 'his best to secure the adoption of our views', but if he should 'find it impossible to secure their adoption he should refer to his Cabinet colleagues for instructions'; according to the Prime Minister, the Cabinet decided that if the other powers 'were immovable the work at the Hague should be considered by Mr MacDonald upon whom was placed the responsibility of final decisions'; and according to Lord Passfield, Secretary of State for the Dominions and Colonies, the Chancellor told the Cabinet that he intended to be rigid about the debt, but the Cabinet decided that 'the degree of rigidity' was to be 'referred to Henderson, the Prime Minister and Snowden to settle'.[4] Of the three Ministers, Snowden held the most extreme position. Concerning Henderson's outlook, Sthamer's

[1] That MacDonald was not first delegate arose out of the French refusal to allow the conference to be held in London. Tyrrell, according to his own account to Stamfordham, 'advised them to give in as they would have Ramsay MacDonald to deal with and anywhere else, Snowden'. The French, however, refused, since 'they were convinced that we [the British] had some Machiavellian plot to hold the Conference in London and ensure that the International Bank would be established there': Stamfordham memorandum of a conversation with Tyrrell, 9 Sep 1929, R.A. GV, M 2232/1.

[2] Selby, *Diplomatic Twilight*, p. 5.

[3] Sthamer to Foreign Ministry, 8 Aug 1929, G.F.M.R., 3375/D 732979–80. The British Cabinet Minutes do not confirm Sthamer's report of Henderson's defeat. But this is not surprising, since it was the custom of the Cabinet Secretariat to record only the conclusions of the Cabinet meetings. On 17 July 1929, however, the Cabinet only agreed to endorse Snowden's approach 'after considerable discussion': Conclusions of Meetings of the Cabinet, Public Record Office (hereafter abbreviated to Cabinet Minutes), Cab. 23/61, 29(29)6, 17 July 1929.

[4] Ibid.; MacDonald to King George V, 14 Aug 1929, R.A. GV, K 2231/8; and M. I. Cole (ed.), *Beatrice Webb's Diaries, 1924–1932* (London, 1956) p. 216.

THE MAN WHO CREATED A FURORE

Mr. Snowden. *They never guessed at home how versatile I am.*

report of the Cabinet encounter has already been cited. Further evidence of the Foreign Secretary's moderation is provided in the following passage from Dalton's diary:

As to the Rhineland Snowden is the most dangerous obstacle to early evacuation. He wants to re-open the Reparations question, haggle over the Young Plan, and abuse the French and Italians and try to claw back some 2 millions a year from each. A hopeless policy! The view of the Office . . . is that a few millions are dust in the balance, compared with the gains of the early and complete evacuation which will also certainly follow swiftly on a general acceptance of the Young Plan. But Uncle, though sound on the principles, is a bit afraid of P. S. [Snowden].[1]

MacDonald appears to have stood somewhere between the Foreign Secretary and the Chancellor. Of him Dawes wrote: 'One senses that he feels that Snowden's attitude creates serious difficulties.'[2]

The first event at the conference was the election of a British civil servant, Hankey, as Secretary-General by general consent. Next, Henri Jaspar of Belgium was nominated to chair the first plenary session. It was understood that the chairmanship would rotate, but in the event Jaspar held the position throughout the conference. After the preliminary speeches, the conference went into secret session, though all the proceedings were subsequently leaked to the Press. Only one important speech was made on the first day, and this appropriately came from Snowden, who was destined to capture world attention as the so-called 'Iron Chancellor' in the weeks that followed. In this speech, according to his own account, he stated unequivocally the essence of the British objections to the proposals in the Young Report:

The British Government had no objection to the volume and the amount of the annuities, but it objected to the proposal to divide the amount into two categories. So long as conditional annuities were being paid it did not matter much, because all nations were getting their money, but unconditional annuities carried the right of mobilisation, and therefore attained greater security than the conditional annuities. The British Government objected to the present proposed division whereby France got five-sixths of the unconditional annuities and Italy had a very considerable sum amounting to £2,000,000 annually,

[1] Dalton Diary deposited at the British Library of Political and Economic Science, entry for 17 June 1929.
[2] C. G. Dawes, *Journal as Ambassador to Great Britain* (New York, 1939) p. 44.

which was much larger than her revenue under the Dawes Plan. There remained a perfectly negligible part to be divided among the other creditor Powers. . . .

The British Government attached the greatest possible importance to the proposed modifications which had been made in the distribution of annuities among the various creditor nations, and which was a departure from agreements which already existed, and, unfortunately, this division was very much to the disadvantage of certain creditor countries and very much to the advantage of other creditor countries. . . .

This was the first time that a suggestion had ever been made that there should be a departure from the Spa percentages. . . . When the Young Committee was convened, it was agreed among the chief creditor Powers that there should be no interference with the Spa percentages.[1]

Snowden also touched upon Great Britain's grievance with regard to inter-allied debts and her objections to the proposals of the Young Plan for payments in kind. He concluded by referring to the state of opinion in Great Britain – something his critics conveniently ignored:

Forgive me if I appear to speak with great firmness in regard to the distribution of annuities. The House of Commons would never agree to any further sacrifices of British interests in this matter. We are agreed – and as you all know, all parties in Great Britain are agreed – upon this.

We are prepared to wipe the slate clean of all international debts and Reparations. That was implied in the Balfour Note. It was the declaration of our Party before we came into power. But so long as Reparations are paid and received, so long as debts are payable, every Government in Great Britain will insist upon Great Britain being treated fairly in this matter.[2]

On the following day, 7 August, the other principal delegates read prepared statements prior to the conference adjourning into commissions to consider the financial and political aspects of the German

[1] Snowden, *An Autobiography*, II 789–90.

[2] Ibid., p. 791. Of this speech Hankey wrote to MacDonald: 'It was most admirably done. I believe Mr Snowden calls himself an Internationalist, but I, who call myself an out-and-out Britisher, really glowed with pride at the way he did it, and I think everybody felt that the presentation was perfectly admirable however much they might disagree about the substance. I have compared notes with Mr Henderson and I find that he too agrees that it was admirably well done': Hankey to MacDonald, 7 Aug 1929, Cabinet: Registered Files, Public Record Office (hereafter abbreviated to C.R.F.), Cab. 21/317.

B 2

problem. The Latin powers took the line that the Young Plan was an indivisible whole and hence could not be amended, whereas the minor powers tended to support the British view.

On 8 August, the Financial and Political Committees commenced their separate deliberations. The former, on which Great Britain was represented by Snowden and Graham, concerned itself with seeking an escape from the impasse created by the proposed departure from the Spa percentages; while the latter, on which Henderson served as the principal British delegate, devoted itself to reaching an agreement on the early evacuation of occupation forces from the Rhineland.

At the first meeting of the Financial Committee, Snowden caused an immediate sensation by opposing a proposal that drafting sub-committees should be forthwith established. Determined to refute rumours that he was bluffing, he repeated his demands for changes in the Young Plan on the three issues of the Spa percentages, deliveries in kind, and the distribution of unconditional annuities. He then brought in once again British public opinion so as to illustrate the futility of the Latin powers putting undue pressure on the British delegation:

> Suppose that we here were to accept it, supposing the British Government were to accept it, what would happen? We might go back to the House of Commons and submit it to the House of Commons, but the House of Commons would not accept it, the country would not accept it, and therefore all the work would have to be begun over again. . . .

Snowden concluded by moving a resolution calling for the establishment of a sub-committee of Treasury experts to consider the points at issue.[1]

It was clear that an impasse had been reached and it was mutually agreed to adjourn until 10 August. Then when the formal sessions were resumed it was found necessary to embark on time-killing tactics in order to allow the principal delegates to seek an off-stage solution. Hence it was expected that the Saturday session of the committee would be devoted to the consideration of the relatively minor issue of deliveries in kind.[2]

The truce was suddenly broken, however, when Henri Chéron, the French Finance Minister, returned without warning to the central issue

---

[1] The full text is to be found in Records of International Conferences, Public Record Office (hereafter abbreviated to I.C.), Cab. 29/111.

[2] In spite of the superficial character of the debate, Graham gave a good account of himself in putting the British case. For the full text, see ibid.

and proceeded to reply to Snowden's speech of 8 August.[1] An even greater shock was in store, for the British Chancellor, clearly nettled both by the timing and content of Chéron's speech, rose to give an immediate and unprepared reply. It was a startling performance, containing echoes of both Palmerston and Beaconsfield. He first attacked Chéron in as undiplomatic a tone as had ever been heard at an international conference, and then went on to threaten in suitably melodramatic fashion the breaking-off of the negotiations and a return to London. His words are worth quoting at some length:

> I am not going to follow M. Chéron on the points he has made, and particularly in the figures he has submitted to the Committee. I will practically confine myself to saying that I do not accept the accuracy of a single figure M. Chéron has put forward. If this were the occasion to go into details on this matter I should refute every one of the constructions M. Chéron has placed upon his figures. It is not true to say that Great Britain did not suffer, in the proposed distribution, under the Young Plan in comparison with the distribution which she received under existing agreements. I hope that the words will not be considered offensive, but M. Chéron's interpretation of the Balfour Note is grotesque and ridiculous to anyone who understands its full character.
>
> It is no good going on arguing day after day in this Committee. . . . I have not come here to spend the rest of my days at The Hague. I want to get back to my own country. . . . The general debate will have to come to a close very soon.[2]

The words 'grotesque and ridiculous' gave particular offence to both the French delegation and domestic opinion in France. Nor did Snowden's tone meet with approval among the German representatives. Julius Curtius, in a conversation with Gustav Stresemann, whom he was soon to succeed as German Foreign Minister, gave it as his opinion that in pre-war days Snowden's language would have led to the immediate rupture of diplomatic relations between Paris and London – an understandable, if perhaps exaggerated, assessment.[3] Hankey, however, sought to convince MacDonald that Snowden's words were not 'in any way

[1] The full text of Chéron's speech is in ibid.
[2] Snowden, *An Autobiography*, II 797. After Snowden had apologised to Chéron, the words 'wholly inaccurate' were substituted for 'grotesque and ridiculous' in the official minutes. See I.C., Cab. 29/111.
[3] Curtius, *Der Young-Plan*, p. 51. Chéron was deeply offended and said of Snowden 'There sits the man who burned Joan of Arc!': Erich Eyck, *A History*

outrageous' but that on translation into French they became 'a perfectly appalling insult'.[1]

In fact Snowden was generally unpopular among the delegates at The Hague at this juncture, and his position was certainly made no easier by the coincidental intervention of MacDonald. After consultation with the international bankers, Montagu Norman and Thomas Lamont, the Prime Minister on 10 August despatched a telegram to his Cabinet colleagues at The Hague in the following terms:

> My information is worsening from all sides: even an adjournment strikes in minds of important people an ominous note. I am relying upon three of you before break occurs to get into touch with me and perhaps we could arrange to meet before any action for adjournment is taken or if you prefer that one of you should meet me in London.[2]

Owing to a blunder by a Treasury clerk the telegram was sent to The Hague *en clair*, and its gist soon became common knowledge among all the delegations. After prompting by Snowden, the Prime Minister sent a further telegram giving full support to the stand taken by the British delegation.[3] But as this telegram was almost immediately issued to the Press and had clearly been extracted from MacDonald, it cannot at first have carried as much weight with other delegates as the original spontaneous and secret communication. For example, on 13 August Philippe Berthelot, Secretary-General of the Quai d'Orsay, told the Germans that the French delegation believed that Snowden had received a letter

---

of the Weimar Republic, 2 vols (Cambridge, Mass., 1962–4) II 206. Snowden also attacked Alberto Pirelli, one of the Italian delegates, who, he alleged, had gone back on a promise made in London not to seek a redistribution in the Spa percentages. Pirelli went white with anger and insisted upon and received a retraction from Snowden: ibid., II 205. Significantly, Snowden made no reference to this particular incident in his autobiography. It is clear that he was carried away with jingoistic fervour during his stay at The Hague. P. J. Grigg, Private Secretary to the Chancellor, recorded how, when the two of them saw a Union Jack, Snowden declared 'I have been a pacifist, I am an internationalist but, somehow or other, whenever I see that flag in a foreign country, I become incredibly imperialist': Grigg, *Prejudice and Judgment*, p. 229.

[1] Hankey to MacDonald, 11 Aug 1929, C.R.F., Cab. 21/317. Vansittart also claimed in his memoirs that he 'suggested the words did not mean the same in English as in French'. He added, however, that 'people will swallow anything if they want to, even an affront': Vansittart, *The Mist Procession*, p. 378.

[2] MacDonald to Snowden; text in Snowden, *An Autobiography*, II 799.

[3] Ibid., II 801.

urging caution.[1] By the 15th, however, the French Minister of Labour, Louis Loucheur, was telling the State Secretary in the German Foreign Ministry, Carl von Schubert, that he 'had asked himself repeatedly whether Snowden was bluffing and had now come to the conclusion that unfortunately he was not'.[2] Then on the 16th Aristide Briand, the French Premier and Foreign Minister, told Stresemann that 'the French delegation knows for certain that Snowden has prevented MacDonald coming to The Hague and that he has even threatened resignation in the event of MacDonald coming'.[3]

MacDonald was meanwhile facing conflicting pressures. The American bankers, eager to see the Young Plan accepted, urged him in the direction of concession, while the bulk of the national Press was strongly supporting Snowden. At the same time, at least one Cabinet Minister was feeling uneasy, as a passage from Beatrice Webb's diary for 13 August illustrates:

> Gentle-natured Parmoor [the Lord President of the Council] motored all the way here to relieve his mind of anxiety about Snowden's pugnacious defence of his country's coffers – which would, so P. thought, endanger the pacification of Europe and good relations with U.S.A. He had even written to J. R. M. [MacDonald] that such an attitude might mean his resignation. Snowden was playing up to the vulgar international individualism of Chamberlain, the Jingo Press, and the City – with the object of superseding J. R. M.[4]

Cecil was also unhappy, as he made clear to Noel-Baker:

> I fear the Hague proceedings, however justified, will not help. The Young proposals may be quite unjust and indefensible. But their failure means the rejection of the advice of an international body and so far is a set-back to internationalism. It is ominous that Snowden has no warmer supporters than the English Die-hards.[5]

---

[1] Hague Delegation to Foreign Ministry, 13 Aug 1929, G.F.M.R., 3375/D 733045.   [2] Schubert to Ministry, 15 Aug 1929, G.F.M.R., 3375/D 733081.
[3] Memorandum of Briand–Stresemann conversation, 16 Aug 1929, G.F.M.R., 4498/E 107863–70. The German ambassador in London had earlier reported that MacDonald was being urged by Norman to go to The Hague in person: Sthamer to Ministry, 10 Aug. 1929, G.F.M.R., 3375/D 733022.
[4] Cole (ed.), *Beatrice Webb's Diaries, 1924–1932*, p. 214. Of course nothing succeeds like success. By the end of August Parmoor was saying that 'it would be superfluous to attempt to express the extent to which Mr Snowden had won the nation's gratitude': *Daily Herald*, 29 Aug 1929.
[5] Cecil to Noel-Baker, 16 Aug 1929, Cecil Papers, Add. 51107.

MacDonald's position, then, was fraught with difficulties, and it is not perhaps surprising that he should have maintained a prolonged period of silence after undergoing the humiliation of having to despatch two contradictory telegrams. This approach, however, had the disadvantage of encouraging rumours and counter-rumours about his supposed attitude.

At The Hague the principal delegates met again on 11 August and agreed to adjourn the formal session of the Financial Committee pending conversations among a number of representative experts. But although many protracted discussions were held, the British expert, Sir Frederick Leith-Ross, was unable to reach agreement with his colleagues. This is understandable, since, according to Leith-Ross, the representatives of France, Italy and Belgium manifested an astonishing lack of diplomatic finesse:

> . . . I received a message asking me to see all these three experts together. . . . Quesnay, acting as spokesman, said that Mr Snowden's attempt to alter the Young Plan was inadmissible and that he must ask me to persuade him to abandon his objections and accept the Plan: otherwise the French Government would feel it necessary to convert all sterling held in London by the Banque de France into gold and transfer it to Paris. I knew that at the time the French assets in London were estimated to amount to something like £240 million and that . . . the French could easily demand gold to an extent which would force us off the gold standard: but I also felt sure that any threat of such action was in the nature of political bluff as the Banque de France would certainly not want to see the collapse of sterling. . . .
>
> Quesnay's demand left me speechless. Without saying a word, I got up . . . to summon a messenger, and when he came I said, 'Kindly show these gentlemen out'. . . . We never heard a word more about the threat to take out the French sterling assets in gold.[1]

On Wednesday, 14 August, Snowden sent what amounted to an ultimatum to the chairman, Jaspar, indicating that some positive proposals would have to emerge by Friday evening.[2] The other creditor powers complied with the letter of Snowden's demand, but their offer

[1] Sir Frederick Leith-Ross, *Money Talks: Fifty Years of International Finance* (London, 1968) p. 124. Leith-Ross's three colleagues were Pierre Quesnay of France, Alberto Pirelli of Italy and Émile Francqui of Belgium.

[2] Cabinet Papers and Memoranda, Public Record Office (hereafter abbreviated to C.P.), no. 238(29) by the British Delegation to the Hague Conference, 31 Aug 1929, Cab. 24/205.

was 'quite unacceptable' and in the view of the British delegation was in some respects 'less satisfactory than the talks between the Experts earlier in the week'.[1]

On Saturday, 17 August, faced with British intransigence, the Latin powers suggested more conversations between experts. That the conference did not break down at this point was perhaps surprising, since Snowden had been threatening to return home and allow a return to the Dawes Plan if serious proposals were not made by the 17th. He and Graham had 'some hesitation' in accepting the new suggestion for keeping the conference going, and only did so on condition that men who had served on the Young Committee should not on this occasion be nominated as experts.[2] It certainly came as no surprise, however, when the changed panel of experts also had to admit failure to agree.

Throughout the week beginning 18 August discussions went on in private and a number of verbal offers were made to Snowden, though none was remotely acceptable.[3] The Latin powers, facing domestic public opinion difficulties, could not bring themselves to alter the broad terms of the Young Plan. Hence concessions to Great Britain clearly had to be made by juggling with such marginal amounts as might be surplus and with the sum Germany had to pay during the transitional phase between the operation of the Dawes Plan and the inauguration of the Young Plan. At first it seemed far from easy to find by these means the £2,400,000 per annum demanded by Great Britain; and such efforts as were made in this direction tended to slacken when it was once again rumoured that the British Cabinet was about to intervene in favour of a compromise or even to hold a meeting in Holland.[4] But when it became clear that Snowden continued to retain his Government's confidence, the negotiations were resumed in earnest.

At this stage, however, even Hankey was beginning to have mixed

[1] Ibid. For further details see also Hankey to MacDonald, 16 Aug 1929, C.R.F., Cab. 21/317.   [2] Snowden, An Autobiography, II 808–9.
[3] For details see C.P., no. 238(29) by the British Delegation to the Hague Conference, 31 Aug 1929, Cab. 24/205.
[4] Such a meeting was indeed suggested to London by the British delegation on 23 Aug, but the Prime Minister rejected this idea. Instead he held a meeting of Cabinet colleagues in London on 24 Aug, as a result of which a telegram was despatched, arguing that 'if a substantial offer, say, 70 to 80 per cent were met, the country would accept it, but leaving the decision in the last resort to the delegation': ibid.

feelings about Snowden's obstinate insistence on making absolutely no concessions. For example, he wrote to the Prime Minister on 23 August:

The Chancellor of the Exchequer is amazing. Never for one moment has he budged from his 100% demand, in public, in meetings with his colleagues, in private or (I ask myself) to himself! He has adopted the trying public rôle of 'bogey man' – so different from his real charming nature. One cannot but admire such fortitude, with all the great politicians in Europe, cajolling, blarneying, threatening. Graham is with him 100%. Henderson . . . [is] stalwartly maintaining the unbroken front . . . but tremendously keen not to break. . . . If you were to ask me what the Chancellor would take, frankly I could not tell you – but I think it would be difficult to refuse 75% of our demand, if we ever got such an offer. . . .

Personally I have always thought in the last resort, before agreeing to a breakdown, we ought to propose an arbitration between the highest offer of the other Creditor Powers and our 100% insistence on the Spa percentages. . . . I believe it would be difficult for anyone to refuse, would give us at least 75% of our demand, would delight all the 'mugwumps' (forgive the term to the reactionary secretary to the C.I.D.). . . . If I were an entirely neutral Secretary General I should propose it myself but I am too good a Britisher![1]

Hankey's plan did not turn out to be needed, for on the night of 27–28 August Snowden at last showed a willingness to make some slight concessions. After prolonged discussion and a series of offers and counter-offers, the British and Latin delegations agreed on a compromise which gave Great Britain around 83 per cent of what she had originally demanded.[2] It is possible to see this outcome as a victory for Henderson, who had consistently deprecated Snowden's totally intransigent attitude. But there is no evidence that Snowden resented the Foreign Secretary's role in the final negotiations, or that he was dissatisfied with the terms of the compromise.[3]

[1] Hankey to MacDonald, 23 Aug 1929, C.R.F., Cab. 21/317.
[2] For details see I.C., Cab. 29/109; and C.P., no. 238(29) by the British Delegation to the Hague Conference, 31 Aug 1929, Cab. 24/205.
[3] At an earlier stage relations between Henderson and Snowden had been somewhat strained. Grigg later wrote: 'Within the British delegation the Foreign Secretary always made it obvious that he disapproved of the obstinate stand we were taking. I remember that the three Ministers – Mr Graham . . . being the third – used to have diminutive Cabinet meetings every day in the presence of Sir Maurice Hankey. Graham always supported the Chancellor for whom he then had a great affection and admiration. One evening, at the height of the

Germany was the principal source of Great Britain's gains, since she was called upon to sacrifice the surplus arising from the transition between the operation of the Dawes Plan and the Young Plan. Her delegates at The Hague agreed with much reluctance to the proposed arrangement at around 2 a.m. on 28 August. They decided that the amount involved was too trivial to risk the complete collapse of the conference, from which Germany had infinitely more to lose than any other power. Even Hjalmar Schacht, the head of the German Reichsbank, having previously shown signs of moving towards the Nationalist position on the reparations issue, felt unable to jeopardise a Rhineland agreement by urging intransigence at this juncture. As he himself wryly commented, 'in the last analysis it was not of decisive importance whether it was 40 billions [marks] or 40.4 billions we would be unable to pay'.[1]

The outcome in financial terms for Great Britain may best be summarised in the words of the *Survey of International Affairs*:

> If we examine the results of the Conference, it would seem that Great Britain obtained: (i) £2,000,000 out of the £2,400,000 increase claimed by her in the total annual payments; (ii) the equivalent of £4,550,000 out of the annual increase of £6,000,000 claimed for the British Empire in the unconditional annuity; and (iii) the return to the conditions laid down in the Dawes Plan . . . with regard to deliveries in kind and the reversal of the new conditions proposed by the Young Plan, although the period of ten years during which such deliveries were to be continued in diminishing amounts was retained.[2]

---

deadlock, Henderson said, hoping to make some dint in Snowden's obstinacy: "Well Philip! you and Willie seem to pay no attention to my views; I might as well go home." But he got entirely the wrong reaction. "That's about it, Arthur!"': Grigg, *Prejudice and Judgment*, pp. 228–9. Dalton, who was not at The Hague, referred to Graham's role in his diary: 'Graham has been particularly weak in the joint conclaves with P.S. [Snowden]. Sitting silently nearly all the time, though voting with P.S. inside and agreeing with Uncle [Henderson] outside that he was pushing things dangerously far': Dalton Diary, entry for 31 Aug 1929. It is not quite clear whether Snowden or Henderson took the leading role in the final negotiations. Henderson's biographer implied that her subject virtually superseded Snowden, while the latter's account suggested that he remained in charge throughout: Hamilton, *Arthur Henderson*, p. 317; Snowden, *An Autobiography*, II 819–21.

[1] Hjalmar Schacht, *The End of Reparations* (New York, 1931) p. 100.

[2] Arnold J. Toynbee et al., *Survey of International Affairs, 1930* (London, 1931) p. 507.

Throughout the period of the deliberations of the Financial Committee, negotiations were continuing simultaneously on the Political Committee. The work of the latter was accorded none of the publicity given to the former, partly because much of it was done in the privacy of Henderson's hotel in Scheveningen and partly because of the absence of any dramatic posturing comparable to that of Snowden. Nevertheless, the overriding question at issue, that of the Rhineland, was of supreme importance and was by no means easily settled. For Stresemann it was the cornerstone of his policy that he should secure the withdrawal of all occupation forces from German soil well in advance of 1935, the date provided for in the Versailles Treaty. It had been his ultimate goal throughout the difficult fulfilment years; and he had certainly suffered too much at the hands of his Nationalist critics to contemplate returning to Berlin without this long-awaited prize. He therefore made it clear from the outset that complete evacuation was a *sine qua non* for Germany's acceptance of the Young Plan, even though the latter was undoubtedly an improvement on the Dawes Plan.[1] The inference was plain: if Stresemann's irreducible minimum was turned down, Germany would return to the 1923 policy of default and non-collaboration – a desperate threat which carried just sufficient conviction seriously to alarm Briand.

Ever since the Thoiry meeting of 1926, Briand had appeared to be torn between a genuine desire to meet Stresemann's wishes and an understandable concern for political self-preservation.[2] In seeking to satisfy both Germany and his own domestic opinion, he had accordingly resorted to procrastinating tactics. Now, in 1929, with Henderson adopting a strong pro-German stand and the ailing Stresemann at breaking point, he cast around for a face-saving formula. This at first took the form of demanding, in return for the evacuation of the Rhineland, the establishment there of a permanent Committee of Verification and Conciliation. Stresemann, however, was adamantly opposed to this scheme and had

[1] Ludwig Zimmermann, *Deutsche Aussenpolitik in der Ära der Weimarer Republik* (Göttingen, 1958) pp. 378–9. See also Henderson to Lindsay, telegram no. 65, 30 Aug 1929, Foreign Office Confidential Prints and General Correspondence, Public Record Office (hereafter abbreviated to F.O.), 408/54.
[2] For details of Briand's attitude towards the evacuation of the Rhineland, see Arnold J. Toynbee, *Survey of International Affairs, 1927* (London, 1929) pp. 109–14, and Toynbee *et al.*, *Survey of International Affairs, 1929*, pp. 167–80.

told the Reichstag on 24 June that rather than agree to any curtailment of Germany's sovereignty in the Rhineland after 1935 he would allow the Young Plan negotiations to collapse.[1] On the Political Committee at The Hague Briand had no better luck with his proposal, but he managed to have it referred to a Committee of Jurists representing each major delegation. Hence when, as had been expected, this committee's report, issued on 19 August, turned out to be unfavourable to the French plan, he was presented with a golden bridge along which to retreat – ostensibly he was bowing to the judgement of international lawyers rather than to German intransigence.[2]

Yet Briand had still not agreed even in principle to an early withdrawal of all French occupation forces. If Stresemann made his acceptance of the financial arrangement dependent on an evacuation plan, the French were determined to insist on the reverse.[3] Hence practically nothing of a decisive nature was achieved by the Political Committee until the Financial Committee had reached a provisional agreement. Briand would go no further than hint at the possibility of the evacuation of a part of the two zones still under occupation – an offer indignantly rejected by the Germans. Briand's equivocating performance now brought Stresemann to 'the verge of despair' and caused even Henderson 'to lose his patience'.[4] Stresemann, generally regarded as a dying man, was driven to sending to Briand on 19 August a letter containing a desperate personal appeal.[5] But in a subsequent meeting between Briand and Stresemann on the same day the former refused to yield, claiming that domestic opinion prevented him from doing so.[6]

In these circumstances Henderson put his influence behind Stresemann. Having begun by insisting that an isolated British withdrawal of her occupation forces was out of the question, he next tried the opposite

---

[1] Toynbee *et al.*, *Survey of International Affairs, 1929*, p. 180. Stresemann took a similar attitude at The Hague, even though on this point Henderson's initial reaction was no better than 'hesitant': Hermann Pünder to Foreign Ministry, 13 Aug 1929, G.F.M.R., 3375/D 733063–5.

[2] The text of the report is in G.F.M.R., 4498/E 108026–7.

[3] See the speeches of Briand and Stresemann to the Political Committee on 12 Aug 1929. The texts are in I.C., Cab. 29/115.

[4] Zimmermann, *Deutsche Aussenpolitik*, p. 379.

[5] Ibid., pp. 379–80. See also Paul Schmidt, *Statist auf diplomatischer Bühne, 1923–1945* (Bonn, 1949) p. 180.

[6] Memorandum of Briand–Stresemann conversation, 19 Aug 1929, G.F.M.R., 3375/D 734950–7.

stratagem of announcing that it was the intention of the British Government to begin the withdrawal of troops on 15 September whether or not a financial settlement was reached at The Hague.[1] Briand's dilemma was painful, since his recently reconstructed Government relied more heavily than hitherto on the forces of the French Right wing. Moreover, as he told the Germans, the French General Staff were against any hasty ('Hals über Kopf') evacuation. He later confided the information that his military advisers opposed any commitment to a final withdrawal from the Strasbourg area prior to the completion of the Maginot fortifications.[2] In the circumstances he was clearly unlikely to come off the fence until the very last minute, since he cannot have been unaware of the fact that the conference might have broken down in the Financial Committee, thereby rendering a decision on the Rhineland unnecessary.

When, however, on 28 August, the Financial Committee reached agreement, Briand was finally cornered. In two days of intense negotiations he, Henderson and Stresemann hammered out the basis of an agreement, which marked a substantial surrender by France. Briand with obvious reluctance named the end of June 1930 as a final date by which all occupation troops would be withdrawn from the Rhineland. In the judgement of a German historian, this represented 'a triumph of goodwill on both sides'.[3] All the same, it appears that the German delegation was still dissatisfied, wanting the final evacuation date considerably advanced. A meeting in Henderson's room at the Grand Hotel, Scheveningen, went on until the early hours of 29 August, but none of the German delegates could wring any further concession from Briand and indeed were compelled to accept additional liabilities of 30 million Reichsmarks as a contribution to the cost of the prolonged period of occupation for which the Young Plan made no provision. Nevertheless, despite German complaints, Briand, constantly muttering 'J'ai mes généraux', had clearly made the larger sacrifice.[4]

[1] Henderson to Lindsay, telegram no. 65, 30 Aug 1929, F.O., 408/54.
[2] Pünder to Foreign Ministry, 9 and 11 Aug 1929, G.F.M.R., 3375/D 733001 and 733029.　　　　　　　[3] Zimmermann, *Deutsche Aussenpolitik*, p. 380.
[4] Curtius's tear-jerking account (*Sechs Jahre Minister der Deutschen Republik* (Heidelberg, 1948) p. 90) was rather less than fair to the French delegates, whose conciliatory conduct was far ahead of the bulk of their compatriots. According to Curtius, a supposedly despairing Stresemann clutched his heart at 1.30 a.m. and cried out 'Ich kann nicht mehr'. But Curtius took no account of the difficulties Briand had to face in justifying his actions to the French Chamber of

The Political Committee issued its report on 29 August and a series of agreements between Germany and the three occupying powers was made on the 29th and 30th.[1] They were all dependent upon the whole of the Hague agreements – financial as well as political – being ratified by the French and German Parliaments. The most important element in the Political Committee's report was the time-table for the evacuation of the Rhineland:

> In the course of the proceedings . . . at The Hague the three Occupy-ing Powers have agreed to begin the evacuation of the Rhineland during the month of September on the conditions laid down in the attached notes. The withdrawal of the Belgian and British forces will be completed within three months of the date on which the operation of evacuation begins. The French forces will evacuate the Second Zone within the same period. The evacuation of the Third Zone by the French troops will begin immediately after the Young Plan is ratified by the German and French Parliaments and put into opera-tion. It will proceed without interruption as rapidly as physical con-ditions permit and in any case will be completed at the latest in a period of eight months terminating not later than the end of June 1930.[2]

The Hague Conference was now brought to a close, on 31 August, with-out all the necessary details of the operation of the Young Plan or of the Bank for International Settlements having been finalised. These were left over for subsequent negotiation and for a further conference, which eventually met in January 1930 after a longer delay than had been expected.

Snowden was accorded a hero's welcome on his arrival in London. The Right-wing Press applauded him; he was presented with the Free-dom of the City; and King George V invited him to Sandringham as a mark of his gratitude. The Conservative and Liberal parties joined in the tumultuous reception accorded to the returning Chancellor. In fact Snowden's only serious critics came from within the ranks of his own party and from within the Foreign Office, some deploring his insistence on 'fair play' for Great Britain as 'jingoistic', others regretting the

---

Deputies. For this see Arnold Wolfers, *Britain and France between Two Wars: Conflicting Strategies of Peace since Versailles* (New York, 1940) p. 82.

[1] The texts of all these agreements were published in Cmd. 3417 of 1929–30.

[2] Toynbee *et al.*, *Survey of International Affairs, 1929*, p. 183.

undiplomatic tone in which he had presented the British case.[1] The foremost public critic of Snowden was H. N. Brailsford, who, writing in the *New Leader*, the I.L.P. weekly newspaper, accepted the French argument that since France had suffered the most actual devastation in the war she was entitled to a larger share of reparations now that the total volume available was being reduced. Brailsford, in common with Norman Angell, also argued that the pacification of Europe should not have been endangered for a mere £2 million per annum.[2] The weakness of these arguments was that they took no account of the vulnerability of a minority Labour administration. With the Liberals strongly opposed to capitulation on the issue of the Spa percentages, and with the Labour Party's reputation in the country as the least 'patriotic' of the major parties, it would probably have meant political suicide if the Labour Government had listened to the counsels of the I.L.P. The criticism of Snowden's undiplomatic behaviour has indeed more substance, but it is arguable that he pushed the Latin powers into concessions in a way that a more orthodox figure could not have done. Certainly there is no evidence that Dalton was correct when he wrote: 'Probably the whole thing could have been settled amicably in a day or two by a skilled and patient negotiator on the British side. But that is not a good description of Mr Snowden.'[3] Again, it has to be asked whether Dalton was accurate

---

[1] The Foreign Office critics were not confined to the political appointees. For example, Lindsay had told Stamfordham that he viewed 'with the greatest apprehension Mr Snowden's attitude' and thought 'that, if he breaks up the Conference, he will do great harm, not only to the Labour Government but to the interests of peace in the whole world. . . .': Stamfordham memorandum of a conversation with Lindsay, 10 Aug 1929, R.A. GV, M 2229/10. Equally critical was Tyrrell, who told Stamfordham that 'though it was quite right to let France . . . know that we refuse any longer to be bled, we should have done so civilly and in a gentlemanly English manner'. He added, '. . . Snowden went to the Hague bent upon hitting the French, a policy which it is said was strongly advocated to him by Lloyd George!': Stamfordham memorandum of a conversation with Tyrrell, 9 Sep 1929, R.A. GV, M 2232/1.

[2] *New Leader*, 16 Aug 1929. Other I.L.P. newspapers, including the *Northern Voice*, gave support to Snowden. At a meeting of the I.L.P.'s National Administrative Council on 28 Sep, P. J. Dollan was defeated by seven votes to two when he sought to disassociate the I.L.P. from the *New Leader*'s attitude. See Robert E. Dowse, *Left in the Centre: The Independent Labour Party, 1893–1940* (London, 1966) p. 170.

[3] Hugh Dalton, 'British Foreign Policy, 1929–1931', *Political Quarterly*, II (1931) 493.

in asserting that Snowden 'did great and needless harm to Anglo-French relations and much increased the difficulties of our foreign policy'.[1] While it is undoubtedly true that Snowden's tone *might* have led to lasting tension between Paris and London, there is no evidence that this did in fact occur.[2] It has also been argued, especially in Germany, that Snowden's conduct led to an increase in Germany's burdens and hence contributed to the failure of the Weimar Republic.[3] In reality, however, the contribution of Snowden to the rise of National Socialism can be dismissed as marginal in the extreme, for, as has been shown, even so unreliable a figure as Schacht recognised that the slight changes made to mollify Great Britain were of a quite trivial character from the German standpoint.

The outcome of the first Hague Conference can be fairly described as an outstanding success for the Labour Government. While domestic opinion was satisfied that British interests had not been sacrificed, the Labour Party's internationalist idealists could reflect that the evacuation of the Rhineland and a substantial reduction in Germany's reparations burden had been achieved; and both patriots and internationalists could feel satisfaction that the Government had stood up to the Latin powers in a firm and independent manner. Nearly two years later Garvin even felt able to write that 'Mr Arthur Henderson, insisting on the speedy evacuation of the foreign garrisons, accomplished the best single stroke for peace that any Foreign Minister has achieved since the armistice'.[4]

Regarding the long-term implications, it has occasionally been argued that the success of the Labour Government's policy of evacuating the Rhineland was the decisive *military* step leading to the Second World War.[5] Certainly it is arguable that if the occupation forces had remained until 1935, they would have deterred or prevented even a National Socialist Government from embarking upon a rearmament programme

---

[1] Ibid., p. 494. For a similar view see Arthur Salter, *Recovery – The Second Effort* (London, 1932) p. 147.

[2] Ironically, Dalton himself confided to his diary a month afterwards that 'the smell after [The] Hague blew off very quickly': Dalton Diary, entry for 1–25 Sep 1929.

[3] See, for example, Eyck, *Weimar Republic*, II 209.

[4] *The Observer*, 31 May 1931.

[5] For example in Quintin Hogg (sometime Lord Hailsham), *The Left was Never Right* (London, 1945) p. 121.

of dangerous proportions. Yet at the time the Labour Government's policy of seeking to conciliate Germany was widely regarded as enlightened; and few could claim without the benefit of hindsight that German revanchism could be seen in 1929 to have reached unmanageable proportions and that all hope of bringing Germany back into the comity of nations ought by then to have been abandoned. In these circumstances, therefore, the Labour Government's policy of appeasing Berlin, while no doubt risky, had much to commend it and cannot fairly be equated with the attitude towards National Socialist Germany later adopted by the National Government.

CHAPTER THREE *The German Problem from the Death of Stresemann to the Opening of the Customs Union Crisis, 1929–1931*

THE outcome of the first Hague Conference marked a watershed in the history of Weimar Germany. The Hague agreements on reparations and the Rhineland were the greatest achievements of the advocates of the policies of fulfilment and seemed to offer hope that international tensions, and especially the long-standing Franco-German feud, might finally be dying away. The last months of 1929, however, saw a sudden deterioration in the prospects for peace, and indeed it might be argued that at this time the situation ceased to deserve the label 'post-war' and merited instead the appellation 'pre-war'.

On 3 October the first blow came with the not unexpected death of Stresemann. Despite his somewhat devious qualities and his connivance at secret rearmament, he was irreplaceable both as a pillar of moderation at home and as a trusted figure on the international stage.[1] Certainly no other German statesman in the Weimar period came nearer to winning the confidence and trust of France. It is, of course, possible that, had circumstances been more favourable, Curtius might have been able to assume Stresemann's mantle. Circumstances, however, could not have been more unfavourable, as Stresemann's death was followed by the onset of an ever-widening world depression. When the famous Wall Street Crash occurred on 24 October 1929 Germany already had a sizeable unemployment problem – the figure stood at 1.76 million.[2] By

[1] On Stresemann's foreign policy, see Henry L. Bretton, *Stresemann and the Revision of Versailles: A Fight for Reason* (Stanford, Cal., 1953), and Hans W. Gatzke, *Stresemann and the Rearmament of Germany* (Baltimore, 1954). A moving tribute to Stresemann by the British ambassador in Berlin appears in Rumbold to Henderson, telegram no. 693, 3 Oct 1929, F.O., 408/54.

[2] For the Wall Street affair and its repercussions, especially in the United States, see John Kenneth Galbraith, *The Great Crash, 1929* (London, 1955). For a more general treatment see Lionel Robbins, *The Great Depression* (London, 1934).

December the number had increased to 3 million, with every indication of a continuing spiral.

Germany's problem was more acute than that of the other victims of the recession, since she was saddled with a reparations burden which could not be modified to take account of the decline in world trade; and she found herself in the unenviable position of having borrowed vast sums on a short-term basis. With international confidence already severely shaken, the German Government was clearly threatened with impending bankruptcy. In order to avoid such a disaster, orthodox financial experts argued for a policy of retrenchment and an end to deficit financing; and it is difficult to believe that in the prevailing climate of economic opinion any alternative policy would have proved viable. Nevertheless, it presented the Coalition Government of Hermann Müller with almost insuperable problems, principally because the Social Democrats were unable to agree to the cutting down of social security, partly on grounds of general policy, and partly from fear of losing electoral support to the Communists.

The Government's plight was made no easier by the irresponsible actions of Schacht, who appeared to be seeking an excuse to go back on his support for the Young Plan. His opportunity came when the German Government reached liquidation agreements with Great Britain and Poland, thereby accepting the permanent loss of a small amount of sequestered property.[1] The British Chancellor, Snowden, unlike the French and the Belgians, had shown characteristic inflexibility on this point and it is therefore arguable that for the sake of a mere £30,000 he furnished Schacht with an opportunity to sabotage the Weimar Republic. There can be little doubt, however, that Schacht would in any case have found some excuse for moving over towards the Nationalist camp as the depression grew steadily worse. As it was, Schacht made his first move on 6 December when he issued his famous Memorandum claiming that the German Government had ceded more than the Young Committee had envisaged and that he could therefore no longer remain silent. He went on to urge stringent financial retrenchment in the new situation.[2]

[1] For the Anglo-German Liquidation Agreement, see Cmd. 3486 of 1929–30; Snowden in *H.C. Deb.*, ccxxxii, cols 699–703, 21 Nov 1929.
[2] Hjalmar Schacht, *Memorandum zum Youngplan* (Berlin, 1929); Harold Nicolson (Berlin) to Henderson, telegram no. 862, 6 Dec 1929, F.O., 408/54.

The Müller administration attempted to deal with the growing financial crisis and accordingly issued, on 11 December, a fourteen-point programme involving a long-term policy of reducing direct taxation. Next, on 16 December, the Chancellor asked for and received a vote of confidence in the Reichstag by 222 votes to 156. But in the course of his appeal to the Reichstag, Müller was compelled to admit the existence of an immediate deficit crisis. This admission, in conjunction with Schacht's agitation, led to the failure of an attempt by Rudolf Hilferding, the Finance Minister, to secure yet another short-term loan, on this occasion from the American finance house, Dillon, Reed and Co. Moreover, the Reichstag on 19 December passed the so-called 'Lex Schacht', which was designed to put an end to further unsupported borrowing of this kind. Instead, it was decided to set up an internal redemption or sinking fund in order to provide a secure base for governmental borrowing.[1]

This victory for Schacht and other orthodox financiers provoked the resignation of Hilferding.[2] Although he was an acknowledged expert in the theory of finance – he was the author of the famous Socialist treatise entitled *Finanzkapital* – he had little success in putting his theories into practice and had long been disliked by non-Socialist members of the coalition.[3] One of these, Paul Moldenhauer, replaced him as Minister of Finance, thereby reducing the Socialists' share of power. In fact, the tension between the S.P.D. and the moderate bourgeois parties was now visibly growing, and it was clearly only to be a matter of time before the Müller coalition collapsed.

Despite the severity of the world depression and its immediate effects upon the stability of Germany, the relations between the major European powers appeared on the surface to be improving. This impression derived in part from the relative ease with which it proved possible to dispose of the problems left unsettled by the first Hague Conference. When the conference adjourned at the end of August 1929, seven committees were appointed to prepare solutions to some of the outstanding

[1] For the inside story of the 'Lex Schacht', see diary entry for 20 Dec in Hermann Pünder, *Politik in der Reichskanzlei: Aufzeichnungen aus den Jahren 1929–1932* (Stuttgart, 1961) pp. 32–37.

[2] Rumbold to Henderson, telegram no. 904, 23 Dec 1929, F.O., 408/54.

[3] *The Times* (23 Dec 1929) claimed that the cause of Hilferding's fall was 'a lethargy which withheld his theoretical brilliance from practical application to the urgent financial problems of the country'.

issues, and the chairman, Jaspar, was instructed to recall the principal delegates when the various reports were completed. During the last months of 1929 a series of meetings was held in Paris, Berlin and Baden-Baden;[1] and sufficient progress was made to justify Jaspar reconvening the full conference on 3 January 1930 – the so-called second Hague Conference.

The principal British delegates on this occasion were Snowden and Graham, Henderson remaining in London. There were also changes in the German and French delegations. The loss of Stresemann and Hilferding meant that Curtius was now the chief German delegate, accompanied by the new Finance Minister, Moldenhauer. The French delegation was led by the new Prime Minister, André Tardieu, who had a reputation for intransigence. The more flexible Briand, now Foreign Minister, was also present but was in such poor health that he made no significant contribution to the proceedings.

The principal outstanding issues were settled within a fortnight, as usual to the disadvantage of Germany. The question upon which the British delegation took the strongest line related to whether or not Germany was to make the required payments on the 15th or on the last day of each month. Snowden insisted upon the former day, since the difference in the interest rate resulted in some slight increase in the British share. The Germans procrastinated on this minor point as well as on the more substantial question concerning whether or not they were to be entitled to announce a moratorium, and, if so, for how many years. Snowden's response was characteristically blunt. He was reported to have told Moldenhauer: 'You do nothing but talk. It is intolerable. Never have there been plenipotentiaries so lacking in full powers of negotiation.'[2] He then threatened to return to London and gave the Germans the option of a return to the Dawes Plan.[3] With the French finding themselves for once in agreement with Snowden, it was now the turn of the German Press to fulminate against the Chancellor's un-

[1] Perhaps the most important of these meetings was the one at Baden-Baden which led to the setting up of the B.I.S. See Henry H. Schloss, *The Bank for International Settlements: An Experiment in Central Bank Co-operation* (Amsterdam, 1958).

[2] *Candide*, 16 Jan 1930, cited in Andréadès, *Philip Snowden*, p. 73. In the official record of the proceedings the same sentiments are attributed to Snowden, though the language is rather more diplomatic: I.C., Cab. 29/109.

[3] Ibid.

diplomatic tone.[1] In spite of the German displeasure, Snowden's intervention did have a salutary influence on the pace of the proceedings.
First, the German delegation, under protest, accepted the 15th of the
month as payment day. Secondly, agreement was reached on the
moratorium problem, whereby the Special Advisory Committee of the
Bank for International Settlements was to advise on matters 'in regard
to the application of the Plan'. But no actual permanent revision of the
agreements could be carried out under the aegis of the B.I.S. Nor could
the Germans suspend payment in marks without giving twelve months'
notice, or for more than two years altogether.

The question of a possible wilful default raised more difficulties, since
Tardieu wished to retain the right to reoccupy the Rhineland in such
circumstances. Article 430 of the Versailles Treaty had pronounced the
Reparations Commission the only competent body to establish wilful
default – and this was now to be abolished. In the French view the
Special Advisory Committee of the B.I.S. should have been accorded the
same right, but this was unacceptable to Germany. The British delegation supported a compromise solution, eventually accepted by all concerned. This took the form of a declaration by the creditor powers of
their intention to appeal to the Permanent Court of International Justice
for a judgement in the event of alleged wilful default. If the verdict went
against Germany, the allies stated that they would assume full freedom
of action. The Germans reluctantly acknowledged the validity of the
allied position.

Further delay was occasioned by the activities of Schacht, who had
persuaded the Reichsbank, of which he was President, to threaten to
refuse to co-operate with the B.I.S. unless certain political and financial
concessions were made by the creditor powers. The Reichsbank attitude
had been foreshadowed in a letter of 31 December 1929 sent to J. P.
Morgan and Co.[2] Yet despite this letter and Schacht's earlier Memorandum, the German delegation summoned him to The Hague as an
adviser. They affected surprise when Schacht threw his so-called
'bombshell' into the conference on 13 January by indicating that the
Reichsbank would not have dealings with the B.I.S. The creditor

[1] See Andréadès, *Philip Snowden*, p. 73 n.
[2] Part of the letter appears in K. R. Bopp, *Hjalmar Schacht: Central Banker*
(Columbia, Mo., 1939) pp. 55–6. For details of the concessions demanded in
January, see Peterson, *Hjalmar Schacht*, p. 95.

powers, especially France, adopted a similarly astonished tone and insisted that the German delegation give a promise that legislation would be passed compelling the Reichsbank to co-operate. For once the German statesmen were happy to fall in with the allies' wishes, for they were at last able to repudiate Schacht. The latter, for his part, seemed no less pleased, since he now had a tenable case for resigning. This he duly did in March 1930.[1] He had successfully manœuvred his departure from the sinking ship of the Weimar Republic. 'There can . . . be no doubt', telegraphed Rumbold, 'that he regards himself as destined to play a considerable role in politics in the future, and his resignation has been timed so as to allow him to appear as the leader of those who believe that the Young Plan imposes an impossible burden on Germany.'[2]

Schacht's Memorandum and the Hilferding resignation had alarmed the French considerably, and they were consequently eager at the Hague Conference to take steps to prevent Germany raising further unsupported foreign loans. Snowden resisted any attempt to place binding treaty obligations upon the Germans, but engineered instead a so-called 'Gentleman's Agreement', whereby the Germans agreed not to raise foreign loans on the strength of revenues already assigned to reparations, nor to take any steps at all in the direction of foreign loans until the first issue of Young Plan bonds had been floated and the B.I.S. consulted.

The only other important business to be dealt with at The Hague concerned non-German reparations. In spite of his occasional use of threatening language, Snowden, on the whole, used his influence on the side of the debtor powers. As a result, Bulgaria's liabilities were substantially reduced, while Austria was excused all further payments.[3]

As the delegates joined together on 20 January for the final ceremonies at The Hague, they doubtless felt that a great act of pacification had taken place and that the reparations problem had been 'solved', at least for a number of years.[4] But their work was largely in vain, for the tides of the financial crisis were soon to sweep aside the whole edifice of the Young Plan and much else besides.

[1] His letter of resignation appears in Bopp, *Hjalmar Schacht*, p. 57.

[2] Rumbold to Henderson, telegram no. 175, F.O., 408/55.

[3] For details of this and other aspects of the Hague Agreement, see Cmd. 3598 of 1929–30.

[4] Even the Germans were pleased. See Pünder, *Politik in der Reichskanzlei*, p. 39. For a hopeful British view, see *New Statesman*, 25 Jan 1930. For further details of the negotiations at the second Hague Conference, see I.C., Cab. 29/109.

The successful outcome of the Hague Conference had no immediately apparent ameliorative effect on the unstable situation in Germany, where the Müller coalition was visibly crumbling, although it had managed to secure the ratification of the Young Plan and the more contentious liquidation agreements. With unemployment figures up to $3\frac{1}{2}$ million, the various social security funds, and especially that for unemployment benefit, were in parlous condition. As was to be the case in Great Britain in 1931, the Socialists were unable to unite on a policy of cutting down expenditure on the social services and hence they felt compelled to go into opposition. The leading S.P.D. figures actually in office were prepared to agree to a compromise put forward by Heinrich Brüning of the Centre Party, but were overruled by their party. Unlike MacDonald in 1931, they loyally accepted the majority verdict,[1] thereby forcing the resignation of the Müller Government on 27 March. The unemployment fund crisis in Germany thus resulted in the collapse of the only viable majority coalition and its inevitable replacement by a minority administration. Paradoxically, a similar crisis in Great Britain a year later had exactly the opposite consequence – except, needless to say, for the unemployed, whose benefits were cut in both cases.

On 1 April Brüning of the Centre Party was appointed Chancellor in succession to Müller. He made it clear that he was prepared to rule without a Reichstag majority and to rely where necessary on Article 48 of the Constitution, at least on a temporary basis. With the support of President Paul von Hindenburg and the Army, his prospects of continuing in office were at the outset by no means negligible.[2]

From the point of view of most foreign observers, Brüning's administration appeared to represent the best available hope for the development of European reconciliation. Curtius was to continue as Foreign Minister and accordingly no basic deviations from the Stresemann pattern were anticipated. That this expectation was to be proved in some respects unsound in no way invalidates the argument that there was no superior alternative to the Brüning Government from the point of view of those who sought pacification on the international scene.

[1] See Pünder, *Politik in der Reichskanzlei*, pp. 45–6, and K. D. Bracher, *Die Auflösung der Weimarer Republik: eine Studie zum Problem des Machtverfalls in der Demokratie*, 2nd ed. (Stuttgart and Düsseldorf, 1957) pp. 296–303.

[2] On the support of the Army for Brüning, see J. W. Wheeler-Bennett, *The Nemesis of Power: The German Army in Politics, 1918–1945* (London, 1953) pp. 201, 204.

In the new circumstances, Henderson's policy was to be one of giving more or less equal support to Briand and Brüning in order to try to maintain both in power. In thus acting as honest broker he may have been attempting the impossible, and certainly it is difficult to escape the conclusion that even such moderate figures as Briand and Brüning held fundamentally incompatible positions which no amount of goodwill could reconcile. Honest brokerage takes two forms – either strictly impartial support for the superior legal or moral case, or support for whichever party is in the greatest need of assistance vis-à-vis its own extremists. Henderson wavered between the two and not infrequently found himself in a rather impotent position as events simply took their course. This, however, was not invariably the case. In the spring of 1930, for example, Henderson intervened strongly on the side of Germany on the issue of Rhineland evacuation. Hearing rumours that the French might use technical and legalistic arguments – a 'frivolous pretext' as Rumbold put it[1] – to delay their departure from the final zone of occupation, the Foreign Secretary made strong representations through the Paris Embassy and also in a personal meeting with Briand to the effect that any delay would have 'unfortunate and dangerous consequences' to the interests of 'international appeasement'.[2] Whether or not the French had originally toyed with the idea of postponing the evacuation, Henderson's action put the matter beyond doubt and the last occupation forces accordingly left German territory on 30 June 1930.

Yet the evacuation of the Rhineland did little to improve the situation, for while the German reaction was one of relief it did not amount to one of gratitude to the French. Even the German moderates refrained from praising Briand and instead began at once to advance further points in the revisionist programme, concentrating at first on the Saar.[3] The French looked at the evacuation through different eyes and affected to find German ingratitude incomprehensible.[4]

At this critical juncture Brüning decided to dissolve the Reichstag and to hold new elections. Whether or not such a course was unavoidable

---

[1] E. L. Woodward and Rohan Butler (eds.), *Documents on British Foreign Policy, 1919–1939* (hereafter abbreviated to *B.D.*), 2nd series (London, 1946 ff.), I, no. 303 (Rumbold to Henderson, 2 May 1930).

[2] *B.D.*, 2/1, no. 301 (Henderson to Tyrrell, 28 Apr 1930) and no. 304, n. 2.

[3] On the German Press reaction to the withdrawal of the occupation forces, see *B.D.*, 2/1, no. 307 (Rumbold to Henderson, 3 July 1931).

[4] *B.D.*, 2/1, no. 313 (Campbell to Henderson, 13 Aug 1930).

is open to dispute;[1] what is abundantly clear is that the decision led to a series of consequences that permanently estranged the Quai d'Orsay. The election campaign from 18 June to 14 September created an extremely unfortunate impression, irrespective of the outcome. All the major parties openly demanded further revision of Versailles, the major differences being about method rather than objectives. In competing for popular support, none of the parties felt able to speak warmly about French moderation or of a continuation of close collaboration with Paris.[2] Naturally these omissions on the part of even the most responsible figures created much ill-feeling and suspicion in French circles. Especially disturbing were the remarks of Gottfried Treviranus, the Minister for Occupied Areas, on the Polish border issue.[3] Next came the great shock of the actual results of the election. The National Socialists increased their support from 12 deputies to 107, obtaining in all 6 million votes; the Communists also gained 23 seats.[4] But although the Brüning administration found itself with even less support than before in the Reichstag, there was no immediate change of government. This did not mean, however, that there was no change in German foreign policy. On the contrary, the Foreign Minister, who at the time was in Geneva attending the League of Nations Assembly, was instructed to take a stiffer line and avoid all mention of a 'policy of understanding'.[5]

[1] Pünder, *Politik in der Reichskanzlei*, p. 57, was convinced of the need to dissolve. G. A. Craig, *From Bismarck to Adenauer: Aspects of German Statecraft* (Baltimore, 1958) p. 86, takes the opposite view.

[2] *B.D.*, 2/1, no. 308 (Rumbold to Henderson, 3 July 1930).

[3] *B.D.*, 2/1, no. 312 (Rumbold to Henderson, 12 Aug 1930).

[4] For the British ambassador's considered reaction to the results, see Rumbold to Henderson, telegram no. 777, 18 Sep 1930, F.O., 408/56. His verdict on the National Socialists was somewhat complacent: 'It would be a mistake to take the National Socialist programme too seriously or even to judge the party too closely by it. . . . Many items in the programme are, indeed, so absurd that they must be revised now that the party has gained such unexpected strength and a disconcerting measure of responsibility. Their programme shows vigour and disrespect. . . . In fact, the National Socialist success may be regarded to a considerable extent as the revolt of impertinent youth against impudent old men . . ., who sit stuffily entrenched in the immutable lists of the older political parties. . . . When one thinks of some of these unhealthy and quarrelsome older politicians, one must confess to an understanding of this spirit of revolt.'

[5] There is some doubt as to why Mgr Ludwig Kaas went to Geneva and whether he had any influence on Curtius. On this, see Edward W. Bennett, *Germany and the Diplomacy of the Financial Crisis, 1931* (Cambridge, Mass., 1962) p. 13, and Curtius, *Sechs Jahre Minister der Deutschen Republik*, pp. 171–2.

C

It has been claimed that Brüning's principal fault in foreign affairs was that he was too inclined to support action simply for its own sake.[1] While this may be correct, it is apparent that this tendency only developed *after* the disastrous dissolution of the Reichstag in June 1930. In practice, of course, Brüning's 'forward policies' were to fail and prove self-defeating. Yet domestic pressures upon him were such that it is difficult to see what alternative he had other than to try even in the face of all the odds to bring off some spectacular success in the foreign context. It has also been argued with considerable ingenuity that Brüning deliberately set out to increase international tension as a means of so exacerbating Germany's financial situation that the creditor powers would be forced to abandon reparations.[2] It seems more probable, however, that, unlike Hitler, Brüning and his colleagues were the somewhat short-sighted pragmatists and improvisers they would have claimed to be.

Whatever the exact motives Brüning may have had, the last months of 1930 saw a marked change of emphasis in German foreign policy. The Western powers were bombarded with a stream of complaints, one revisionist claim after another being brought forward with apparently little consideration for the effect on relations with France. To this attitude Henderson gave no encouragement, as is clear from the following lines written to Rumbold:

> As for our own role in existing circumstances, it is quite clear. We shall continue to exert all our influence in Paris to strengthen the hand of those statesmen such as Briand who are in my belief sincerely desirous of pursuing a policy of pacification, but Germany must be made to realise that there are limits to the extent of our influence and that without the wholehearted co-operation of her leaders of opinion we cannot be held responsible for a hardening of French opinion against her. What this would mean in terms of loss and disadvantage to Germany I need not emphasise.
>
> The consequences would be far-reaching indeed and not such as I care to contemplate.[3]

Characteristic of the new turn in German policy were the remarks of the Minister of the Interior, Joseph Wirth, in connection with the newly-evacuated Rhineland. Rumbold informed London that Wirth had been

---

[1] Craig, *From Bismarck to Adenauer*, pp. 84–5.

[2] Wolfgang J. Helbich, 'Between Stresemann and Hitler: The Foreign Policy of the Brüning Government', *World Politics*, XII (1959–60) 24–44.

[3] Henderson to Rumbold, 11 Nov 1930, Henderson Papers, F.O. 800/282.

reported as saying that 'the Rhineland was not really free owing to its being subject to certain servitudes'[1] – meaning the permanent demilitarisation provision in the Versailles Treaty. This and other reports made a considerable impression on the British Foreign Office, for in the words of a permanent official, Orme Sargent, 'the question affects us indirectly moreover since "undemilitarisation" would cut at the roots of Locarno'.[2]

More German complaints arose over the work of the Preparatory Commission on Disarmament. Berlin urged a meeting of the full General Disarmament Conference before the end of 1931 and refused to be deflected from this demand in spite of Henderson's argument that full preparations were a prerequisite for success. Curtius claimed that 'it was intolerable that the nations all round Germany should be increasing their armaments whilst Germany herself remained disarmed'.[3] The Germans' attitude was such that they seem to have been less concerned with achieving a *successful* Disarmament Conference than with providing for themselves an excuse for rearming beyond the Versailles limit. With perhaps more justification, they also showed great resentment at the Preparatory Commission's rejection of a German amendment on the subject of trained reserves.[4]

Clearly the French were determined to retain certain advantages over Germany even if an agreement was reached on the limitation and reduction of land armaments. The British attitude at this time was to try to wear down French obstinacy and persuade them to accept at least some measure of arms control. In this realistic effort no assistance was forthcoming from the Brüning Government, which insisted on equality of status to a wholly impossible degree. No nation at Geneva was prepared to encourage such an approach, and it is not therefore surprising that a British observer was to conclude that 'the general attitude of Germans towards the Commission continues to be half mistrustful, half defiant'.[5]

The German attitude towards disarmament and towards revisionism in general, however, caused more irritation than alarm in the later months of 1930. The same could not be said of Germany's persistent attempts to suspend or even terminate the payment of reparations, since

[1] Cited in *B.D.*, 2/1, no. 327 (Sargent to Rumbold, 14 Oct 1930).
[2] Ibid.   [3] *B.D.*, 2/1, no. 331 (Rumbold to Henderson, 27 Oct 1930).
[4] *B.D.*, 2/1, no. 337 (Basil Newton (Berlin) to Henderson, 17 Nov 1930). See also below, pp. 95–6.
[5] *B.D.*, 2/1, no. 337 (Newton to Henderson, 17 Nov 1930).

moves to this end threatened to bring about a deepening of the already serious international financial crisis. The success of the extremists in the September elections had led in any case to a considerable loss of confidence on the part of foreign investors in Germany. But even worse in its implications was an irresponsible speech on 16 October by Brüning, who hinted at the possibility of a moratorium on the Young Plan payments.[1]

The French reaction was entirely and predictably hostile. The British, to whom the Germans looked with some hope, adopted a more friendly tone, but Henderson made it clear that he disapproved of any immediate move to declare a payments moratorium even though there had been 'a catastrophic fall in world prices, which has had the effect of increasing the real burden of all gold obligations, including the reparation liabilities of Germany, and which has accordingly diminished the value of the concessions embodied in the Young plan'. Henderson went on to argue that Great Britain did not think that these facts constituted 'any justification either for a suspension of transfers or for any revision of the Young Plan'.[2] He pointed out that, contrary to the German view, the Special Advisory Committee of the B.I.S., even if all its members were in agreement, had no power under the terms of the Hague Agreement to recommend any revision in the Young Plan. His conclusion was:

> While, therefore, the declaration of a moratorium or a request for the convening of the Special Advisory Committee seems most unlikely to result in any alleviation of the burdens on Germany, the dangers to Germany of any such action are exceedingly grave. Such dangers are both financial and political. . . .
>
> The net result would be to inflame nationalist and chauvinist feelings throughout Europe with ultimate consequences on the political and economic situation which would involve direct and indirect losses both to Germany and to other countries far greater than any advantages which the German Government could hope to obtain from the action which they had set on foot.

He told the Germans firmly that if they did call for a moratorium 'they must expect no support or help from this country in the inevitable difficulties which they will bring upon themselves'.[3]

---

[1] For details of this speech, see Bennett, *Germany and the Diplomacy of the Financial Crisis*, pp. 20–1. The withdrawals at this time amounted to around one-third of the total; for a detailed discussion, see ibid., pp. 16–17.

[2] *B.D.*, 2/1, no. 338 (Henderson to Rumbold, 2 Dec 1930).   [3] Ibid.

One writer has claimed that this warning from Henderson amounted to a *démarche*, and that 'Whatever may be said of later British foreign secretaries . . . it cannot be claimed that he failed to take up the cudgels against revisionism'.[1] It is equally arguable that Henderson was passing no judgement on the desirability or otherwise of revisionism but was rather pointing out to the Germans how the calling of the Special Advisory Committee would at that time have had detrimental rather than salutary effects. It was significant that by the New Year Henderson's views were being echoed by no less a figure than Hermann Pünder, State Secretary in the Chancellery.[2] It is thus possible that Henderson's advice may have played an important part in deterring the Germans from adopting an ill-considered course.[3]

Having recognised that the machinery provided by the Young Plan was unlikely to lead to any alleviation in their burden, the Germans turned next to the idea of an international conference independent of the Young Plan terms. Encouraged by Frederic Sackett, the American ambassador in Berlin, Brüning attempted, in the first months of 1931, to persuade President Herbert Hoover to call a World Economic Conference to discuss the depression, war debts and reparations. It came as no surprise, however, when these overtures met with negative and discouraging reactions from the Western democracies. The attitude of the French was predictably that they would only consider assisting Germany in return for the abandonment of revisionist objectives – a totally unacceptable condition for Berlin; Hoover was polite but unhelpful; and the British response was also cool, Henderson taking the view that it was 'clearly premature for His Majesty's Government to associate themselves with any attempt to press for such a conference'.[4]

In spite of the uncertainty created by these desperate manœuvres on the part of Brüning, Germany's financial position became less acute in the early months of 1931. International financiers had gradually recovered from the shock of the 1930 elections and drew encouragement from the withdrawal of the Nationalists and the National Socialists from

[1] Bennett, *Germany and the Diplomacy of the Financial Crisis*, p. 29.
[2] Ibid., p. 36. For evidence that Curtius had been similarly convinced, see *B.D.*, 2/1, no. 353 (Rumbold to Henderson, 4 Mar 1931).
[3] Henderson had no such opportunity to counsel prudence with regard to the later Customs Union affair, since no preliminary soundings were taken.
[4] *B.D.*, 2/1, no. 350 (Henderson to Rumbold, 19 Feb 1931).

the Reichstag.[1] Moreover, in spite of coolness on certain issues, Brüning was assured of the general goodwill of the British. As Henderson put it:

The fall of the Brüning Government in the present period of political and economic strain might easily have far-reaching detrimental effects on international relationships. If, therefore, there is a real danger of its not being able to weather the storm to which it is likely to be exposed in the near future, it ought, I consider, to be the policy of His Majesty's Government to give it such support and encouragement as they properly can, in order to fortify its position.[2]

Rumbold was an even more enthusiastic supporter of Brüning than his chief, and it is therefore not surprising to discover that the proposal for a visit by the German Chancellor to Chequers originated in the British Embassy in Berlin.[3] Henderson issued an invitation to Brüning and Curtius through Konstantin von Neurath, the German ambassador in London, the principal objectives being to reassure Brüning of British sympathy and to settle some outstanding aspects of the disarmament issue. Henderson was not to know that when the visit eventually took place the financial plight of Germany would have forced itself to the top of the agenda. Nor was he aware that the news of an Austro-German Customs Union project was about to break; had he known of it, he would surely have withheld the invitation if only in deference to French susceptibilities.

The main preoccupation of Henderson for the first two months of 1931 was in fact with the disarmament problem and in particular with the German attitude towards it. Curtius, in spite of his gain in international prestige as a result of judgements on the League Council against Poland's treatment of German minorities, did little to strengthen the hand of Henderson. Instead, by demanding an earlier opening of the World Disarmament Conference than Henderson believed to be practical, Curtius gave encouragement to those in Germany whose attitude to Geneva was hostile and impatient. In spite of a personal talk between the two Foreign Ministers on 17 January,[4] the German attitude was not significantly modified. On 12 February Henderson therefore instructed Rumbold to complain to Curtius in forthright terms. Revealing

[1] B.D., 2/I, no. 349 (Rumbold to Henderson, 13 Feb 1931).
[2] B.D., 2/I, no. 350 (Henderson to Rumbold, 19 Feb 1931).
[3] B.D., 2/I, no. 354 (Rumbold to Henderson, 6 Mar 1931).
[4] B.D., 2/I, no. 347 (Henderson to Vansittart, 17 Jan 1931).

something of his thinking on the disarmament problem as a whole, as well as on the specifically German role in it, the British Foreign Secretary wrote in the following vein:

> The German Government must be aware that the ideal of complete, or anything like complete, disarmament, is not at the present moment within the sphere of practical politics. Disarmament can at best be a gradual process, achieved by degrees at successive conferences. The degree of actual disarmament, i.e., of the reduction of existing armaments, which can be attained at the first Disarmament Conference, will depend in large measure on the psychological atmosphere which can be created during the year which will intervene before the conference meets. . . . A policy of endeavouring to extort disarmament by menaces is one which, on sober reflection, can scarcely commend itself to the German Government.[1]

Henderson hoped the Germans would abandon 'the somewhat cynical attitude of detachment which they have felt obliged to adopt during the past months'.[2] In conveying the Foreign Secretary's views to the Germans, Rumbold modified the phrase 'cynical attitude of detachment' to 'cold and detached'. Nevertheless, Curtius affected to be offended even at this and claimed that Germany was for disarmament and not rearmament.[3] He went on to hint at German suspicions that the British had accepted the French view on various aspects of the land armaments problem in an attempt to secure a naval disarmament agreement.[4]

By March Curtius was fulminating against the Draft Convention elaborated by the Preparatory Commission. Claiming that this would be a means of maintaining a permanent distinction between the victors and the vanquished of the war, he went so far as to say that if the Draft Convention was to be the only basis of discussion at the World Disarmament Conference, 'Germany would have no interest in attending this Conference'.[5]

As well as encountering this discouraging attitude to disarmament in Berlin, Henderson was also aware that the Germans were seeking to rearm up to, and even beyond, the limits of what they were allowed.

[1] B.D., 2/1, no. 348 (Henderson to Rumbold, 12 Feb 1931).　　　[2] Ibid.

[3] B.D., 2/1, no. 351 (Rumbold to Henderson, 24 Feb 1931).

[4] Ibid. For a good general account of the German attitude to disarmament, see also B.D., 2/1, no. 352 (Rumbold to Henderson, 26 Feb 1931).

[5] B.D., 2/1, no. 356 (Rumbold to Henderson, 18 Mar 1931). For a description of the Draft Convention see below, pp. 95–8.

Notwithstanding their financial difficulties and the state of French suspicions, the German Government had insisted on going ahead with its
plans for building four 'pocket battleships' between 1931 and 1934, and
as early as January 1930 Sir George Milne, the Chief of the Imperial
General Staff, had prepared a memorandum in which he indicated a
number of ways in which the Germans appeared to be evading the
military provisions of Versailles.[1] But though he knew of these developments, Henderson chose, for a time, to turn a blind eye in the interest of
general European reconciliation. The turning point for him was to come
in March 1931 with the launching of the project for a Customs Union
between Austria and Germany. This move decisively demonstrated that
the German Government was determined to take selfish and irresponsible actions whatever the consequences. Henderson, unlike many of his
compatriots, was not slow in modifying his attitude when faced with
clear evidence of the changed character of German policy.

[1] See *B.D.*, 2/1, appendix II, for the full text of this memorandum. See also a
memorandum by John Balfour of the Foreign Office, 11 Nov 1929, F.O., 408/54.

CHAPTER FOUR

Geneva, 1929–1931: The Disarmament, Arbitration and Security Questions

THE programme adopted by the Labour Party in 1928, entitled *Labour and the Nation*, contained an important section on international affairs, and this, unlike the other parts, was taken quite seriously once the party had assumed office, Dalton even having copies of it circulated to various heads of department in the Foreign Office.[1] Yet *Labour and the Nation*, along with other Labour Party declarations of the time, was in some ways out of line with Henderson's personal position and reflected the definite change of emphasis that had occurred in the party's foreign policy in the years following the electoral defeat of 1924.[2] In particular, the party gave more attention to arbitration and to disarmament and rather less to security and the possibility of sanctions.[3] In 1924, for example, the Geneva Protocol, largely the work of Henderson and Parmoor, had gone a long way towards meeting French requirements for security, and if it had been carried through it might well have improved the chances of a disarmament agreement. However, the Conservatives took office before the Protocol had been ratified, and it was not surprising that, with their customary aversion to 'fighting other people's wars', they dropped the

[1] See *Labour and the Nation* (London, 1928) pp. 40–3; Dalton's unusual way of bringing it to the attention of the Foreign Office is noted in *Call Back Yesterday*, pp. 223–4. He adds with obvious relish that the Foreign Office had to pay the Labour Party for the copies it received.

[2] Other statements issued by the Labour Party just prior to the 1929 General Election included *Labour's Appeal to the Nation* (the actual election manifesto) and *Arbitration: Tory Record and Labour Policy* (London, 1929).

[3] For a similar view, see George W. Shepherd, 'The Theory and Practice of Internationalism in the British Labour Party with Special Reference to the Inter-War Period', unpublished London University Ph.D. thesis, 1952, p. 347. For a differing interpretation, see Henry R. Winkler, 'The Emergence of a Labor Foreign Policy in Great Britain, 1918–1929', *Journal of Modern History*, XXVIII (1956) 247–58.

project. Not that the Labour Party's position was entirely beyond doubt in this respect; for the Labour Cabinet of 1924 did not reach the stage of signifying its approval for Henderson's work, and it has since been suggested that it never would have done so.[1] Certainly MacDonald's position on the matter was such as to suggest that he was closer to the semi-isolationist, Austen Chamberlain, than to the internationalist, Henderson.[2] In addition to the veiled opposition of some of the party's Right-wingers, Henderson and the supporters of collective security faced difficulties from two distinct groups on the far Left. One section, the out-and-out pacifists, refused to consider sanctions at all even on behalf of the League; while a second group clung to the view that Geneva was the seat of a 'league of burglars' and that any support for it implied acceptance of the 'criminal peace of Versailles'.[3]

In view of the existence of these various conflicting strands of opinion on sanctions, it was clearly in the interest of party unity for the Labour leaders, during the years 1924 to 1929, to concentrate attention on the less contentious issues of arbitration and disarmament.[4] At all events, any idea of reviving the Geneva Protocol was tacitly dropped; and all Henderson's efforts in office after 1929 to give to the French alternative guarantees – usually of a partial character – met with stiff resistance from MacDonald.

On returning to power, MacDonald asked Cecil to return to his former position as a specialist adviser on the League of Nations, but this did not mean that the Prime Minister was to be a strong League supporter. He was not only opposed to Cecil's line on the desirability of constructing an international system based on collective security and

---

[1] Richard W. Lyman, *The First Labour Government, 1924* (London, 1957) pp. 176–80; and Catherine Ann Cline, *Recruits to Labour: The British Labour Party, 1914–1931* (Syracuse, N.Y., 1963) pp. 91–3.

[2] See above p. 27.

[3] Those holding the latter position were at this period members of a contracting group. See Cline, *Recruits to Labour*, pp. 97–8. They were later to become more important again in the mid-1930s when Sir Stafford Cripps adopted their point of view.

[4] For useful accounts of the development of the Labour Party's foreign policy between 1925 and 1929, see Kenneth E. Miller, *Socialism and Foreign Policy: Theory and Practice in Britain to 1931* (The Hague, 1967) chap. 5; and Eleanor Farrar, 'The British Labour Party and International Organisation: A Study of the Party's Policy towards the League of Nations, the United Nations and Western Union', unpublished London University Ph.D. thesis, 1952, pp. 88–101.

effective sanctions against aggression, but he was also a sceptic with regard to other aspects of the League's work. In particular, he showed little sympathy for the endeavours of the League Committees dealing with arbitration and disarmament, although these subjects had figured prominently in *Labour and the Nation*. MacDonald, it is true, attended the Tenth Assembly in Geneva, but he showed less enthusiasm than most of his colleagues in the British delegation and generally used his influence privately in favour of caution. This impression must have conveyed itself to the bulk of the assembled delegates, for his major speech to them on 3 September was accorded a less rapturous welcome than his oratorical flights normally produced; whereas Henderson and Graham, though both more pedestrian in manner, were acclaimed as 'successes'.[1]

The most notable achievement at the Tenth Assembly came when Great Britain and the Dominions signed the Optional Clause accepting compulsory arbitration of all justiciable disputes. The British example was followed by many other states with the result that, whereas previously the Optional Clause had obtained only nineteen signatures, it was soon to be accepted by some forty-two nations. Behind the scenes Henderson had an extremely difficult task to secure British accession to the document, having to face degrees of opposition from the Dominions, the Foreign Office, the Admiralty, the Chiefs of Staff, and inevitably, the Prime Minister. Permanent officials in Whitehall, representing various interested ministries, originally suggested that Great Britain should sign but with as many as nine reservations, a course which would probably have created a worse impression than not signing at all.[2]

Eventually, however, the Foreign Office prepared a memorandum for the Cabinet in which only three reservations were suggested. Henderson,

[1] For criticisms of MacDonald's performance see, for example, Cecil, *A Great Experiment*, p. 202; and Arthur Salter, *Slave of the Lamp: A Public Servant's Notebook* (London, 1967) p. 55. Sections of French opinion, in particular, expressed disquiet at MacDonald's plea to the delegates 'to face the problem of disarmament "on the assumption that the risk of war breaking out is far less than the hope of peace being permanently observed"': Nevile Henderson (Paris) to Arthur Henderson, telegram no. 136, 6 Sep 1929, MacDonald Papers.

[2] The full list of reservations may be seen in Minutes of a meeting of representatives of the Foreign Office, the Dominions Office and the India Office, 20 June 1929, Dalton Papers deposited at the British Library of Political and Economic Science.

when forwarding this document to his colleagues, included a personal note explaining that he would prefer to sign the Optional Clause without any reservations. He added that he was particularly uneasy about one of the reservations in the memorandum, namely a vague reference to areas of vital British interest.[1] For different reasons this particular reservation was also unacceptable both to the Admiralty and to the Air Staff, which considered that the areas of vital interest should be explicitly named. The Admiralty also argued that a further reservation was necessary on the subject of belligerent rights.[2]

In these circumstances the Cabinet decided to establish a Cabinet Committee under the Prime Minister.[3] On this committee Henderson continued to resist any reservation regarding areas of vital interest, as is made clear in the following minute:

> I would emphasise the extreme undesirability of asserting the so-called British Monroe Doctrine in any explicit form by way of reservation. To assert it as our predecessors did in connexion with the Kellogg Pact, by reference to certain unnamed regions, is plainly inconsistent with the repeated declarations, and the whole internationalist outlook, of the Labour Party. To assert it, on the other hand, with Egypt specifically named, would be to advertise the fact that our legal status in Egypt was untenable. We should thereby encourage the Egyptians to refuse to conclude a treaty by friendly negotiations and to insist on a reference of our legal rights to arbitration, which it would be very damaging for a Labour Government to refuse.[4]

Despite resistance from Alexander, Henderson succeeded in carrying the Cabinet Committee both on this point and also on belligerent rights. But further difficulties for the Foreign Secretary were now raised by various Commonwealth statesmen. In particular the Government of Stanley Bruce in Australia 'persistently obstructed any departure from the policy of the Baldwin Government'.[5] In these circumstances

[1] C.P., no. 192(29) by Henderson, 3 July 1929, Cab. 24/204.

[2] C.P., no. 200(29) by Alexander, 9 July 1929, Cab. 24/204; and C.P., no. 237(29) by Sir Hugh Trenchard, July 1929, Cab. 24/205.

[3] Cabinet Minutes, Cab. 23/61, 28(29)6, 10 July 1929. The other members of this committee were Henderson, Parmoor, Passfield, Alexander, Lord Sankey (the Lord Chancellor) and William Wedgwood Benn (the Secretary of State for India).

[4] Minute by Henderson, 24 July 1929, Records of Cabinet Ad Hoc Committees (hereafter abbreviated to C.A.H.C.), Cab. 27/392.

[5] Passfield to Beatrice Webb, 10 Sep 1929, Passfield Papers deposited at the British Library of Political and Economic Science. Much to the relief of the

MacDonald at first took the view that without Dominion concurrence Great Britain should not sign the Optional Clause, but 'under pressure from Henderson' he weakened.[1] The result was that, after much acrimonious debate, all the Dominions (with the exception of Ireland) were persuaded to unite on the policy of signing the Optional Clause with the following three reservations:

1. Disputes in regard to which the parties to the dispute have agreed or shall agree to have recourse to some other method of peaceful settlement.
2. Disputes with the Government of any other member of the League which is a member of the British Commonwealth of Nations, all of which disputes shall be settled in such a manner as the parties have agreed or shall agree.
3. Disputes with regard to questions which by international law fall exclusively within the jurisdiction of the United Kingdom.[2]

MacDonald announced the British intention to sign on 3 September, and Henderson followed him three days later with a detailed analysis of

---

Labour Government in London, the Bruce Government fell shortly afterwards. For further details of Australian and other Dominions' objections to the Labour Government's attitude to the Optional Clause, see various telegrams in Records of the Prime Minister's Office (hereafter abbreviated to Premier), 1/72.

[1] Cecil, *A Great Experiment*, p. 202. At the height of the controversy Cecil wrote to MacDonald on the constitutional implications of an Australian veto on British policy: 'if no step can be taken till all are unanimous our Constitution will be even more unworkable in foreign affairs than that of the U.S.A. For we shall have to obtain not a two thirds majority of a Senate but unanimity from our Dominions': Cecil to MacDonald, 21 Aug 1929, Premier, 1/72. In this connection it is worth recalling that Labour's election manifesto had simply stated that a Labour Government intended to sign the Optional Clause. It made no mention of Dominion support being essential; nor did it suggest that there would be any need for reservations.

[2] Cmd. 3421 of 1929–30. For a careful study of the implications of these reservations, see H. Lauterpacht, 'The British Reservations to the Optional Clause', *Economica*, x (1930) 137–72. For the differing attitudes of the Dominion Governments, see Gwendolen M. Carter, *The British Commonwealth and International Security: The Role of the Dominions 1919–1939* (Toronto, 1947) p. 127. For further detail, see also C.A.H.C., Cab. 27/392, and Cecil to Henderson, telegram no. 49, 25 Sep 1929, F.O., 411/10. The Irish refused to agree to any limitation on their right to bring an inter-Commonwealth dispute before the Permanent Court of International Justice. They accordingly signed the clause with a declaration of their own.

the reservations.[1] The Optional Clause was accordingly signed by Great Britain on 19 September. This move, however, had still to be ratified at Westminster. When the matter duly came before the House of Commons on 27 January 1930, the Government had to face a Conservative amendment regretting the omission of a further reservation concerning the laws of the sea. In the debate Austen Chamberlain claimed that Labour had changed its line on the laws of the sea since 1924 when, he alleged, it had contemplated signing the Optional Clause with a reservation on this subject; and he could not accept Henderson's argument that the Pact of Paris had fundamentally changed the international situation, since the Covenant remained unaltered. Henderson did his best to justify the abandonment of a reservation on the laws of the sea by pointing out that 'only another Member of the League could bring our naval action before the Permanent Court under the Optional Clause'. The Foreign Secretary also felt obliged to justify the three reservations actually made, since some members of his own party clearly thought them unnecessary. He tried hard to convince them – and perhaps himself also – of the need for a less than total adherence to the arbitral principle, but he revealed his true feelings when he referred in an unguarded moment to the fact that Ireland had differed from the other Dominions in having unreservedly accepted the Optional Clause. 'Not for the first time,' he said, 'they went one better than the rest of us.'[2] The Conservative amendment was eventually rejected by 278 votes to 193.

Apart from action on the Optional Clause, the British delegation to the General Assembly of 1929 drew attention to the need for amendments to Articles 12 and 15 of the Covenant to bring it into line with the Kellogg Pact; for an investigation into the pay and conditions of the Secretariat of the International Labour Office and the League of Nations; and for a two-year tariff truce. In addition, Henderson indicated that Great Britain welcomed the Convention for Financial Assistance to States in Danger of Aggression, which the Foreign Office had been studying since the spring. British support, however, was to extend only to states adhering to a comprehensive Disarmament Treaty. This reservation was clearly

[1] The speeches of MacDonald and Henderson are recorded in League of Nations, *Official Journal*, Special Supplement no. 75, pp. 33–6, 56–60.

[2] For this and other quotations from the debate, see *H.C. Deb.*, ccxxxiv, cols 653–778, 27 Jan 1930.

a concession to the Conservative, isolationist viewpoint of avoiding further commitments to collective security. But even this was insufficient for certain elements on Fleet Street, and accordingly a violent campaign was launched against Henderson's limited and conditional statement. The matter was raised in the Cabinet, and as a result MacDonald wrote a critical letter to the Foreign Secretary.[1] The latter's scathing reply revealed something of his resentment at the Prime Minister's attitude towards him:

Thanks for your favour received this morning. I am somewhat at a loss to understand why members of the Cabinet should be disturbed by the stunt press. . . .

Such attacks we expect, but what we do not expect, and what we resent, is the leakage which enables the Press to get busy with huge headlines about a split in the Cabinet. . . . I do not forget that I had a similar experience in 1924, but there was some small justification, then. In my opinion, there is none, on this occasion. . . . To enable you more fully to understand my position, I enclose a letter from the Treasury dated July 13th, together with an extract from the memorandum of policy to be pursued at Geneva relating to our attitude on the financial

[1] The Cabinet Minutes are unusually uninformative about what took place. They merely record that 'the attention of the Cabinet was called' to the hostile Press reports and that 'the Prime Minister undertook to write to the Secretary of State for Foreign Affairs on the subject': Cabinet Minutes, Cab. 23/61, 32(29)3, 9 Sep 1929. But Passfield wrote of this meeting that 'needless to say there is no truth in newspaper reports that it was about a "split" over Henderson's statements at Geneva': Passfield to Beatrice Webb, 10 Sep 1929, Passfield Papers. It seems possible, therefore, that the Prime Minister in his letter to Henderson may have failed to give an accurate representation of the views of the Cabinet. The tenor of MacDonald's letter, which the present writer has failed to trace, may be judged from Henderson's indignant reply. In this connection it is worth noting that T. P. Conwell-Evans, a historian, subsequently wrote to Rose Rosenberg, the Prime Minister's private secretary, arguing that the Convention for Financial Assistance was 'not a very good idea, and is not strictly in line with the Prime Minister's speech at the Assembly'. He added: 'There has been during the last five years a movement away from Article XVI [the most drastic provision in the League Covenant for the deployment of military sanctions against an aggressor], and Mr MacDonald's speech at the Assembly was a culminating expression of that movement.' A secretary informed Conwell-Evans that MacDonald had said that this letter was 'quite in accord with his views; but the pledge had already been given by Sir Austen Chamberlain or Lord Cushendun and its renewal slipped through in the great rush of work which has been going on . . .': Conwell-Evans to Rose Rosenberg, 14 Sep 1929, and H. B. Usher to Conwell-Evans, 17 Sep 1929, MacDonald Papers.

assistance proposal, which was submitted to you personally, and returned to the Foreign Office ticked by you. . . . After perusing the documents, I am sure you will agree that my authority was unquestionable, and that I have disposed of any suggestion that I have acted precipitately.

Yet your letter and the Cabinet minute place me in a position of considerable embarrassment. You say, 'I suppose the Convention will not be produced, but if it is you ought to let us have it at once, so that it may go through the usual examination.' The Convention was issued last March, and, as the letter from the Treasury shows, has been examined. . . .

Surely we shall stultify our whole attitude if, on being confronted with the first issue that gives us an opportunity of giving some effect to our policy, we turn back because a few hostile and ill-informed critics elect to make a fuss. . . .

I write strongly, because, as the result of my experience in 1924, and now, as evinced in the Cabinet minute, your letter, and the telephone message from No. 10, there is not that confidence when working in the international sphere one is entitled to expect.[1]

Henderson also gave support to the idea of a General Convention to Improve the Means of Preventing War – originally a German proposal. Negotiations on this project dragged on throughout the term of the Labour Government and appear to have played no important part in Henderson's policy.[2]

Although Great Britain had played an outstanding part in the 1929 General Assembly's public deliberations, there were notable contributions from other nations also.[3] For example, Briand advanced his controversial proposal for European union, of which mention will be made later. Then Stresemann, making the last major speech of his life, appears

[1] Henderson to MacDonald, 12 Sep 1929, cited in full in Hamilton, *Arthur Henderson*, pp. 327–8. For the subsequent development of the Convention for Financial Assistance, see Toynbee *et al.*, *Survey of International Affairs, 1930*, pp. 82–91. The British Government eventually acceded to the Convention on 2 Oct 1930 on the condition stipulated by Henderson in 1929. See Cmd. 3906 of 1930–1.

[2] For details of later developments, see Arnold Toynbee *et al.*, *Survey of International Affairs, 1931* (London, 1932) pp. 254–9; and Jean Schwœbel, *L'Angleterre et la sécurité collective* (Paris, 1938) pp. 204–9.

[3] Great Britain's contribution to making 1929 one of the League's most successful years was widely acknowledged at the time and since. See, for example, F. P. Walters, *A History of the League of Nations*, 2 vols (London, 1952) II 412.

to have made an unforgettable impression in his appeal for European pacification.

Life at Geneva did not consist, however, solely of great speeches to the Assembly; still more important work was proceeding on the various committees. The British became especially involved in the work of the Third Committee, that concerned with disarmament, which met in 1929 to consider the progress being made by the Preparatory Commission for the General Disarmament Conference.[1] The Commission at the time stood adjourned, partly in order to await the outcome of the five-power naval conversations. However, at its last session in April 1929 it had reached a number of surprising decisions which tended to facilitate the drafting of a formal agreement but only at the expense of not dealing with the realities of the problem so far as land disarmament was concerned. The United States and Great Britain (then under the Conservatives) had accepted the French thesis that there should be no limitation on trained reserves; nor were war materials to be directly limited by enumeration. Moreover, in deference to British and American opposition, budgetary limitation and international verification plans were dropped. All that remained was an American proposal for a 'declaration' of arms expenditure.[2] Needless to say, the Germans were greatly aggrieved by these decisions, as also were those who were eager to see a meaningful disarmament agreement, including the new Labour Government which, under pressure from Cecil, was persuaded to seek a reopening of the issues in question on the League's Third Committee. On 28 August Cecil wrote to MacDonald:

> I have read some minutes of yours on various papers urging caution so as not to scare the Fighting Services or the Dominions. Need I say that I appreciate this point most fully. . . . But there are certain considerations on the other side which I should like to submit to you. First (and this most nearly concerns my work) the last meeting of the

---

[1] The task of the Preparatory Commission was to draw up a framework of methods and principles of arms limitation. All actual figures were to be left for filling in at the Disarmament Conference proper.

[2] For a bitter summary of these developments, see Temperley, *The Whispering Gallery*, pp. 119–22. For a description of the work of the Preparatory Commission from its inception in 1925 to the advent of the second Labour Government, see J. W. Wheeler-Bennett, *Disarmament and Security since Locarno, 1925–31: Being the Political and Technical Background of the General Disarmament Conference, 1932* (London, 1932) pp. 43–74.

Preparatory Commission took certain provisional decisions which unless corrected may do much harm. In particular they decided against all forms of International supervision and any form of limitation of material whether by direct enumeration or budgetary limitation. . . . Now what I am afraid of is that if we simply allow the Assembly to approve generally the proceedings of the Preparatory Commission we may when that body meets again be met with the objection that the question was decided.[1]

The outcome was that in due course Cecil obtained Cabinet permission to move the following resolution in the Third Committee:

The Assembly . . . expresses the hope that the Preparatory Commission will finish its labours at the earliest possible moment, and considers that in concluding the draft disarmament convention it should consider how far the following principles have been or ought to be adopted:

1. The application of the same principles to the reduction and limitation of personnel and material, whether in sea, land or air forces.
2. The limitation of the strength of a force either by limiting its numbers, or its period of training or both.
3. The limitation of material either directly by enumeration or indirectly by budgetary limitation, or by both methods, and the recognition of a competent international authority to watch and report upon the execution of the treaty.

This motion provoked strong opposition from France and her allies, and it seemed to be too near to the German position to carry the support of all the neutrals. Facing possible defeat or more probably a victory at the cost of French anger, Cecil retreated and decided to accept a compromise amendment moved by Nikolaos Politis of Greece. This simply stated that the minutes of the Third Committee should be placed before the next meeting of the Preparatory Commission, thereby abdicating responsibility for making any clear recommendation on controversial subjects while at the same time providing an opportunity for the questions at issue to be reopened on the Preparatory Commission.

Cecil received a letter of strong support from Henderson:

I hasten to say that I am in the fullest agreement with what you did and to congratulate you warmly upon the result which you secured. My principal desire, as I told Benes, when I saw him, was that we should be free in the Preparatory Commission to raise any element

[1] Cecil to MacDonald, 28 Aug 1929, Cecil Papers, Add. 51081.

of importance for the limitation of national armaments. Since the Politis resolution, as it was adopted, gives us the right to do this, I feel sure we have got what we wanted and I am delighted with the success which you obtained.[1]

The Foreign Secretary's sense of satisfaction sprang essentially from relief that an open breach with Paris had been avoided. From the outset he had recognised that nothing of value with regard to land disarmament could be achieved without French co-operation; and Cecil, in deciding to accept the Politis compromise, had been greatly influenced by the knowledge that the Foreign Secretary 'had seemed very nervous about any controversy with the French'.[2] As will be seen, this same realistic consideration dominated British policy again when, in November 1930, the Preparatory Commission eventually resumed its deliberations.

An interesting episode concerned the Briand project for European unity first launched officially at Geneva on 5 September 1929. The French Premier in his initial speech on the subject made the following observations:

> I think that among people constituting geographic groups, like the peoples of Europe, there should be some kind of federal bond. . . . That is the link I want to forge. Obviously, this association will be primarily economic, for that is the most urgent aspect of the question, and I think we may look for success in that direction. Still I am convinced that, politically and socially also, this federal link might, without affecting the sovereignty of any of the nations belonging to such an association, do useful work. . . .[3]

The next development came when the French called a meeting, to which they invited all the European nations represented at Geneva. Briand again outlined his plan and promised to provide a more detailed memorandum at a later juncture.

The first British Minister to comment on the proposal was Graham, who welcomed it as a sign that Europe was ready for a move towards

---

[1] Henderson to Cecil, 27 Sep 1929, ibid. Cecil's accounts of the proceedings at Geneva are in Cecil to Henderson, letter, 23 Sep 1929, Henderson Papers, F.O. 800/284, and Cecil to Henderson, telegram no. 31, 25 Sep 1929, F.O., 411/10.

[2] Cecil to MacDonald, 23 Sep 1929, Cecil Papers, Add. 51081.

[3] The full text of Briand's speech is in League of Nations, *Official Journal*, Special Supplement no. 75, p. 52.

freer trade. He went on in a remarkable and detailed speech, made without a single note, to urge a two-year tariff truce and an international agreement on the coal industry.[1] The outcome of this initiative by the President of the Board of Trade was the largely abortive International Economic Conference of 1930.[2] However, British opinion, though favouring a breakdown of trading barriers, quickly appreciated that the Briand plan had several less attractive features: it would make Great Britain's relations with the Commonwealth difficult; it might undermine still more the authority of a League of Nations containing neither the Soviet Union nor the United States; and it might arouse the suspicions of other continents. Moreover, pro-German elements in Whitehall alleged that the French had an ulterior motive in sponsoring such a plan, namely that of seeking an 'Eastern Locarno'.

The promised French memorandum took many months to prepare and was only despatched from the Quai d'Orsay on 17 May 1930.[3] The British were asked to let the French have their observations on the memorandum not later than mid-July. Reaction in London was cautious in the extreme, and particular care was taken to sound out the views of other European governments, especially that of Germany. Brüning's attitude was reported to be as follows:

> Assuming that the political idea underlying the memorandum meant that the European nations must agree, as a pre-condition of an economic federation of Europe, that the present *status quo* as regards frontiers must be accepted, he said quite definitely that no Government in Germany, however socialist in complexion, could subscribe to such a condition.[4]

[1] Graham's speech is given in full in ibid., pp. 77–81.

[2] This conference first met in March 1930, when its only positive achievement was the drafting of a Commercial Convention, to which accession before November 1930 was invited. For the text see Cmd. 3539 of 1929–30. Although the terms of this convention consisted only of high-sounding aspirations, signatures were received from a mere twenty-five states, the United States being a prominent non-signatory. Following upon resolutions at the Eleventh General Assembly, a further session of the conference was held at Geneva in November 1930. But the only significant sentence in the Final Protocol of the conference was one recording that the delegates were 'unable to agree upon a date for putting the Commercial Convention into force': Cmd. 3885 of 1930–1.

[3] The full English text was published in Cmd. 3595 of 1929–30 and reprinted in John W. Wheeler-Bennett (ed.), *Documents on International Affairs, 1930* (London, 1931) pp. 61–73.

[4] *B.D.*, 2/1, no. 188 (Rumbold to Henderson, 28 May 1930).

Schubert in the Foreign Ministry took much the same line, adding that the economic aspect of the plan was 'a very good kernel'. He also stressed the fact that 'if the idea was to come to anything England must join'.[1]

By 30 May the British Foreign Office had drawn up a preliminary and private memorandum on the subject. While affecting to believe that the French proposal was well-meaning and sincere, those responsible for the British memorandum did not fail to point out that Briand's attitude had undergone some modification, and that in particular the French memorandum differed from Briand's speech at Geneva in that the emphasis was now on the primacy of the political rather than the economic aspects of the plan. British policy, it was suggested, should be based on 'caution, though cordial caution'.[2] While clearly unenthusiastic, the Foreign Office's advice was to the effect that the British Government, hoping to avoid direct French condemnation, should wait for other governments to show up the deficiencies of the scheme. The fundamental British position, however, was to be based on the following six principles:

i. We can agree to no proposals which in practice (whatever their intention) may damage the prestige and authority of the League;
ii. If therefore, there is to be new machinery, it should be built into the existing framework of the League;
iii. We warmly desire to improve the co-operation between European countries for the promotion of their common interests or [sic – and?] will help to bring it about;
iv. We cannot, however, help to create any political or economic group which could in any way be regarded as hostile to the American or any other continent, or which would weaken our political co-operation with the other members of the British Commonwealth;
v. We believe that in economic and technical matters much might be done which would not be open to objection in these respects which would promote British interests;
vi. We must not antagonise Latin-America, Asia or any other section of the League. This being so, M. Briand's proposals should not be discussed in a 'European' Conference run as a rival meeting outside the Assembly, but rather in the Committees of the Assembly itself.[3]

Henderson appears to have agreed with these recommendations. For example, he told his colleagues on a Cabinet Committee, established to consider this question, that 'M. Briand's proposals, in their present

[1] Ibid.   [2] B.D., 2/1, no. 189 (memorandum, 30 May 1930).   [3] Ibid.

form, are unacceptable and that, if adopted, they would be detrimental
to the satisfactory development of the League of Nations'.[1]

Although the British Foreign Office had rapidly decided on its attitude,
there was no immediate move to reply to the French. Instead, in accord-
ance with Foreign Office advice, the British stood aside and waited for
foreign criticisms to commence, being no doubt gratified to learn, for
example, at the end of May that Italy was strongly opposed to the
scheme.[2] Indeed, only on the last possible date, 16 July, was their reply
to reach the French ambassador in London. Even then they claimed that
their response was 'preliminary and tentative in character' because of the
need for consultation with Commonwealth members – as always a convenient excuse for temporising or increasing British demands.[3] The
British attitude to the Briand plan, then, was superficially friendly but
in reality hostile. Cold water was poured, for example, on the idea of
new institutions being established outside the League framework; nor
were possible French ulterior motives concerning Germany's eastern
frontiers ignored.[4] But if the British reaction was tepid, that of many
other European nations, excluding those in the French camp, was not
dissimilar – the only real distinction being that the British gave a particularly skilful demonstration of diplomatic hypocrisy.[5] Several nations
regretted the non-inclusion of Turkey, and Germany even deplored the
absence of the Soviet Union from Briand's plan.[6]

At the Eleventh General Assembly in September 1930, Briand appeared to be on the point of publicly abandoning his project – partly
because of the disappointing response, partly because of the German
election results – but instead he moved an innocuous resolution calling
for the establishment of a Commission of Inquiry for European Union

[1] Memorandum by Henderson, 3 July 1930, C.A.H.C., Cab. 27/424. No
minutes were kept of the proceedings of the Cabinet Committee.

[2] B.D., 2/I, no. 190 (Graham to Henderson, 30 May 1930).

[3] B.D., 2/I, nos 193 and 194 (memorandum, 3 July 1930, and Henderson to
de Fleuriau, 16 July 1930).   [4] B.D., 2/I, no. 194.

[5] For hostile and bitter reactions to the conduct of 'Perfidious Albion', see the
French writers J. F. Charvet, L'Influence britannique dans la S.D.N. (Paris, 1938)
pp. 131–8; and Jacques Bardoux, L'Île et l'Europe: La Politique anglaise (1930–
1932) (Paris, 1933) pp. 284–95.

[6] For summaries of the replies of foreign governments to the Briand project,
see B.D., 2/I, no. 195 (22 Aug 1930), and Wheeler-Bennett (ed.), Documents on
International Affairs, 1930, pp. 74–9. For the full text of the replies, see League
Document A 46 (1930) VII 17–76.

within the League.[1] The Commission duly held a number of meetings, but the Briand plan at least was obviously a lost cause and the Commission merely a face-saving device.

Anglo-French differences sparked off at the Tenth Assembly were not confined to the European union project. Another controversy arose out of the British suggestion that amendments to the Covenant were required, in particular to Articles 12 and 15. After the introductory reference to the matter of 'closing the gap' by MacDonald and Henderson in the Assembly, the matter was taken up on the First Committee where Sir Cecil Hurst, the chief legal adviser to the Foreign Office, put the British case for eliminating passages suggesting that nations might in certain circumstances have recourse to war, that is three months after arbitration or in the event of lack of unanimity on the League Council. A sub-committee recommended that the League Council should establish a Committee of Eleven to study how the Covenant could be brought into harmony with the Kellogg Pact and report back to the next assembly. On 24 September 1930 this suggestion was endorsed by the Assembly.[2]

The Committee of Eleven eventually began its deliberations on 25 February 1930 at Geneva, at a time when the issue of international security was being separately considered at the London Naval Conference. The French, who had consistently argued that increased security provisions were an essential prerequisite for any radical measures of arms limitation and reduction, sought to promote success at London by urging upon the Committee of Eleven far-reaching Covenant amendments. They were gratified to discover that the British nominee to the committee, Cecil, was in broad sympathy with their viewpoint; but they were quickly disabused of any expectations they may have had that the British Government would react in a similar fashion.

By 5 March the Committee of Eleven had completed its work, and presently published a majority report making a series of recommendations but not concealing that considerable differences of view still existed.[3] The report recommended changes to Articles 12, 13 and 15 to take account of the British desire to close the Covenant gap as

[1] Enclosure in Henderson to Vansittart, telegram no. 48, 22 Sep 1930, F.O., 411/12.
[2] For details of these developments, see enclosures in Cecil to Henderson, telegram no. 38, 25 Sep 1929, F.O., 411/10.
[3] For details, see Cmd. 3748 of 1930–1, pp. 19–37.

suggested by MacDonald, Henderson and Hurst at the 1929 General Assembly; but it also went further than the British position by urging that Article 15 should be amended to allow the League Council to require the implementation of arbitral awards in circumstances where no military clash had occurred. This move towards compulsory international arbitration was essentially a revival of the Geneva Protocol scheme of 1924, and as such was endorsed by Cecil, who rejected all Foreign Office advice in the contrary sense.[1] Cecil argued defiantly that as a British nominee and not a delegate to the committee he was free to act independently of London. 'Had you desired merely a gramophone mouthpiece', he wrote, 'you ought to have sent somebody else. . . .'[2] He then sent to Dalton the following justification of his conduct:

> The majority of the Committee desired to provide for compulsory arbitration in all cases and all of them except perhaps the Japanese and myself wished to go further than we have done.
>
> I believe it will be quite hopeless to expect the Continental mind to tolerate the idea of taking away the right of war without putting something in its place.[3]

The report of the Committee of Eleven was certainly most unwelcome to the Labour Government, which was under strong pressure from its permanent officials not to meet French demands for security to any worth-while degree. The position was made no easier by the simultaneous controversy on sanctions conducted in the columns of *The Times*. On 20 February Philip Kerr fired the first serious shot by urging that the Government should not consent to any extension of its military obligations under the Covenant. He was apparently opposed even to the Hurst proposals of 1929 for closing the Covenant gap, on the ostensible grounds that this might alienate the United States and thereby undermine the Kellogg Pact of 1928.[4] The affair took a more serious turn on

[1] The Foreign Office view is contained in two telegrams dated 3 and 4 Mar 1930, Cecil Papers, Add. 51104. Cecil was urged not to go beyond Hurst's proposals of 1929.

[2] Cecil to Noel-Baker, 4 Mar 1930, Cecil Papers, Add. 51107.

[3] Cecil to Dalton, 4 Mar 1930, Cecil Papers, Add. 51104.

[4] *The Times*, 20 Feb 1930. Kerr, later Marquess of Lothian, first rose to prominence as a member of Lloyd George's secretariat. He was later a prominent appeaser and British ambassador in Washington. A good picture of the man emerges from A. L. Rowse, *All Souls and Appeasement: A Contribution to Contemporary History* (London, 1961). For a pedestrian official biography, see J. R. M. Butler, *Lord Lothian (Philip Kerr), 1882–1940* (London, 1960).

27 March when Austen Chamberlain joined in the controversy in support of Kerr. He concluded:

> The more the League concentrates on the application of sanctions after war has broken out the weaker it will be. The more it concentrates on the prevention of war, the greater success it is likely to obtain.
>
> Prevention, not punishment, is its true line of advance, and its friends should work in the spirit of the missionary rather than of the hangman.[1]

This move was a clear warning to the administration that it might have to face opposition in Parliament if it went ahead with its policy of closing the Covenant gap.

Cecil, in particular, was extremely angry at these developments. He was especially contemptuous of the spurious argument that the Americans were likely to take offence at any extension in sanctions among League members. As he wrote to his Private Secretary, William Arnold-Forster:

> What rot Austen wrote! Neither he nor anyone else seems to be able to understand that there is a vital difference between trying to put the Pact into the Covenant and the Covenant into the Pact. The latter might offend the United States and would be a very foolish thing to do. I do not see how the former could have any such results, unless you look at the curious will o' the wisp which Philip Kerr seems to regard as a reality, to summon all the signatories to the Kellogg Pact in the event of a threat of war. Such a folly seems to me worthy of Alexander I of Russia. I doubt whether literary people should be allowed to take part in politics.[2]

Cecil presently met Secretary of State Henry Stimson and Dwight Morrow of the American delegation to the London Naval Conference and was gratified to find them in complete agreement with his interpretation of the American attitude. He kept the following record of the conversation:

> . . . Mr Stimson asked me what I had been doing in Geneva. I then explained to him that I had been trying to devise means by which the Pact could be put into the Protocol. He then referred to Philip Kerr, and spontaneously said that it seemed to him to make all the difference whether we were trying to put the Pact into the Covenant, or the Covenant into the Pact. I entirely agreed and disclaimed all intention

---

[1] *The Times*, 27 Feb 1930.
[2] Cecil to Arnold-Forster, 3 Mar 1930, Cecil Papers, Add. 51140.

of putting the Covenant into the Pact which would have been an insane project. . . . I explained that . . . in my view the ambit of the Covenant would remain very little altered from what it was now, and that though there was on paper some extension of the sanctions of Article 16 in practice it was difficult to believe that any Covenant-breaking Power which desired war would not go to war immediately instead of waiting the six or nine months provided by the Covenant. He fully agreed with this. . . . Mr Dwight Morrow then interposed that he thought the real anxiety with the French was whether the Covenant would work, and that it had been very much increased by the recent letter from Sir Austen Chamberlain to the Times. I said that I thought Chamberlain's letter most unfortunate. . . .[1]

Although they had quite misjudged the American attitude, Kerr and Chamberlain were, however, the real victors of the sanctions controversy in that they succeeded in putting the radical recommendations of the Committee of Eleven beyond the realm of practical politics. They were not without assistance from other quarters. For example, the *New Statesman*, referring to demands for French security, declared in an unsigned article:

It is our old friend Security and it is asking as usual for cream and more cream – or whatever it is that prudent cats need to fortify themselves with against the aggressiveness of Mickey Mouse! . . . It is a demand which appears to have been met with the absolute refusal that it deserves.[2]

MacDonald, prompted by Hankey, fully shared these sentiments, as he repeatedly made clear at the London Naval Conference. It is not therefore surprising that the British Government refused to endorse the Committee of Eleven's recommendations and thereby greatly damaged the prospects of French participation in any disarmament agreement.

It is interesting to discover that Cecil was always doubtful about the wisdom of the British decision to open the Pandora's box of Covenant revision. On 27 February 1930 he wrote privately to Kerr as follows:

To my mind, the objection to the policy in which we are engaged is that as a matter of actual practical effect the result is not likely to be very great. I have always believed that if the Covenant were fully and loyally carried out there is practically no danger of war, and I therefore

[1] Record of a Cecil conversation with Morrow and Stimson, 13 Mar 1930, ibid., Add. 51100.   [2] *New Statesman*, 15 Mar 1930.

personally have believed that from that point of view the importance of the Kellogg Pact has been greatly exaggerated. Holding that view, I was in favour of not raising the matter, simply on the ground that its practical importance was not sufficiently great to justify the possibility of controversy. . . .[1]

In the light of events, Henderson must have come to regret that he had not followed Cecil's original advice.

The failure of Great Britain and France to reach agreement on the Covenant meant that each was to block the other's proposals, thereby creating an impasse. The Eleventh Assembly in September 1930 considered the reports of the Committee of Eleven and of a sub-committee of the League's First Committee, which had drawn up a compromise formula. It was decided that the two reports should be circulated to governments for their observations, but the outcome was clear: none of the recommendations would be implemented. Henderson informed the Assembly that Great Britain would consider accepting the amendments and similar measures of security only on condition that a Treaty for General Disarmament was signed – with the result that the 'closing of the gap' was put off to the Greek Calends.

The League Assembly of 1930 was rather less of a success than that of the previous year, although the contrast lay more in the realm of atmosphere than actual achievements. In particular, the result of the German elections cast a sinister shadow over the proceedings; and in any case, even before this event, the deterioration in the economic and political stability of the world had become increasingly apparent.

The British delegation to Geneva, though not including the Prime Minister, was again a strong one. Henderson made almost as good a personal impression as in 1929, but nothing he could say could hope to bridge the obviously widening chasm between Paris and Berlin. Moreover, the British attitude was unmistakably more cautious than hitherto. In addition to showing coolness towards the Briand plan for European union, Henderson had to make it clear that British undertakings in the matter of sanctions would not be extended without disarmament measures.[2] Whatever his personal views may have been, Henderson

[1] Cecil to Kerr, 27 Feb 1930, ibid., Add. 51107.
[2] In particular, a disarmament agreement was to be a precondition for any radical revision of the Covenant and for the coming into operation of the Convention for Financial Assistance. For a contemporary account of the British

accordingly emphasised the need for progress with regard to disarmament and arbitration rather than security.[1] For example, on 11 September he appealed to the Assembly with these words:

> The Assembly will forgive me if I say quite frankly what is in my mind. We can never fulfil the purpose for which the League has been created unless we are prepared to carry through a scheme of general disarmament by international agreement. The authors of the Covenant never believed that international co-operation could succeed if national armaments should remain unrestricted, and if armament competition should revive. . . . It was only two years ago that a solemn resolution was adopted which declared that the present system of security as set up by the Covenant, by the treaties of peace and by the reductions in the armaments of certain countries under those treaties, and also by the Locarno agreements would allow of the conclusion at the present time of a first general Convention for the reduction and limitation of armaments. Yet . . . two years have gone by, and we have not yet made that general Convention. The pace is slow, and the peoples of the world are growing impatient and doubtful, in many cases, of our good faith.[2]

The immediate response was not hopeful. Within a week, the French were with good reason thrown into a state of acute alarm by the German election results. Curtius, meanwhile, had been instructed to step up German demands for an early disarmament conference and to avoid remarks liable to disturb the Nationalists at home.[3] Next, Italy for the first time came out on Germany's side, not it would seem because of the justice of the latter's case but simply as a consequence of Benito

---

delegation's contribution to the Eleventh Assembly, see Cmd. 3771 of 1930–1. See also Hugh Dalton and Mary Hamilton, 'The Eleventh Assembly of the League of Nations', *Journal of the Royal Institute of International Affairs* IX (1930) 758–82.

[1] To what extent Henderson was secretly out of sympathy with the Cabinet's attitude at this time is unclear; but certainly he was later to adopt the French view. When asked by Sir Norman Angell to account for the collapse of the Disarmament Conference, he was to reply instantly 'The failure to tackle security effectively before we started on disarmament': Norman Angell, *After All* (London, 1951) p. 252.

[2] League of Nations, *Official Journal*, Special Supplement no. 84, p. 42.

[3] The extent of Curtius's volte-face is open to doubt. The account given by Curtius himself has recently been challenged by an American historian who has examined the German documents with immense care. See Curtius, *Sechs Jahre Minister der deutschen Republik*, pp. 171–2; and Bennett, *Germany and the Diplomacy of the Financial Crisis*, p. 13.

Mussolini's increasing bitterness towards Paris.[1] The result of these developments was to make disarmament less likely than ever, Henderson and his utopian colleagues being clearly impotent in the face of increasing tension.

On arbitration the outlook was considerably brighter, and Henderson was able to announce to the League Assembly that Great Britain intended to sign the General Act of Arbitration, Conciliation and Judicial Settlement as soon as negotiations with the Dominions were completed. The Imperial Conference met in October 1930 and, as Dalton minuted, 'agreed on this, if on little else'.[2] The one exception was South Africa, which refused to adhere to the General Act under any circumstances because of the danger that the situation of Asiatic immigrants in that country might be made the subject of international jurisdiction.[3] All the other Dominions with the exception of Ireland accepted the same reservations as those that had applied in the case of the Optional Clause.[4] The British decision to adhere to the arbitral principle, even for non-justiciable disputes, was authorised by the House of Commons on 9 March 1931, the Liberals again supporting the Government against the Conservatives. The Opposition view was put by Chamberlain, who argued that non-justiciable disputes would be more suitably settled by the League Council than by an Arbitral Tribunal 'of accidental establishment, with no jurisprudence built up by its own decisions'.[5] Apart from the Conservative objections, some doubts were also expressed by Left-wing I.L.P. members, who regretted that no provision was being made for the revision of the unjust aspects of the Versailles Treaty.[6] In the end a Conservative amendment was defeated by 231 votes to 139 and the

[1] For the shift in Mussolini's foreign policy, see H. Stuart Hughes, 'The Early Diplomacy of Italian Fascism, 1922–1932', in Craig and Gilbert, *The Diplomats*, pp. 230–2.

[2] Dalton, *Call Back Yesterday*, p. 253. He also claimed that some of the permanent officials in the Foreign Office adopted an obstructionist attitude.

[3] General Herzog told Cecil that while he regarded the international danger 'as extremely remote', he held that within South Africa 'it was conceivable that a great agitation would arise based on anti-Asiatic feeling, and that would do a great deal more harm than any good that might be achieved by his signing the General Act': Cecil memorandum for Henderson, 31 Oct 1930, Cecil Papers, Add. 51081.   [4] See Cmd. 3803 of 1930–1. The Irish made no reservations.

[5] *H.C. Deb.*, ccxlix, col. 837, 9 Mar 1931.

[6] See, for example, the views of Fenner Brockway, *H.C. Deb.*, ccxlix, cols 863–9, 9 Mar 1931.

Government was free to go on to formal accession to the General Act on 21 May. Dalton wrote exultantly: 'A Historic event! Now we have done everything in *Labour and the Nation* (international policy), except General Disarmament.'[1]

General disarmament, however, presented quite exceptional difficulties, as became painfully apparent in November 1930 when the Preparatory Commission resumed its meetings. Forced to recognise that the French were most unlikely to give up their superiority over Germany, the Labour Government was faced with an agonising choice: either to go on vainly crusading for complete equality of treatment for Germany, or to turn instead to the pursuit of partial measures and in effect to the appeasement of the French desire to maintain military superiority. Temperley told a German diplomat in Geneva that the British Government 'after a long debate and with a heavy heart' had decided to favour the French view as the only way of getting any kind of World Disarmament Conference into existence.[2] This British decision, which clearly amounted to a volte-face, inevitably disappointed the Germans. Even so, Henderson appears to have hoped that Berlin would not press for complete equality of treatment vis-à-vis Paris but that, in practice at least, Brüning would take the 'realistic' line that the situation required. His optimism was soon to be dispelled, since Brüning showed no inclination to make any concessions.[3]

Great Britain was represented at the Preparatory Commission meeting by Cecil who, it was rumoured, was 'most unhappy about his role'.[4] His instructions were 'not to put forward any scheme of direct limitation but with liberty to accept any such scheme' proposed by another delegation which he considered 'practicable'.[5] 'Practicable' in the context clearly

---

[1] Dalton, *Call Back Yesterday*, p. 254.

[2] Albert Dufour to Bülow, 29 Nov 1930, G.F.M.R., 9126/H 245837–43. An interesting theory was held in German circles that Great Britain gave way to France for a less honourable reason, namely under financial pressure from the Bourse, at that time the most stable money market in the world. But in the absence of any clear evidence of such pressure, the theory can only be regarded as malicious speculation.

[3] It has been shown above (pp. 70–1) that Henderson responded to the German attitude with (for him) stiff reprimands. Indeed, so irritated was his tone that it is tempting to wonder whether he was not really feeling pangs of conscience at having in effect stabbed the Germans in the back.

[4] Dufour to Bülow, 29 Nov 1930, G.F.M.R., 9126/H 245837–43.

[5] Cecil to Wilson Harris, 29 Nov 1930, Cecil Papers, Add. 51167.

implied that the plan must be acceptable to France, and hence there was little hope that such a plan would be forthcoming.

Although he was required to capitulate to Paris on the fundamental points at issue, Cecil nevertheless took the lead in securing a reopening of discussion on the Preparatory Commission of various problems already dealt with at the previous session in the spring of 1929. It was finally decided, however, in the face of French protests, that only specific issues could be raised and that no further general discussion was to be tolerated. In spite of this ruling, Maxim Litvinov of the Soviet Union bored the Commission with a lengthy diatribe against all 'capitalist' nations without producing any meaningful practical proposals. That the Soviets were not serious about disarmament but sought only propaganda advantages was widely suspected at the time. For example, Cecil wrote of them:

> As for the Russians, they are only concerned to show that nothing is to be hoped for from capitalist governments, and they have put forward various more or less dishonest proposals – which they know we cannot accept – in order to enable them to make with wearisome reiteration the same speech about the wickedness of all governments except themselves.[1]

The first relevant contribution to the proceedings came from the embittered German representative, Count Johann Heinrich von Bernstorff, who moved an amendment on trained reservists, demanding a limitation on the number of conscripts. The French responded by insisting on the maintenance of their system of universal conscription, making use of the somewhat casuistic argument that anything else would be socially unjust. The German amendment was defeated by twelve votes to six, with Great Britain abstaining. Cecil made it clear that he had at no time wished to reopen this aspect of the conscription problem. He did favour, however, a limitation on the length of compulsory service and sought French agreement to a reduction in the two-year period then in force. When the French showed no signs of consenting to this, a compromise was reached whereby a limitation was approved in

[1] Ibid. Cecil was also personally repelled by the Soviet representatives with whom he came into contact at Geneva. As he wrote to Noel-Baker: 'I have done my best to get into relations with the Russians as far as I can bring myself to do so, but I must say they give me a shiver down my back whenever I look at them': Cecil to Noel-Baker, 11 Nov 1930, Cecil Papers, Add. 51107.

principle, but what this was to be in terms of months was to be left for the General Disarmament Conference to determine.

On 11 November a still more acrimonious debate commenced on the question of materials for land warfare. Germany, with the enthusiastic backing of Italy, called for a strict limitation of war stock and restriction by the enumeration method. In the face of determined French opposition, Cecil concluded that this scheme was not 'practicable', and in the vote he accordingly abstained. As the result was a tie, with nine votes on each side, the resolution had to be declared not carried. Hence the British could have cast a decisive vote and thereby significantly altered the course of negotiations. Certainly the Germans would have felt less aggrieved; but, on the other hand, the French would probably have boycotted any General Disarmament Conference if their point of view had been voted down. Cecil instead favoured budgetary limitation, claiming rather unconvincingly that this method was superior to enumeration, since it prevented a competition in quality. He pointed out that the Germans, subjected by the Versailles Treaty to limitation by enumeration, had spent huge amounts on the 'pocket battleship', the *Ersatz-Preussen*. What Cecil failed to do was to answer the argument that budgetary limitation by itself did nothing to end the disparity between the position of France, with her mighty arsenal, and all her rivals, who for one reason or another had only small resources of war materials.[1] Cecil's proposal for budgetary limitation was carried overwhelmingly after it was seen that the enumeration supporters could not command a majority. But both the Americans and the Germans, though for different reasons, indicated their dissent by abstaining.

[1] It is an open question whether the Labour Government favoured the budgetary method solely because of the need to secure French concurrence. Certainly this was not the factor that counted for most among a number of permanent officials. Their reason for preferring the budgetary rather than the enumeration method was later explained by Temperley: 'It [budgetary limitation] was certainly the less drastic method of the two; acceptance of the other rendered investigation on the spot by an International Commission necessary, and this neither we nor the Americans were, at that stage at any rate, prepared to accept': Temperley, *The Whispering Gallery*, p. 133. The Americans, however, were also opposed to budgetary limitation, since that too would have involved at least a degree of verification. It was for this reason that the British Air Ministry wanted Great Britain to adopt the same policy. See C.P., no. 339(30) by Trenchard, 14 Oct 1930, Cab. 24/215. The Cabinet overruled the view of the Air Ministry: Cabinet Minutes, Cab. 23/65, 66(30)5, 6 Nov 1930.

The drawing up of draft articles referring to naval and air armaments caused less trouble. The London Naval Treaty was taken as the basis for the former; while with regard to the latter the only real difficulty arose out of a French desire to keep a check on the number of civil aircraft in existence. The Germans, having the rare privilege of being free from any Versailles restriction in this respect, resisted the French proposal, which was, however, endorsed by a large majority.

A significant feature of the Draft Convention was the provision whereby a state might derogate from its obligations in the event of threats to its security.[1] But at the suggestion of the Americans, it was agreed that in such an eventuality 'the other High Contracting Parties shall promptly advise as to the situation presented'. It was certainly possible to interpret this initiative of the Americans as a modification of the line they had adopted on a consultative pact at the London Naval Conference, but whether, on the other hand, it marked any really significant change of heart in Washington seems dubious indeed.[2] The British, in particular, appear to have been excessively delighted that the United States had taken a step away from the extreme isolationist position.

More far-reaching conclusions might have been drawn by British observers from a later incident in the drafting process, when the Germans were so thoroughly humiliated that the likelihood of their supporting a disarmament treaty virtually disappeared. The British were, moreover, indirectly responsible for this development in that they proposed the following article:

> The present Convention shall not in any way diminish the obligations of previous treaties under which certain High Contracting Parties have agreed to limit their land, naval and air armaments and have thus

[1] This provision had to be included, since the Draft Treaty obviously did not offer alternative protection to potential victims of aggression. A 'Permanent Disarmament Commission' was to have been established, with the duty 'of following the execution of the present convention', but its powers were likely to have been extremely limited both in the matter of verification of compliance with the terms of the treaty and in the provision of sanctions in the event of a violation of either the treaty or the general peace.

[2] For evidence of American motives, see United States Department of State, *Papers Relating to the Foreign Relations of the United States* (Washington, various years – hereafter abbreviated to *F.R.*), 1930, I 194–5 (Stimson to Gibson, 20 Nov 1930). For a somewhat different assessment, see Walter Lippmann, *The United States in World Affairs, 1931* (New York, 1932) p. 241. For the American attitude at the London Naval Conference see below, pp. 128, 130–1.

D

fixed in relation to one another their respective rights and obligations in this connection.

Cecil apparently had in mind only the naval treaties. The French, however, seized on this article as a means of securing a renewed German recognition of the disarmament clauses of Versailles, and they accordingly moved this addendum:

> The following High Contracting Parties, signatory to the said treaties, declare that the limits fixed for their armaments are accepted by them in relation to the obligations referred to in the previous paragraph, the maintenance of such obligations being for them an essential condition for the observance of the present Convention.

Bernstorff's reaction was predictable and bitter. 'Germany', he declared, 'will not renew her signature to the disarmament clause of Versailles. I beg you, Gentlemen, to renounce any such illusion.'[1] He threatened that Germany would reject the whole Draft Treaty rather than yield on this point. In an electric atmosphere Cecil reproached Bernstorff in a highly intemperate fashion and was made to appear rather petulant when the latter replied in a much more courteous and dignified tone.[2] Cecil then voted for the French amendment, which was duly adopted. Even one of Cecil's closest collaborators, Temperley, was to aver that 'we ought never to have voted for it'.[3]

Apart from their profound dissatisfaction with the Draft Treaty, the Germans also felt aggrieved that their demand for the naming of an opening date for the World Disarmament Conference was turned down by the Preparatory Commission. By 25 January 1931, however, a date was at last fixed, the League Council deciding in favour of February

[1] Temperley, *The Whispering Gallery*, p. 139.

[2] Relations between Cecil and Bernstorff had never been good. Echoes of the tension between them are to be found in *The Memoirs of Count Bernstorff* (London, 1936) pp. 315–16.

[3] Temperley, *The Whispering Gallery*, p. 140. It was probably this incident and its repercussions which led Cecil to write many years later that at this time he had had a difference of opinion with Henderson, who thought he 'had given away too much to the French': Viscount Cecil of Chelwood, *All the Way* (London, 1949) p. 196. For Cecil's full-length description of all the proceedings at the final session of the Preparatory Commission, see his numerous despatches in F.O., 411/13. The full text of the Draft Convention is reprinted as an appendix to Wheeler-Bennett, *Disarmament and Security since Locarno*, pp. 364–76.

1932.[1] Even this did not give satisfaction to Berlin, since Germany had consistently urged that a start ought to be made before the end of 1931.

It is rather surprising that in these unpromising circumstances Henderson placed such high hopes on the World Disarmament Conference that he took no persuading to accept the chairmanship in addition to his many other duties when the League Council offered him the post in May 1931. The idea met with initial resistance from MacDonald, who would have preferred Smuts; but in the end the Prime Minister capitulated and Henderson was formally appointed on 22 May. The stage was now set, therefore, for the tragic World Disarmament Conference, and Henderson, in accepting the chairmanship, had taken the decisive step along the road towards his personal 'martyrdom'.[2]

[1] Cmd. 3804 of 1930–1.

[2] The pathos of Henderson's tenure of the chairmanship of the World Disarmament Conference is well captured by Winkler, 'Arthur Henderson', in Craig and Gilbert, *The Diplomats*, pp. 340–2.

CHAPTER FIVE

Anglo-American Relations prior to the London Naval Conference, 1929

IN the opening months of 1929 MacDonald, then Leader of His Majesty's Opposition in what was certain to be a General Election year, felt obliged to draw attention to the strained state of Anglo-American relations.[1] No doubt the Labour leader hoped that the question might become an election issue and help to catapult him into power; but he was also in all probability genuinely anxious to see an improvement in Anglo-American relations quite apart from any electoral considerations. In those days it was fashionable for British Left-wingers to feel strong affection for the United States; for not only had Woodrow Wilson stood very close to the Union of Democratic Control point of view in the First World War and to some extent in the peacemaking that followed, but the United States had also retained sufficient of its pioneering mystique to cast a spell over progressive elements in Great Britain.[2] It is therefore readily understandable that MacDonald should have seen it as his mission in 1929 to bring about a diplomatic *détente* with Washington on his return to Downing Street.

Undoubtedly the major cause of the coolness between London and Washington arose out of the events of 1927 and 1928 relating to naval disarmament. To explain the complexities of this subject it is necessary to trace the course of events during the immediately preceding years.[3]

[1] *The Times,* 25 Jan 1929. See also J. Ramsay MacDonald, 'America and England', *Nation,* 30 Jan 1929.

[2] On the relations between British 'progressives' and the United States, see Henry Pelling, *America and the British Left from Bright to Bevan* (London, 1956), and Laurence W. Martin, *Peace without Victory: Woodrow Wilson and the British Liberals* (New Haven, 1958).

[3] For further details on the issue of naval limitation in the 1920s, see Merze Tate, *The United States and Armaments* (Cambridge, Mass., 1948); Gerald E. Wheeler, *Prelude to Pearl Harbor: The United States Navy and the Far East,*

The greatest breakthrough in arms limitation known to history had occurred at Washington in 1922, when all the principal naval powers had agreed to limit their battleship fleets to specified sizes until the year 1930. Some of the powers – and especially the United States – then became eager to extend the agreement to auxiliary naval craft, both for reasons of economy and out of a genuine belief that an uncontrolled arms race might help to sow the seeds of a future war. Accordingly, the issue of further naval limitation was repeatedly raised both in inter-governmental negotiations and in the more public forums of the League of Nations and its various disarmament commissions.

The only powers whose ardour for further drastic naval reduction could be called into question were Great Britain and France. In the case of Great Britain, many elected politicians – in addition to the professional naval experts, whose ultra-patriotic and ultra-cautious attitude to these questions varied little from country to country – were suspected of taking a pessimistic and cynical view of any disarmament conversations. At any rate, even if they did not all openly attack the idea of disarmament, many highly-placed Conservatives insisted on the so-called 'doctrine of requirements', which denied the right of the United States to mathematical parity with Great Britain in certain categories of auxiliary craft on the grounds that the United States had fewer global commitments to meet. In the case of France, there was very great reluctance to agree to enter upon any naval negotiations at all unless these were directly linked to the question of land armaments and the alleged need for concrete guarantees of security against aggression. It was therefore only with the greatest difficulty that the French could be persuaded to advance their views on the isolated consideration of naval arms, and these views, when obtained, were generally unhelpful. They refused to agree to parity with the Italians, since the latter had fewer seas to defend; they did not wish to see any limitations on small so-called defensive submarines; and they preferred limitation by overall tonnage rather than by category of auxiliary craft.

1921–1931 (Columbia, Mo., n.d., 1963?); R. A. Chaput, *Disarmament in British Foreign Policy* (London, 1935); Stephen Roskill, *Naval Policy between the Wars*, vol. 1: *The Period of Anglo-American Antagonism, 1919–1929* (London, 1968); David Carlton, 'Great Britain and the Coolidge Naval Disarmament Conference of 1927', *Political Science Quarterly*, LXXXIII (1968) 573–98; and David Carlton, 'The Anglo-French Compromise on Arms Limitation, 1928', *The Journal of British Studies*, VIII (1968–9) 141–62.

The Italians and Japanese were less difficult to satisfy from Washington's point of view, but they nevertheless presented certain problems. Italy demanded, seemingly for reasons of prestige, the right to complete equality with France; while Japan sought a 10 per cent increase in her ratio vis-à-vis her rivals compared with that which had been accorded to her at Washington in 1922. All the same, the Italians and the Japanese were genuinely on the American side in that they were both eagerly seeking a sharp reduction in expenditure and were in favour of putting an end to the possibility of a ruinous arms race.

The tension between the two sides came to a head in 1927 when President Calvin Coolidge called a naval conference at Geneva. The French – and hence the Italians – simply refused to attend, while the British, who did participate, adopted an attitude unacceptable to the Americans. Lord Jellicoe made it clear at an early stage that the British Empire had an 'absolute need' for fifty-five small and fifteen large cruisers and that she could not agree by treaty to the United States being permitted to exceed the British total number of units in either type of vessel. The Americans, apprehensive of the potential power of British armed merchantmen, wished to concentrate upon the construction of large rather than small cruisers and to equip all of them with guns of 8-inch calibre. They therefore greatly resented the British 'take-it-or-leave-it' approach. All hope of agreement finally vanished when the British Cabinet adopted an equally inflexible attitude on the gun-calibre question, the British delegation being firmly instructed to insist that no small cruiser was to mount a gun exceeding 6-inches in calibre. The conference accordingly broke up amid mutual recriminations on 4 August 1927.

A year later the Americans had even more cause for irritation when the so-called 'Anglo-French compromise' was negotiated. This extraordinarily inept plan seemed to Coolidge to be a gratuitous insult, since it was difficult to believe that its authors could have entertained any serious expectation of its winning acceptance in Washington. The offensive proposals were those providing for a limitation of all auxiliary vessels except for small cruisers and coastal submarines. It was clearly no coincidence that many small cruisers were required by Great Britain and that France wished to construct large numbers of coastal submarines. Needless to say, neither of these categories of vessel held any appeal for United States naval planners.

After these damaging setbacks to his prestige, it is hardly surprising that Coolidge 'could scarcely bear mention of the word "disarmament" '.[1] Fortunately, however, he decided to retire in 1929 and hence there remained the possibility that a fresh start might be made under the new President. At the same time, the Americans pressed ahead with their plans to construct a large and adequate Navy as the only effective response to Anglo-French intransigence. The Cruiser Bill, eventually passed by the Senate on 5 February 1929, provided for the building of fifteen large cruisers and an aircraft carrier over a period of three years.

Thus it was that at the beginning of 1929 Anglo-American relations had sunk to a level of mistrust and coolness quite unacceptable to MacDonald. By June, however, when he came to power, the situation had taken a turn for the better, and indeed it may be said that circumstances have rarely been more propitious for the achievement of a dramatic *détente* between two states formerly estranged. The inauguration of the new President, Herbert Hoover, provided the main grounds for optimism, since he made it clear that he was willing, as Coolidge had not been, to overlook the events of 1927 and 1928. For good measure, there was also to be a new American ambassador to London, the popular General Charles Dawes. The other major factor making for a new approach on both sides of the Atlantic arose, paradoxically enough, out of the progress of the American Cruiser Bill. In Great Britain the Conservative Government were jerked back to reality when they perceived that the United States could, if it so desired, rapidly outstrip all other nations in naval construction; while in the United States Hoover and his colleagues were naturally anxious to avoid the necessity for a naval race and may also have been disturbed on the domestic scene by mounting pacifist protests which had threatened to cripple the Cruiser Bill and seemed to augur ill for any subsequent measures of naval expansion. Thus it might be said that both governments had strong incentives to reach an accommodation – the United States because she feared that in the face of popular agitation it would not be possible to carry out her naval programme over a protracted period; Great Britain because she feared the opposite.

In fact a number of preliminary feelers had been put out by Hoover prior to the British General Election, and there appears to have been

[1] R. H. Ferrell, *American Diplomacy in the Great Depression: Hoover–Stimson Foreign Policy, 1929–1933* (New Haven, 1957) p. 73.

some possibility that Baldwin would have visited the United States if he had been returned to office.[1] However, nothing of a far-reaching character had been completed when the Prime Minister went to the country. All the same, it is worth noting that the Conservatives were expected to respond to Hoover's overtures if re-elected, and hence it is by no means certain that Labour's victory at the polls was of decisive importance in bringing about an improvement in Anglo-American relations. The British ambassador in Washington, Howard, in conversation with the Secretary of State, Stimson, on the eve of the General Election 'ventured to think that whatever Government might be in power in Great Britain after the elections the attitude towards the new American proposals regarding naval disarmament would be equally sympathetic'.[2] The judgement of an American writer on this point is worthy of repetition here:

> It seems therefore that the most important factor in bringing about the change in Anglo-American relations was the election of Mr Hoover rather than the election of Mr MacDonald. Yet the Labour victory undoubtedly hastened the tempo of the negotiations and produced more quickly the agreement which might have come eventually under the previous Government. Mr MacDonald undertook with relish what Mr Baldwin had reluctantly come to see was necessary.[3]

The most important psychological breakthrough came from the American side when on 22 April 1929 Hugh Gibson, the American ambassador to Belgium and representative on the League of Nations Preparatory Commission, made a notable speech at Geneva. In it he dramatically abandoned the former United States demand for mathematical parity in all naval categories and instead argued that a yardstick formula might serve to reconcile conflicting needs.[4] This acceptance of a degree of elasticity in the calculation of ratios, although an important concession by Washington, was accorded a welcome out of all proportion to its significance.[5] In fact the yardstick was to be a source of

[1] Raymond G. O'Connor, *Perilous Equilibrium: The United States and the London Naval Conference of 1930* (Lawrence, Kans., 1962) p. 32.

[2] *B.D.*, 2/1, no. 1 (Howard to Chamberlain, 23 May 1929).

[3] P. M. Sheppard, 'Anglo-American Relations during the Administration of Herbert Hoover, with particular reference to Europe', unpublished London University M.A. thesis, 1955, p. 53.

[4] For the full text of Gibson's speech, see *F.R.*, 1929, I 91–6.

[5] For an account of world reaction, see O'Connor, *Perilous Equilibrium*, pp. 26–7.

considerable embarrassment to Hoover over a period of many months, for while he saw it as a rather minor instrument for oiling the wheels of negotiation, the other rival powers, and especially Great Britain, seemed to expect him to produce a magic formula which would somehow obviate altogether the need for hard bargaining. Yet Gibson's intervention in the Geneva debate was invaluable, if only because it served to bring naval disarmament once again into serious consideration in both Washington and London.

From the outset the statesmen on both sides of the Atlantic were resolved to learn the lessons arising out of the failures of 1927 and 1928. For example, it was agreed that nothing should be done without careful preparation: no hasty actions were to be taken that might result in dashing the hopes of the over-enthusiastic. In this the two powers were avoiding the pitfall into which Coolidge had stumbled in 1927 and, significantly, it was the Americans who now acted as the brake on an impatient MacDonald. For example, Dawes had to begin his mission to St James's by informing the new British Prime Minister that a visit to the United States before a preliminary understanding on the naval issues had been reached would be premature and probably harmful. MacDonald bowed to the inevitable, but it must have been damaging to his pride to be told bluntly on 24 June that a visit by him might enable the American Senate to engage upon 'demoralising and demagogical discussion' of the naval negotiations.[1] The British Press was also an extreme embarrassment at this time to both the ambassador and to the sensitive Prime Minister, for it was generally supposed that the American visit would be arranged without delay.[2] The Americans were also to show considerable good sense in resisting British pressure for an early non-technical conference. Though much criticised at the time for dragging their feet on this point, the Americans were undoubtedly correct in

[1] Dawes, *Journal*, p. 16. After presenting his credentials to the King on 15 June, the ambassador stated that 'he was the mouthpiece in England of the President and the American Government and, were the Prime Minister to go to America, it would arouse all sorts of suspicions . . .'. The King surprisingly indicated that he was of the same opinion and 'begged him [Dawes] . . . to dissuade him [MacDonald] from what, apparently, is his present fixed intention': memorandum by Stamfordham, 15 June 1929, R.A. GV, M 2217/1.

[2] Dawes apparently lost his temper with one persistent journalist and is alleged to have snapped, 'Mac will get his invitation when I'm good and ready to give it to him and not before': Drew Pearson and Constantine Brown, *The American Diplomatic Game* (New York, 1935) p. 80.

D 2

arguing that careful preparation ought to be a *conditio sine qua non* for any conference, however informal.[1]

The British, on the other hand, showed commendable tact in their attitude towards the other three major naval powers. They repeatedly drew attention to the paramount need to avoid giving the impression to these nations that they were to be faced with an Anglo-American *fait accompli*. Having themselves suffered such a blow to their *amour-propre* in 1928, the Americans were quick to appreciate the point. The result was that both parties went out of their way to conciliate the ambassadors of the other interested parties without at the same time revealing all that took place in the conversations. Great Britain, in particular, made a special effort to reassure France on the question of the status of the Preparatory Commission to which so much importance was attached in Paris, Alexander Cadogan, the British diplomat, informing the French representative on the Preparatory Commission that 'there is no desire to take the matter of naval disarmament out of the hands of the Preparatory Committee, and we at any rate, for our part, would wish to do nothing that might cause any embarrassment to that Committee'.[2] Inevitably the bilateral talks were bound to cause some uneasiness among the other interested powers, and it was perhaps a measure of the tact employed by both Washington and London that no strong resentment resulted.

Yet while paying every possible attention to the susceptibilities of the other powers, Great Britain and the United States early arrived at the conclusion that French and Italian co-operation in a final treaty was far from certain, and they accordingly reached a provisional understanding that they might have to settle for a tripartite agreement with Japan. Leading Foreign Office diplomats were quick to point out that in the case of French and Italian abstention from any agreement the emphasis in

[1] *F.R.*, 1929, I 137–9 (Stimson to Dawes, 27 June 1929).

[2] *B.D.*, 2/1, no. 11 (Cadogan to René Massigli, 6 July 1929). Cecil's view of the British position was a rather different one. 'The Foreign Office', he told Noel-Baker, 'are all for getting on with the Five Power conference quickly and leaving the Preparatory Commission to look after itself. They say agreement on actual Naval reductions will help the other negotiation. But I have my doubts. It may be that subconsciously they think that by pressing the Anglo-American negotiations alone they will get a definite result which will be good, and if it is a small one that will be still better. Anyhow, Naval reductions *by themselves* will do little or nothing to secure peace': Cecil to Noel-Baker, 13 Aug 1929, Cecil Papers, Add. 51107.

the negotiations would have to be placed upon limitation rather than reduction.[1] No doubt 'the He-man old salt-sea dogs' of the Admiralty, as Hoover called them,[2] also grasped eagerly at this argument for obstructing the course of the pacific idealists. Neither MacDonald nor his First Lord, Alexander, however, seems to have put up any vigorous opposition to the reasoning of the pessimists, even though it should have been apparent to them that in any event France and Italy were likely to remain very much second-class naval powers. The American political leaders, by contrast, seemed to prefer substantial reduction rather than mere limitation whether or not the Latin powers were prepared to sign a formal treaty. They favoured ignoring verbal intransigence until such time as this found reflection in an actual increase in the size of the Latin fleets, at which point, they argued, the British, American and Japanese strength could be adjusted accordingly.[3]

In spite of these differences of approach, the Anglo-American conversations continued to make progress during the first month after MacDonald's accession to power, although the emphasis continued to lie in the field of generalities. It was, for example, quickly established that the politicians would handle the negotiations and that in any naval conference the experts and professionals would be restricted to a purely advisory role.[4] This decision arose out of a possibly mistaken belief that the intractability of the latter had been responsible for the collapse of the 1927 Geneva Conference. Again, it proved surprisingly easy to persuade the United States to restrict the negotiations to the subject of the control of naval vessels; other allied problems such as the laws of war, the 'freedom of the seas' question and the military potential of merchant shipping were to be left out of account.[5] This marked a surprising

[1] B.D., 2/I, no. 6 (memorandum by Craigie, 26 June 1929).

[2] Herbert Hoover, Memoirs: The Cabinet and the Presidency, 1920–1933 (London, 1952) p. 341.

[3] F.R., 1929, I 174–6 (Stimson to Dawes, 2 Aug 1929).

[4] B.D., 2/I, no. 5 (minute by Lindsay, 25 June 1929). The Americans, it seems, wanted to take even stronger action against the experts at this stage, though they were soon to modify their position in this respect as the technical aspects increased in complexity. The British experts were far from happy at the prospect of demotion. For example, Admiral V. H. S. Haggard, the Fourth Sea Lord, thought that the politicians would find it far from easy to draw up a yardstick. He added sadly, 'However everything points to a reduction of armaments and I think we will have to face it': Daily Herald, 22 June 1929.

[5] B.D., 2/I, no. 3 (Henderson to Howard, 24 June 1929).

concession by Washington and one that was unpopular with the Navy General Board and the Navy League, as well as with those like Senator William E. Borah, who perversely chose to argue that a settlement of the controversial issue of the freedom of the seas was likely to help pave the way to an early agreement. Whether or not Hoover's policy was the result of his relative ignorance of the issues involved, it undoubtedly went a long way to making an accommodation possible.

To this end, Hoover's contribution was undoubtedly more important than MacDonald's declaration that he accepted in principle Anglo-American parity in naval strength. It is certainly difficult to follow the reasoning of one writer, who has said with respect to a MacDonald telegram of 28 June confirming that Great Britain accepted parity in principle:

> This voluntary surrender of control of the sea was fundamental to a successful outcome to the negotiations. . . . MacDonald's acceptance of this principle was probably the most important concession made by any statesman during the negotiations that preceded the London Naval Conference of 1930.[1]

In fact there is some evidence that even the outgoing Conservative Government had already gone a long way to accepting the principle of mathematical parity, and it had never once been denied by MacDonald whether in opposition or in office.

The outstanding problem throughout the summer months of 1929 did not in fact turn upon such statements of principle; the fundamental difficulty was rather that of bringing the two powers to the point of bargaining over concrete figures. In this connection the British could not be faulted, since they had been told by Gibson at Geneva that a yardstick formula was 'ready in the President's safe',[2] and quite naturally they wanted to know the secret in order to see whether they could concur. Dawes, in his Pilgrims' Dinner speech of 18 June, did nothing to dispel the impression given by Gibson,[3] and in private he told MacDonald

---

[1] O'Connor, *Perilous Equilibrium*, p. 36. As one acute writer put it, 'The issue was not parity – it was the level of parity': Conyers Read, 'More Light on the London Naval Treaty of 1930', *Proceedings of the American Philosophical Society*, XCIII (1949) 293.

[2] *B.D.*, 2/1, no. 6 (memorandum by Craigie, 26 June 1929).

[3] For the full text of Dawes's Pilgrims' Dinner speech, see Dawes, *Journal*, pp. 17–23.

that a yardstick would be produced which would change the problem 'from one of tonnage to one of points'.[1] Time after time MacDonald was to ask to be allowed to see the formula, but he met with nothing except delaying tactics of a most irritating character.[2]

In point of fact a settled and agreed American yardstick simply did not exist in the form that Gibson's Geneva speech had implied, but Hoover did not have the courage to admit this openly. It is true that he endeavoured to arrive at one with the assistance of his naval advisers, but the latter in turn used delaying and obstructionist tactics. They attempted always to complicate the issue further and then asserted that the imponderables were too great to allow any trustworthy formulae to be produced. There was a sense in which they were correct, but Hoover and Stimson were concerned not with the complete *certainty* of parity in naval strength but only with some kind of approximation that could be presented with reasonable credibility to the public opinions of several nations. In this it was the statesmen who were the realists and not the experts.[3] It was the former, for example, who understood the need to keep to a minimum the factors under consideration. Notwithstanding the objections of the Navy General Board, they suggested that only displacement, guns and age should be taken into account. In their estimate 'protection, speed, habitability, etc., are entirely relative to the other factors and do not require special consideration'.[4]

However, none of this brought a firm agreement much nearer. Nor for that matter did the unilateral goodwill gestures made by each country during July. On the 24th MacDonald announced to the House of Commons that he intended to halt work on the construction of two cruisers, the *Surrey* and the *Northumberland,* and to cancel two submarines

---

[1] *B.D.*, 2/I, no. 3 (Henderson to Howard, 24 June 1929).

[2] See, for example, *B.D.*, 2/I, no. 19 (MacDonald to Dawes, 17 July 1929). As late as 1 August MacDonald wrote to Dawes: 'I trusted much to your device of a yardstick and am sorry to see that it has disappeared from recent despatches. I still trust to it and wish we had it . . .': MacDonald to Dawes, 1 Aug 1929, MacDonald Papers.

[3] In his memoirs Hoover failed to indicate that there was any clash between the statesmen and the experts in Washington. He drew attention to MacDonald's troubled relations with the Admiralty and then surprisingly added: 'I had no such difficulties. Admirals Pratt, Hepburn and Jones genuinely supported what we were trying to do': Hoover, *Memoirs: The Cabinet and the Presidency*, p. 341.

[4] *B.D.*, 2/I, no. 16 (Dawes to MacDonald, 12 July 1929).

and one submarine-depot ship.[1] He also intended to slow down work at Singapore. Hoover, who had been apprised of the intended British action as early as 11 July,[2] responded with alacrity – work on three cruisers was suspended. As Howard wrote to MacDonald, 'it was an act of no little courage on his part to reply right away to your naval armament cut in the way he did. . . .'[3]

These gestures were, however, a substitute for a concrete agreement, since the real negotiations had at this stage reached something of an impasse. Great Britain continued to ask to see the Hoover 'yardstick', and the United States continued to temporise. While never stating clearly that they did not intend to produce their formula, the Americans instead began to indicate alternative lines on which they preferred to proceed. As early as 27 June, Gibson suggested that Great Britain should announce her minimum needs and then the United States would attempt to adjust her fleet accordingly.[4] The British gradually came to see that this was the way that the 'yardstick' was going to operate: it was to be a mere veneer upon any settlement reached rather than the basis of it. Thus the two sides began to consider the question of minimum British requirements, and it was only in this way that serious negotiations really got under way.

By 22 July it had been agreed that the then British level in submarines and destroyers would be taken as standard and that the Americans, who had a preponderance in these categories of vessels, would scale down to this level by the end of 1936, provided only that a satisfactory arrangement was reached with regard to cruisers.[5] It was on the latter issue that accord was to prove so elusive, for here at any rate exact parity was out of the question owing to the supposedly very different needs of the two countries. Clearly some agreement involving elasticity was essential.

The United States began by estimating that the total British tonnage in cruisers amounted to some 402,800 tons, while that of the United States stood at no more than 300,000 tons.[6] This gap in total tonnage was, in the American view, too wide to be considered equivalent, notwithstanding the fact that much of the British total was accounted for

---

[1] *H.C. Deb.*, ccxxx, cols 1304–7, 24 July 1929.
[2] *B.D.*, 2/I, no. 14 (MacDonald to Dawes, 11 July 1929).
[3] Howard to MacDonald, 25 July 1929, MacDonald Papers.
[4] *B.D.*, 2/I, no. 7 (memorandum by Craigie, 27 June 1929).
[5] *F.R.*, 1929, I 149–52 (Stimson to Dawes, 22 July 1929).   [6] Ibid.

by small cruisers and those of a police character. The Americans did not accept that any yardstick formula would convince their nation that actual parity in fighting strength existed between two fleets of such widely divergent total tonnages. On this point the State Department repeatedly drew attention to the limitations of any yardstick. For example, Stimson telegraphed to Dawes in the following terms:

> parity must not only be substantially real but must be recognisable as such by the people of both countries. It must not be a matter of such difficult technique that each people will think the other is outwitting it. For this reason we can never get very far away from the quantitative aspect of parity which has hitherto been used in such negotiations.[1]

If the existing tonnage gap between the two powers was too great, how was it to be closed? Since the United States wanted naval limitation or even reduction, she was reluctant to consider building up her cruiser fleet to the British level. The British were therefore asked to state their minimum requirements. The result at first was so disappointing to the Americans that the talks appeared to be in danger of breaking down. On 29 July MacDonald claimed that Great Britain would need fifteen large and forty-five small cruisers,[2] and among the latter were to be counted four of the *Hawkins* class whose gun calibre, in the American view, almost qualified them for the former category. The reaction in Washington was extremely unfavourable, Stimson concluding that MacDonald might be 'trying us out'.[3] Dawes accordingly conveyed to MacDonald the substance of the American objection:

> Obviously the proposals are not for reductions but increases in cruiser programmes both for Great Britain and the United States. In proposing 15 and 45 as the number of cruisers you desire, you are proposing a total of 60 cruisers against 52 which are in service today. . . .[4]

'I emphasise', replied MacDonald, 'that naval armaments are not what is built but what, things remaining as they are, must be built,

[1] *F.R.*, 1929, I 190–5 (Stimson to Dawes, 15 Aug 1929).
[2] *B.D.*, 2/I, no. 26 (MacDonald to Dawes, 30 July 1929).
[3] *F.R.*, 1929, I 168–70 (Stimson to Dawes, 31 July 1929).
[4] Dawes to MacDonald, 1 Aug 1929, MacDonald Papers. MacDonald later told the Cabinet that Dawes and Gibson had accepted his proposal for sixty cruisers but that Washington had disagreed: Cabinet Minutes, Cab. 23/61, 33(29)1, 13 Sep 1929. See also memorandum by Stamfordham of a conversation with MacDonald, 31 July 1929, R.A. GV, K 2231/1.

and when we use the word "reduction" that must be taken into account.'[1]

This line of argument by the Prime Minister suggests that he had fallen under the influence of the Admiralty. But he soon modified his position, informing Dawes on 8 August that he was prepared to reduce his claim for small cruisers from forty-five to thirty-four.[2] This was indeed a most significant concession and meant that the differences between the two sides were now quite small. Nevertheless, the talks dragged on and the United States was still unwilling to favour an immediate MacDonald visit to Washington. The trouble arose out of the desire of the United States for as many as twenty-three large cruisers – later modified to twenty-one – compared with fifteen for Great Britain. At the end of July, when they had been calling for a total of sixty cruisers, MacDonald and Alexander had indicated to Dawes that they were not worried how many large cruisers the United States acquired.[3] In August, however, the British leaders changed their minds on two grounds. First, they were convinced that 8-inch guns were worth 'almost an infinity' of 6-inch ones.[4] Secondly, they realised that there were other powers involved, especially Japan, which had been calling for an increase in her ratio compared with that accorded to her at Washington. As MacDonald was later to write to Dawes:

> although in our talks with each other we assume that the discussion takes place between us two, that is not really the case. There are shadowy entities behind me. A spirit photograph would show you

[1] MacDonald to Dawes, 1 Aug 1929, MacDonald Papers.

[2] *B.D.*, 2/1, no. 28 (MacDonald to Dawes, 8 Aug 1929). By 17 September MacDonald, with characteristic vacillation, had become afraid that even this modification was too modest and that the critics would say 'that we have not been nearly bold enough'. As he wrote to Alexander: 'Generally my suspicion is that the Admiralty is getting from us not only 50 ships, which of course is quite a good reduction, but is increasing the fighting efficiency of the Navy so that, from that point of view, it is more formidable than it would be if we had more ships with a total efficiency for war purposes of a decidedly lower level than our fleet will be in 1936': MacDonald to Alexander, 17 Sep 1929, Alexander of Hillsborough Papers deposited at Churchill College, Cambridge, A.V.A.R. 5/3.   [3] *F.R.*, 1929, I 176–81 (Dawes to Stimson, 4 Aug 1929).

[4] *F.R.*, 1929, I 186–8 (Dawes to Stimson, 9 Aug 1929). Throughout the naval discussions of 1929–30 it was tacitly accepted, even by the Americans, that small cruisers should mount only 6-inch guns. This provided a sharp and perhaps vital contrast with the negotiations of 1927.

Ramsay MacDonald and Arthur Henderson, 1929

The second Labour Cabinet descend to the garden at 10 Downing Street

On the steps from left to right: Lord Parmoor (Lord President), Ramsay MacDonald
(Prime Minister) and Arthur Henderson (Foreign Secretary). *Back row from left to
right:* Lord Thomson (Secretary for Air), Arthur Greenwood (Minister of Health),
Thomas Shaw (Secretary for War), Lord Noel-Buxton (Minister of Agriculture),
Philip Snowden (Chancellor of the Exchequer), J. R. Clynes (Home Secretary),
William Adamson (Secretary for Scotland), J. H. Thomas (Lord Privy Seal) and
George Lansbury (First Commissioner of Works).

*The British delegation to the first Hague Conference sign the
Rhineland Evacuation Protocol, August 1929*

Seated: Philip Snowden and William Graham (President of the Board of Trade).
Standing in the middle: Arthur Henderson.

The London Naval Conference of 1930

Left to right: Dino Grandi (Italy), Henry L. Stimson (United States), Aristide
Briand (France), Ramsay MacDonald (Great Britain) and André Tardieu (France)

*Ramsay MacDonald receiving a ticker-tape welcome in Broadway,
New York, October 1929*

Ramsay MacDonald and President Herbert Hoover outside the White House, October 1929

Gustav Stresemann

Aristide Briand

Montagu Norman

Viscount Cecil of Chelwood

The Seven-Power London Conference, July 1931

Front row: Andrew Mellon (United States), Pierre Laval (France), Aristide Briand (France), Ramsay MacDonald (Great Britain), Henry L. Stimson (United States) and Arthur Henderson (Great Britain). *Second row in the middle:* Heinrich Brüning (Germany).

unaccompanied, but round me would be the ghosts of the other nations.[1]

On reflection the British therefore came to the conclusion that they wanted the United States to have no more than eighteen large cruisers.[2]

A further British offer on 30 August to scrap her controversial *Hawkins*-class cruisers was still insufficient to tempt Washington.[3] But on 9 September the decisive breakthrough came when MacDonald suggested that the United States should fit a number of their desired 10,000-ton cruisers with 6-inch guns. Without finally accepting this offer, Hoover now decided that the gap was sufficiently narrow to justify allowing MacDonald to visit Washington.[4] The final details could be left, if need be, to the actual conference. However, it was typical of his cautious and reserved attitude towards Great Britain that he avoided giving MacDonald a direct invitation even at this stage; he merely agreed that the Prime Minister might now invite himself.[5]

The impending tête-à-tête between the President and the Prime Minister prompted both the British and the Americans to reconsider the position of the other three naval powers. In a bid to avoid the appearance of a *fait accompli* arising out of MacDonald's visit, it was agreed between Washington and London that the British Government should issue formal invitations to a five-power naval conference before the end of his visit to the United States.[6] This was duly done on 7 October, after the Prime Minister had arrived in the United States, though its final form had been agreed when he was still at sea.

[1] *B.D.*, 2/1, no. 67 (MacDonald to Dawes, 23 Sep 1929).
[2] This policy was unsuccessfully challenged in the Cabinet by Shaw, who pleaded for a compromise. Asked by Alexander if his remarks were to be taken as authorising the Prime Minister to settle on a figure of twenty-one cruisers for the United States, in which case 'the Admiralty would say the Prime Minister had passed the point of safety', Shaw replied 'that he would risk a little Admiralty opposition rather than a break-down'. Shaw did not press his point when Passfield and Parmoor 'both expressed the view that the wholehearted support of the Admiralty was indispensable': Cabinet Minutes, Cab. 23/61, 33(29)1, 13 Sep 1929. [3] *B.D.*, 2/1, no. 41 (MacDonald to Dawes, 30 Aug 1929).
[4] *B.D.*, 2/1, no. 49 (MacDonald to Dawes, 9 Sep 1929); *F.R.*, 1929, I 220–3 (Dawes to Stimson, 10 Sep 1929; and Stimson to Dawes, 11 Sep 1929).
[5] Ferrell, *American Diplomacy in the Great Depression*, p. 79. See also Lord Howard of Penrith (Sir Esmé Howard), *Theatre of Life* (London, 1935–6) II 540.
[6] American resistance to this plan was finally broken down by MacDonald. See *B.D.*, 2/1, nos 61, 64 and 70 (MacDonald to Dawes, 17 Sep 1929; Dawes to MacDonald, 18 Sep 1929; and Henderson to Craigie, 2 Oct 1929).

MacDonald sailed from Southampton on 28 September and arrived in New York on 4 October. It does not appear that he spent much time preparing for the diplomatic conversations he was to have, since in the event Hoover was to take the initiative on every issue and MacDonald's off-the-cuff responses were more than once to be repudiated by London. In fact it would appear that the Prime Minister was primarily interested in making a good impression on the American people as a whole. According to one somewhat jaundiced observer, MacDonald's main concern on the voyage across the Atlantic centred upon the question of his attire:

> He consulted the staff of advisers he had with him on the boat ... they did not feel entirely competent to decide the question on their own responsibility. . . . Urgently they radioed the Foreign Office. The Prime Minister, they said, wanted to know whether he should wear a top-hat or a cloth cap in the Keir Hardie manner. With hardly a few seconds hesitation the Foreign Office replied that the Prime Minister should certainly wear a morning coat and top-hat. This he did.[1]

On arriving in New York, MacDonald duly received an enthusiastic welcome, complete with ticker-tape. He delivered several public orations in New York and Washington, culminating in an address to the Senate. Everywhere his somewhat flowery phrases and revivalist oratory created a good impression and, considering his connections with Socialism, the overall impact he had on the United States was remarkably favourable.[2]

Certainly the public aspect of the visit was incomparably more successful than the private talks between the President and the Prime Minister, which took place principally on 6 October at the former's Rapidan retreat. Hoover dominated the conversations from the outset and made a number of proposals primarily designed, as he subsequently admitted in his memoirs, 'to test MacDonald's views'.[3] The principal questions covered were naval limitation, food ships in times of war, British bases in the Western hemisphere and the possible extension of the Pact of Paris.

[1] Claud Cockburn, *In Time of Trouble: An Autobiography* (London, 1956) p. 171. The present writer regrets that he has been unable to locate documentary confirmation of this account.

[2] For a detailed description of the public aspect of MacDonald's visit, see Ferrell, *American Diplomacy in the Great Depression*, pp. 79–80. For a much more hostile account, see Cockburn, *In Time of Trouble*, pp. 171–3.

[3] Hoover, *Memoirs: The Cabinet and the Presidency*, p. 345.

The talks on naval limitation centred on two matters, first the possibility of an extension of the battleship agreement of 1922, and secondly
an examination of the remaining gap between London and Washington
with regard to cruisers. On battleships MacDonald was eager for a
reduction in tonnage and gun calibre but not for a complete holiday in
new construction because of fear of 'dislocation in the yards'.[1] Since
Hoover, by contrast, was interested only in a reduction in numbers, an
impasse on the battleship issue was quickly reached. Similarly, no real
progress was made on the cruiser question, but this was not altogether
unexpected. The Prime Minister had in fact deliberately refrained from
bringing any Admiralty representatives with him so as to avoid making
the success of his visit in any way appear to depend upon a solution to
this problem being found.[2] In the circumstances the President could only
make the modest claim that, as a result of a Navy Board concession on the
age factor, the gap was rather nearer to being bridged than hitherto.[3]

The subject of food ships and the freedom of the seas was raised by
Hoover in spite of an earlier agreement that it should not be linked to the
naval limitation discussions. The President hinted at the need to appease
the Senate if subsequent naval agreements were to be ratified, and in
particular he thought that a British willingness to treat food ships like
hospital ships would be sufficient to bring the freedom of the seas

[1] B.D., 2/I, no. 77, p. 106 (memorandum by MacDonald on his conversations
with President Hoover). There was perhaps a certain irony in the erstwhile
near-pacifist resisting disarmament measures in the interests of the well-being
of a capitalist economy. MacDonald may also have been influenced by the
determined opposition of the Admiralty to a battleship holiday. For the
admirals' view, see Alexander to MacDonald, 30 July 1929, MacDonald Papers.

[2] MacDonald had been strongly urged to adopt this course by Dawes before
leaving London: Dawes, *Journal*, pp. 71, 73. The Admiralty had taken a very
different view. Alexander had asked the Prime Minister to take a naval officer
with him, while Sir Charles Madden, the First Sea Lord, had written to
MacDonald urging that Alexander should accompany him: Alexander to Mac-
Donald, 17 Sep 1929, and Madden to MacDonald, 21 Sep 1929, MacDonald
Papers.

[3] B.D., 2/I, no. 77, p. 107 (memorandum by MacDonald). Hoover's problem
with regard to large cruisers had been greatly accentuated by the Navy General
Board's meeting of 11 September. The latter's uncompromising insistence on
twenty-one large cruisers left Hoover little room for mœanuvre: O'Connor,
Perilous Equilibrium, pp. 43–4. Not until the London Naval Conference had
actually commenced did the President and the Secretary of State feel that the
time had come to ignore the General Board.

controversy to an end.[1] MacDonald was initially impressed by this idea and told Stimson that he thought the Labour and Liberal parties together with the younger Conservatives would support it.[2] However, in the face of unexpected opposition from London, the Prime Minister felt unable to accept Hoover's proposal without further consultations with his colleagues. Hoover next requested that his initiative in bringing up the matter should be recorded in the final communiqué on the talks with the understanding that this did not commit MacDonald to anything. But even this was rejected in London by both Henderson and the Chiefs of Staff, who laid stress on the findings of the Belligerent Rights subcommittee of the Committee of Imperial Defence, which had reported on 6 March 1929 after two years' study in favour of continued adherence to the traditional British attitude of maintaining complete freedom of action.[3] MacDonald therefore again disappointed Hoover, making use of Henderson's astute argument that a food-ship embargo might be necessary to deal with an aggressor under Article 16 of the League Covenant.[4] The Prime Minister, however, pointed out to his colleagues that there were no means of preventing Hoover raising the matter publicly after the end of the visit.[5] The result was that once this had happened – in the President's Armistice Day speech – the British Government were to be faced with criticism from those sections of the Labour Party to which sentimental appeals were well calculated to be irresistible.[6]

On the subject of bases in the Western hemisphere, Hoover proposed that, in return for a similar American undertaking with respect to the Eastern hemisphere, Great Britain should undertake not to maintain any capable of menacing the United States. He did not pretend that the United States would be conceding very much, since the only American

[1] *B.D.*, 2/1, no. 77, p. 110 (memorandum by MacDonald).

[2] *F.R.*, 1929, III 3–7 (memorandum by Stimson, 7 Oct 1929).

[3] *B.D.*, 2/1, no. 77, appendix A, nos 5 and 6 (Henderson to Howard, 8 Oct 1929, 2.50 p.m., and Henderson to Howard, 8 Oct 1929, 4 p.m.). For the report of the C.I.D. subcommittee, see C.P., no. 304, 4 Nov 1929, Cab. 24/206.

[4] *B.D.*, 2/1, no. 77, appendix A, no. 6 (Henderson to Howard, 8 Oct 1929).

[5] *B.D.*, 2/1, no. 77, p. 112 (memorandum by MacDonald).

[6] The *Daily Herald*, 13 Nov 1929, for example, produced a characteristically idealistic editorial fully approving Hoover's supposedly humanitarian appeal. The full text of the President's speech is given in an enclosure in Ronald I. Campbell (Washington) to Henderson, telegram no. 2129, 14 Nov 1929, F.O., 414/264.

bases in the East were in the Philippines and restrictions concerning fortifications there had been laid down in the 1922 Naval Treaty. Nevertheless, MacDonald was sympathetic and believed that a declaration in the sense Hoover requested would have great psychological importance. This view, however, did not appeal to the Chiefs of Staff in London and, on hearing their protests, the Prime Minister once again had to disappoint the Americans whose hopes he had earlier raised.[1] It is also of interest to note in connection with British bases in the West Indies that Hoover made a verbal offer to purchase Bermuda, Trinidad and British Honduras as part of a debt settlement. The President later recorded in his memoirs that MacDonald 'did not rise to the idea at all . . . I had a hunch he did not take the payment of the debt seriously'.[2]

Nor was any accord possible on Hoover's suggestion for an amendment to the Pact of Paris designed to provide for consultation and possible mediation by neutrals in the event of a dispute. Surprisingly, MacDonald was unenthusiastic at this prospect of breaking down American isolationism. He appears to have been warned that such a move would only succeed in weakening the authority of the League of Nations.[3]

The talks at Rapidan were therefore unsuccessful in that no agreement was reached on any of the specific questions raised. This was confirmed by the vague character of the joint statement issued at their conclusion.[4] In some ways, moreover, Hoover appears to have been rather unscrupulous in his efforts to take advantage of MacDonald. It is therefore difficult to appreciate what led the latter to say of the former on his return to London: 'his powerful way of furthering an argument made me almost smile in his face and exclaim to him out of the happiness of my own soul "Oh you dear old Quaker".'[5]

In fact the only success MacDonald had in the United States was in obtaining popular acclaim at his public appearances. Important as this may have been in psychological terms, it was not so entirely unexpected

---

[1] *B.D.*, 2/1, no. 77, pp. 114–15 (memorandum by MacDonald). For further details and background information on this subject, see D. C. Watt, 'American Strategic Interests and Anxieties in the West Indies: An Historical Examination', *Journal of the Royal United Service Institution*, CVIII (1963) 224–32.

[2] Hoover, *Memoirs: The Cabinet and the Presidency*, p. 346.

[3] *B.D.*, 2/1, no. 77, p. 116 (memorandum by MacDonald).

[4] The text of the communiqué, issued on 19 Oct 1929, appears in *F.R.*, 1929, III 33–5.   [5] *Daily Herald*, 8 Nov 1929.

as to merit the lyrical and extravagant praise it was accorded by some British Socialists. Beatrice Webb wrote in her diary that 'a feat of endurance and triumph in political activities had been J. R. M.'s visit'; and Dalton, not normally an enthusiast for the Prime Minister, wrote in his diary on 1 November that MacDonald had 'made for himself an eternal niche in the temple of history'.[1] After the fall of the Labour Government, the same writer contended that MacDonald's 'American visit was his greatest contribution to foreign policy during the period of his second administration'.[2]

In order to place these judgements in perspective, it is worth recalling the slightly sardonic forecast of Lord Thomson. He had told Beatrice Webb on 23 September that MacDonald 'would come back after a magnificent reception in the U.S.A., with absolutely *no* reduction of expenditure on naval armaments'.[3] That had to wait until more serious negotiations commenced at the London Naval Conference of 1930.

[1] Cole (ed.), *Beatrice Webb's Diaries, 1924–1932*, p. 223; Dalton, *Call Back Yesterday*, p. 246.

[2] Dalton, in *Political Quarterly*, II 499.

[3] Cole (ed.), *Beatrice Webb's Diaries, 1924–1932*, p. 220. Thomson also alleged that MacDonald had been drawn into 'a maze of figures by [Sir William W.] Fisher [Deputy Chief of Naval Staff] – and he had no head for figures': ibid.

CHAPTER SIX

The London Naval Conference and its Aftermath, 1930–1931

T HE London Naval Conference was one of the most distinguished international gatherings of the twentieth century, being attended *inter alios* by the Prime Ministers of France and Great Britain, and by the Foreign Ministers of Great Britain, France, Italy and the United States. Moreover, the conference was conducted in the grand manner, continuing in all for three months.[1] But, as is so often the case, the mere presence of distinguished delegations did little to promote far-reaching agreements, although considerations of prestige may have led some of the statesmen to accept paper formulae of somewhat doubtful value. At all events, the results of the conference were of a limited character and were clearly disappointing to contemporaries, even if to some modern historians they may now seem rather more impressive in the light of the knowledge that no other comparable agreement on arms limitation has since been negotiated.

The conference was officially opened by King George V on the morning of 21 January in the elegant Royal Gallery of the House of Lords, the event being only slightly marred by the fact that an extremely thick fog delayed the arrival of many of those invited to attend.[2] After the departure of the monarch the first plenary session settled questions of procedure and established the necessary working committees. But, as is usual at such gatherings, the important decisions were to be reached not in the official sessions but in private meetings between delegation leaders. These critical private conferences, because of the unstable Parliamentary situation in London, often had to take place in cramped rooms in the Palace of Westminster rather than in St James's Palace,

---

[1] It was perhaps a measure of the importance then attached to disarmament negotiations that Stimson felt justified in being absent from the Department of State for the whole of this period.

[2] For a graphic description of the opening ceremony, see Ferrell, *American Diplomacy in the Great Depression*, pp. 88–90.

the official headquarters of the conference – a constant reminder to the delegates that the Labour Government might fall at any time.

In spite of the fog and the dangers so obviously facing the MacDonald administration, the omens at the opening of the conference were not all inauspicious. In particular, a meeting between Stimson and Tardieu on 20 January gave rise to optimism in that French hostility to Anglo-American plans appeared to have been modified. A French memorandum of 20 December had laid stress on her paramount requirement for adequate security arrangements, particularly in the Mediterranean, and it seemed to link a naval disarmament agreement to a successful outcome to the land disarmament discussions being held at Geneva.[1] By 20 January, however, Tardieu was expressing a willingness to consider a naval treaty in isolation from land disarmament.[2] On the other hand great difficulties remained, since the French still wanted increased security guarantees and in addition refused to consider the possibility of parity in naval strength with the Italians, who in turn appeared to regard a declaration of parity as essential to their prestige. Moreover, differences also existed among the other three naval powers. The United States and Great Britain were still divided on the cruiser issue both in terms of total tonnage and of gun calibre; and both these countries were at odds with Japan in that they did not wish to concede Tokyo's claim for an improved ratio in auxiliary vessels compared with that which had been agreed in capital ships in 1922.

It was not surprising, in view of the protracted negotiations of 1929, that the Anglo-American differences were the first to be resolved at the 1930 conference. Although the British did not adopt an entirely inflexible position on every issue and actually conceded a good deal to Washington with regard to battleships, the decisive concession leading to agreement came from the American side. The most important point on which Stimson and his colleagues yielded to the British was on the number of large cruisers to be allotted to the United States. When it became clear that MacDonald would not and could not accept the Navy General Board's demand for twenty-one such cruisers, the American delegation met on 4 February and unanimously agreed to settle for eighteen.[3] If the delegates were united on this, their naval advisers were

[1] F.R., 1929, I 299–304 (copy of French memorandum, 20 Dec 1929).

[2] F.R., 1930, I 5 (Stimson to Joseph Cotton (Washington), 20 Jan 1930).

[3] F.R., 1930, I 13–17 (Stimson to Cotton, 4 Feb 1930).

not, for while Admiral William Pratt agreed with making the concession, Admiral Hilary Jones adhered to the General Board's view.[1]
But it was with the full support of Hoover that the American delegates
decided to inform the British of their intention to ignore the General
Board recommendation.

The British response to this gesture was a concession on the battleship
issue. At Rapidan, MacDonald had resisted Hoover's proposal for a
complete naval holiday in the construction of capital ships down to 1936
on the grounds that failure to replace obsolete vessels would cause 'dislocation in the yards'.[2] Hoover, on the other hand, had not responded
to MacDonald's request for a cut in the maximum tonnage of new
capital ships.[3] The first sign the Americans had that MacDonald might
be yielding to them came on 15 January, when at a Press conference he
said that in the opinion of the British Government

> the battleship, in view of its tremendous size and cost and the develop-
> ment of the power of attack in the air and under water, is a very doubt-
> ful proposition and they would wish to see an agreement by which the
> battleship would in due time disappear altogether from the fleets of
> the world. Until that is possible the Government would like the Con-
> ference to consider whether agreement cannot be reached that no
> immediate replacements should be made and the life of the existing
> battleships extended.[4]

This represented a much greater policy shift on MacDonald's part
than was generally appreciated at the time. He had earlier persuaded a
Cabinet Committee, despite some resistance from Henderson, to endorse an Admiralty-approved document, known as 'The Blue Print',
which reaffirmed his Rapidan stand on battleships.[5] This document
had then been sent to the Dominions for consideration without the

[1] Ibid. For details of the arguments deployed by the various naval advisers,
see Wheeler, *Prelude to Pearl Harbor*, pp. 171–3. Admiral Jones had to return
home from London suffering from ulcers, but he recovered sufficiently to
testify against the terms of the treaty when it came before the Senate Committee
on Foreign Relations.

[2] *B.D.*, 2/1, no. 77 (memorandum by MacDonald, Oct 1929).

[3] Ibid.   [4] *The Times*, 16 Jan 1930.

[5] Minutes of the fifth meeting of the London Naval Conference Cabinet
Committee, 9 Jan 1930, I.C., Cab. 29/117. Henderson suggested a 'bolder offer'
regarding battleships. MacDonald, however, said that 'if a holiday were to occur
until 1936, it would then mean a building rush after that period which must if
possible be avoided'.

Cabinet being consulted. The story of MacDonald's subsequent volte-face is told in the following extracts from Dalton's diary:

> On Wednesday [15 January] J. R. M. made his statement to the journalists. Something had made him move sharply to the left on battleships. . . . Anyhow he threw over the Admiralty and the Blue Print Doctrines without a word of warning or consultation. . . . [Henderson] said to Phil [Noel-Baker] afterwards 'Now we've got them on the run !' The Admiralty were furious, not without reason. Here was a completely new policy, a clear reversal. They prepared a violently argumentative document. . . . But Phil has come into his own. J. R. M. has been ringing him up to produce counter arguments and to demolish the Admiralty case. He has been round to No. 10 in Conference with J. R. M. and King Albert [Alexander], who doesn't know where *he* stands (!), and Craigie.[1]

The most decisive reason for MacDonald's volte-face, in Dalton's view, was that Snowden, based at The Hague and 'furious' at not having seen the 'Blue Print' before it was sent to the Dominions, had submitted a written protest to the Prime Minister.[2] The Chancellor stated:

> I think it would be a great mistake to submit these proposals to the Conference as a minimum of our demands. . . .
>
> If they go through, in a few years' time both we and the other Great Powers will have Navies which are not less numerous, and are positively more powerful, more up to date, and far more costly than the present Fleets. . . .
>
> . . . reduced Naval Estimates depend on a reduction of the size of the British fleet *pari passu* with other Powers. I urge that we should lead the way with a scheme designed to secure this object.
>
> I hope that this will include a plan for reducing the number of Capital ships. . . .
>
> In no circumstances can I approve the Admiralty proposals that the future size of capital ships should be settled here and now at 25,000 tons, and that replacement should commence at the rate of one a year before 1936. . . .
>
> The U.S.A. are clearly right in proposing that this question should be postponed until 1936, and that meanwhile no new ships be laid

[1] Dalton Diary, entry for 19 Jan 1930. Dalton's claim that on 15 January MacDonald acted without warning is not strictly accurate, since on 14 January he had secured Cabinet agreement to a reversal of policy on battleships. There is, however, no evidence that he had consulted the Admiralty experts before suddenly making this suggestion to the Cabinet. See Cabinet Minutes, Cab. 23/63, 1(30)2, 14 Jan 1930.   [2] Dalton Diary, entry for 21 Jan 1930.

down. . . . We cannot allow the Dockyard situation to determine our building programme. . . . To spend money on shipbuilding to find work is the most wasteful form of expenditure. . . .[1]

Henderson's influence may also have counted for something, although it is clear from the following passage in Dalton's diary that the Foreign Secretary's methods did not take a spectacular form:

> Uncle made a fight against battleships, but, I gather, found J. R. M. and King Albert sticky. . . . Uncle said tonight after putting, as his growing habit is, the points on the other side . . . 'after all I have to remember that I'm only Second Delegate. I may have to choose between going on with the others, or dropping out and leaving them to it.'[2]

Cecil was also active in the campaign to persuade MacDonald to over-rule the Admiralty's demand for battleships. In a memorandum for the Prime Minister, dated 17 December 1929, he argued that vessels under 10,000 tons were preferable to battleships since they were cheaper to construct and easier to maintain. Battleships were also inconvenient because they required unusually large harbours, the provision of which, as in the case of Singapore, could prove disproportionately expensive. Cecil went on to reject the Admiralty view that battleships had a sub-stantially better prospect than a cruiser of surviving a submarine or air-craft attack; and he was equally unimpressed by fears that armed merchantmen might be a serious menace to any naval vessel smaller than a battleship.[3]

The shift in British policy first indicated on 15 January was confirmed by MacDonald in a talk with Stimson on the 18th, 'although he was really worried by the industrial aspect of the matter'.[4] A further develop-ment came on 7 February when a British White Paper was published suggesting a reduction in both the tonnage and the number of capital ship replacements.[5] The American response was at first disappointing,

---

[1] For the text of Snowden's letter to MacDonald, dated 12 Jan 1930, see Cabinet Minutes, Cab. 23/63, 1(30), appendix 1, 14 Jan 1930. Snowden claimed to have the full support of Graham, who was also at The Hague.

[2] Dalton Diary, entry for 9 Jan 1930.

[3] Cecil memorandum for MacDonald, 17 Dec 1929, Cecil Papers, Add. 51081.

[4] F.R., 1930, I 2–4 (Stimson to Cotton, 19 Jan 1930).

[5] Cmd. 3485 of 1929–30. It is reprinted in B.D., 2/1, no. 142. If Henderson had had his way the British would have proposed more far-reaching reductions. In a memorandum to the Commonwealth delegations he had written: 'it must

since Stimson, while still eager for an agreement on capital ships, for a time attempted to obtain the right to build one new American battleship to compensate for the British possession of two post-war vessels, the *Rodney* and the *Nelson*. Eventually, however, the Americans gave way on this point and in return the British decided on 14 February to settle for a complete holiday in battleship construction until 1936.[1] Once this had been tentatively agreed, the British call for a reduction in the maximum tonnage level became *ipso facto* an irrelevancy.

The only other important difference remaining between Washington and London concerned the total tonnage in cruisers. Were the Americans to be allowed 327,000 or only 320,000 tons? The dispute was finally resolved on 27 February by splitting the difference at 323,500 tons and by an understanding that either power would have the option of duplicating the fleet of the other.[2] At this stage the Anglo-American settlement was based on the assumption that a satisfactory agreement would be reached with France and Italy. When this later proved unobtainable, Great Britain and the United States, following up a suggestion by Hoover, decided to overcome the difficulty by adopting an accelerator clause whereby new vessels could be constructed in the unlikely event of the Mediterranean powers undertaking a greatly increased building programme.[3]

The problems raised by the Japanese demands were less easily settled and at one time appeared to be completely intractable. That a

---

always be borne in mind that the purpose of the London Conference is to make agreements that shall create a new equilibrium of naval strength at lower levels of armament than now exist . . . if very low levels of naval armament were reached, British sea-power would be much increased, for the fast armed merchantmen, in which we should have a great preponderance over other nations, would become an important factor in any war that might subsequently occur': Henderson memorandum, 23 Jan 1930, I.C., Cab. 29/134. The Admiralty, however, had successfully resisted most of Henderson's specific proposals on the grounds that Great Britain's supply lines were particularly vulnerable and that she therefore had 'an absolute need' for certain levels of tonnage in fighting vessels: Minutes of the Third and Fifth Meetings of the Delegations o ;the British Commonwealth, 31 Jan and 6 Feb 1930, I.C., Cab. 29/133.

[1] *B.D.*, 2/1, no. 146 (notes of a meeting between British, French and American representatives, 14 Feb 1930).

[2] *F.R.*, 1930, I 32 (Stimson to Cotton, 28 Feb 1930).

[3] For the origin of the accelerator clause, see *F.R.*, 1930, I 31 (Cotton to Stimson, 26 Feb 1930).

AT THE BAR OF THE FIVE NATIONS;
OR, A *CONSOMMATION* DEVOUTLY TO BE WISHED.

M. Briand. *I want something sustaining. Can you give me a 'Military Commitment'?*

Mr. MacDonald. *Sorry, we don't serve it. Against the rules of the house. But I can recommend our 'No. 16 Old Geneva Clarified.'*

[In order to appease the desire of France for guarantees of security, persistent research has been made for a formula based on a "clarifying" interpretation of Article No. 16 of the Covenant of the League of Nations.]

three-power agreement eventually emerged owed much to the willingness to retreat by both the British and the Americans. Considering that in 1929, in their negotiations with the Americans, the British had repeatedly emphasised their concern about the size of the Japanese fleet, they played a curiously passive role on this question at the London Naval Conference. For example, at a vital meeting between the representatives of the three nations on 17 February 1930, Henderson feigned neutrality between Tokyo and Washington, claiming that 'his Delegation were just interested spectators'.[1] This kind of diplomatic tactic was not entirely uncharacteristic of Henderson. What is more surprising is that neither MacDonald nor Alexander apparently showed any signs of serious displeasure at Henderson's failure to stand up for British interests; and later on they willingly fell in with the so-called compromise solution which in fact represented an almost total victory for Tokyo. Henderson at least showed that he was well aware of the shift in British policy when he wrote to Sir John Tilley, the British ambassador in Tokyo, giving details of the latest offer made to the Japanese. He stated:

> the above compromise represents a considerable departure from our original attitude, and during the negotiations we have made concession after concession to Japan before reaching the present position. It is useless for the Japanese Government or the Japanese delegation here to think that we can go any further.[2]

The Americans had begun their talks with the Japanese confidently enough by first attempting to link a renewed battleship agreement, for which Tokyo was known to be eager, to a settlement of the cruiser question.[3] As the weeks passed, however, it became increasingly obvious that overwhelming domestic pressures alone ruled out any possibility of Japan accepting a simple extension of the 1922 'Rolls-Royce: Rolls-Royce: Ford' ratio to auxiliary categories. Once this had been grasped in Washington, the Americans bent over backwards to reach a formal three-power agreement, and eventually on 13 March they offered terms which they persuaded the Japanese delegation to recommend to Tokyo.[4]

[1] *B.D.*, 2/1, no. 147 (notes of a meeting between British, American and Japanese representatives, 17 Feb 1930).

[2] *B.D.*, 2/1, no. 156 (Henderson to Tilley, 15 Mar 1930).

[3] See for example *B.D.*, 2/1, nos 133, enclosure, and 147 (memorandum of American-Japanese conversation, 26 Dec 1929; and notes of a meeting between British, American and Japanese representatives, 17 Feb 1930).

[4] *F.R.*, 1930, I 61 (Stimson to Cotton, 13 Mar 1930).

After prolonged hesitation, these terms were accepted by the Japanese Government on 2 April. The Japanese were given parity in submarines and destroyers, and a 70 per cent ratio in small cruisers. In large cruisers they were accorded a 70 per cent ratio for the bulk of the six years during which the treaty was to be in operation, although at the very end of the period they were to be reduced in theory to a 60 per cent level. The only other meaningful concession required of Japan concerned submarines, for although accorded parity, the total tonnage she was permitted (52,700 tons) was considerably smaller than she would have preferred.[1] But taken as a whole, the agreement was very much a triumph for the Japanese, even though some militant domestic elements could not be brought to see it in that light.[2]

As was to be expected, the most difficult negotiations at the London Naval Conference centred not, however, on Japan but rather on the attitude of France and Italy. Rome insisted on parity between the two Latin nations while Paris was equally determined to deny it. In addition, the French wanted at least a reaffirmation, and probably an increase, in their security guarantees from the British, whom they correctly suspected of having developed isolationist tendencies. The Americans found themselves involved in this complicated situation not because they themselves cared much about the size of the French and Italian fleets but simply because they realised that the ratification of their agreement with the British might be jeopardised by a failure to reach a settlement in the Mediterranean theatre.[3] However eager MacDonald may have been to stabilise his fleet and crown his new approach to Washington with a striking agreement, he could not lightly dismiss the European situation in view of the Admiralty doctrine, known as the two-power standard, which in effect required British naval strength to be equivalent to the combined fleets of the two most powerful continental naval powers.

[1] For details of the final modifications, see *B.D.*, 2/1, no. 175 (notes of a meeting between British, American and Japanese representatives, 2 Apr 1930).

[2] The London Naval Treaty in fact appears to have played some part in undermining the position of the liberal element in Japanese politics. See Takehiko Yoshihashi, *Conspiracy at Mukden: The Rise of the Japanese Military* (New Haven, 1963) esp. pp. 61–79. A symbolic gesture occurred on the return of Admiral Takeshi Takarabe to Tokyo from London – he was presented with a dagger by angry militants: O'Connor, *Perilous Equilibrium*, p. 118.

[3] See *F.R.*, 1930, I 2–4, 62–3 (Stimson to Cotton, 19 Jan 1930 and 14 Mar 1930).

As has been noted, the French, prior to the opening of the conference, had agreed to abandon the link between naval and land disarmament. But this did not in itself solve any problems of detail. In fact the outlook appeared to be grave when on 12 February the French announced the size of the fleet they would require in the event of no agreement with Italy being achieved and no satisfactory security arrangements emerging. The total tonnage France deemed essential in the various categories of auxiliary craft amounted to 483,076 tons.[1] The British reaction to the French figures was to state frankly that they were 'far too high'.[2] Yet there appeared to be no initial inclination in Whitehall to make any serious concession on security in order to secure a reduction.[3]

By contrast, the American delegation, and in particular the Secretary of State, sought to promote negotiations for a consultative pact as a means of placating the French. Stimson believed that MacDonald might not otherwise be able to secure the acceptance of the Anglo-American agreement.[4] Although there was at this stage no intention on the part of the American delegates to suggest the participation of their own country in any consultative arrangements, extravagant rumours to this effect alarmed the President in Washington. He was acutely aware that enemies of naval limitation on Capitol Hill would seize upon any arrangements, however innocuous, as being a move towards military entanglements in Europe. For this reason he took the view that it would be inadvisable at this time to consider even an amplification of the Kellogg Pact, although he himself had suggested this at his Rapidan meeting with MacDonald. The President now felt that the link between such an arrangement and a naval treaty might prove fatal to the latter's chances in the Senate.[5] The American delegates in London at first agreed with Hoover's assessment, and on 8 March Stimson told Briand that 'any blending of a successful naval treaty and the Kellogg Pact now would be disastrous to both', and that he was 'a friend of both'.[6] It was even decided that a formal public statement to this effect was necessary in order to prevent any misunderstanding, and this was duly made on 11 march by Stimson.[7]

[1] For a breakdown of this total, see O'Connor, *Perilous Equilibrium*, p. 88.
[2] *B.D.*, 2/1, no. 144 (note of a conversation between Craigie and Massigli, 13 Feb 1930).   [3] Ibid.   [4] *F.R.*, 1930, I 36–9 (Stimson to Cotton, 3 Mar 1930).
[5] *F.R.*, 1930, I 39–40 (Hoover in Cotton to Stimson, 3 Mar 1930).
[6] *F.R.*, 1930, I 55–6 (Stimson to Cotton, 10 Mar 1930).
[7] *F.R.*, 1930, I 57–9 (Stimson to Cotton, 12 Mar 1930).

Meanwhile Great Britain had given the French no real encouragement on security. On 26 February the French presented the draft of a
Mediterranean Pact to the British, but it was a foregone conclusion
that this would not evoke a favourable response, at least in the context
of the London Naval Conference, since the British had given an undertaking as early as 1 January to the Spanish ambassador that no such pact
would be negotiated in Spain's absence.[1] The French and the British
accordingly gave consideration to a possible consultative pact not confined to the Mediterranean. But French hopes of any worth-while
arrangement were undermined on 9 March when MacDonald, in a
broadcast to North America, declared that 'we shall not agree to any
treaty which may result in entangling military alliances'.[2] At the same
time, as has been shown elsewhere, the British Government were unwilling to accept all the radical Covenant amendments which the
Committee of Eleven, meeting in Geneva, had favoured.[3] A further
decisive blow to French hopes came on 19 March, when the Prime

---

[1] B.D., 2/1, nos 151 and 131 (French draft of a Mediterranean Pact given to
Craigie, 26 Feb 1930; and minute by Lindsay, 1 Jan 1930). For a further undertaking to Madrid, see B.D., 2/1, no. 140 (memorandum for the Spanish ambassador, 17 Jan 1930). Despite these assurances to Spain, Cecil unsuccessfully
sought to encourage Henderson to promote a Mediterranean Pact: 'I gather . . .
that the Government may feel it advisable to do something to satisfy French
anxieties with regard to the Mediterranean in return for an adequate reduction
in their naval programme. . . . I should like you to know that if the Government
should decide on anything of that kind, I would do my best to secure that the
League of Nations Union come out strongly in your support. I have spoken to
Gilbert Murray and Maxwell Garnett on the subject, and they both fully agree
with me. In these circumstances I have little doubt that we should carry with us
at any rate the majority of the Executive Committee, unless indeed you propose
something of a very extreme character. Even so, you could count on my support
for what it is worth': Cecil to Henderson, ? Mar 1930, Henderson Papers,
F.O. 800/281.

[2] Dawes, Journal, p. 168. At this time MacDonald was receiving strong
encouragement for his anti-French stand from Garvin of The Observer, who
wrote: 'Last August I told General Dawes my conviction that the French dogma
of security meant rocks ahead. But nobly nobly have you played your own part
and you stand higher in the whole world's eyes. If we save Anglo-American
friendship we save all in the end. This I believe in my soul. What you have done
for that cause I never can forget; and though we may differ on other questions,
I shall never write an unchivalrous or hurtful word about you personally while I
live': Garvin to MacDonald, 14 Mar 1930, Rosenberg Papers.

[3] See above, pp. 87-91.

E

Minister told Briand that 'it was quite impossible to add to our military commitments'.[1]

By 22 March Briand was back in Paris, where the atmosphere was so gloomy that the British ambassador, Tyrrell, sent home an extremely pessimistic report on the prospects of the conference continuing.[2] The substance of this report was made known to Stimson, who promptly decided that spectacular moves were required to save the conference from collapse. Accordingly, on 24 March, in a meeting of the British and American delegations, he abandoned his previous position concerning American participation in a consultative arrangement. He now declared a willingness to negotiate on the matter provided it was clearly understood that no American *military* involvement could possibly arise. He also hinted that the Americans might reconsider their attitude to the freedom of the seas problem in the special case of the British fleet becoming involved in a 'League War'.[3] For his volte-face he failed to obtain Hoover's advance approval. But he maintained that the situation was too urgent to permit delay and he claimed that, with MacDonald and Henderson divided on security, he had to seize the opportunity to strengthen the hand of the Foreign Secretary, who wished to meet Briand half-way on security.[4] In view of Stimson's move, MacDonald instructed Henderson on the next day to ask Briand to come over for further discussions.

Briand agreed with alacrity, and as a result the Paris Press of the same day was tempted to publish optimistic rumours some of which attributed more to the Americans than even Stimson had offered.

[1] As reported to a meeting of the American and British delegations. See *B.D.*, 2/1, no. 168, 24 Mar 1930.

[2] The present writer has been unable to trace the text of Tyrrell's message, but it is referred to in *F.R.*, 1930, 72–3 (Stimson to Cotton, 22 Mar 1930).

[3] *B.D.*, 2/1, no. 168 (notes of a meeting between British and American representatives, 24 Mar 1930). MacDonald was particularly interested in the hint about the freedom of the seas.

[4] *F.R.*, 1930, I 92–5 (Stimson to Cotton, 29 Mar 1930). At a meeting of the British delegation on 24 March Henderson hinted at sympathy with the French view on security and 'recalled that the French had never abandoned the Geneva Protocol'. He added that he himself had always maintained that 'the provisions of Article 11 of the Protocol merely emphasised what was already in the Covenant, but did not commit us to any new obligation'. None of Henderson's colleagues, however, revealed any willingness to consider a revival of the Protocol: Minutes of the Meetings of the British Delegation, 24 Mar 1930, I.C., Cab. 29/128.

Realising that these rumours would prove acutely embarrassing to the administration in Washington, Stimson felt obliged to make a dramatic midnight statement explaining publicly the views he had earlier expressed in confidence to the British delegation. Meanwhile Hoover had decided that the departure from the position announced on 11 March could not be tolerated, and in a confidential telegram virtually repudiated Stimson.[1] The episode did not improve Stimson's standing in Hoover's eyes, for clearly the matter had been handled in a rather inept fashion. Yet it remains true that Stimson's action secured the return of the French to London and thereby paved the way for a tolerable three-power settlement.[2]

The renewed conversations on security were inevitably somewhat overshadowed by the tacit withdrawal of Stimson's proposal for a consultative arrangement. The British, however, tried to save the situation by offering a reaffirmation of previous obligations and, in particular, Annex F of the Locarno Treaty.[3] Less hopefully, talks were continued on the possibility of an Anglo-French declaration on the interpretation of Article 16 of the Covenant. The French wanted to include the following sentence:

[The Signatory Governments] hereby declare that, so far as they are concerned, a State resorting to hostilities in violation of the Pact of Paris shall, unless the Council decides otherwise, *ipso facto*, be deemed to have committed an act of war against them within the meaning of the first paragraph of Article 16; they would in consequence immediately take against the aggressors the measures provided by the said paragraph.[4]

This idea the British found totally unacceptable and instead they offered a draft declaration which was so ambiguous as to be scarcely worth

---

[1] See *F.R.*, 1930, I 85–6 (Cotton to Stimson, 26 Mar 1930). The President's words were not quite so unequivocal as he implied in his memoirs: Hoover, *Memoirs: The Cabinet and the Presidency*, p. 348.

[2] Briand himself was later to praise Stimson for 'having given the push that broke the jam between the British and the French': *F.R.*, 1930, I 101 (Stimson to Cotton, 3 Apr 1930).

[3] This idea was apparently the brainchild of Noel-Baker and Cecil: Harold Nicolson, *Dwight Morrow* (London, 1935) p. 391. It was first taken up by MacDonald at the crucial meeting with the Americans on 24 March: *B.D.*, 2/I, no. 168.

[4] *B.D.*, 2/I, p. 295, n. 2.

making.[1] Briand took the British draft to Paris for consultations and presently returned with the news that it had been received 'with a certain amount of disappointment'.[2]

Meanwhile, on 7 April, MacDonald had shown the British draft to his Cabinet and had also taken soundings of Opposition leaders. On the next day he told the French that the declaration would have to

> provide that at the effective point in the discussion of the recommendation Parliament should have a chance of intervening. In any event, Parliament would have to be consulted because before any move could be made to carry out a recommendation, the Government would have to obtain credits from Parliament.[3]

Here, then, was the erstwhile Union of Democratic Control demand for Parliamentary control of foreign policy being used to assist MacDonald to avoid strengthening the provisions for collective security.

The inadequacies of the British draft, taken together with a further public statement by MacDonald on 30 March to the effect that there would be no extension in British military obligations, served to discourage the French from making any concessions on naval disarmament.[4] The value as a bargaining counter of the proposed joint declaration was, moreover, greatly reduced by the British decision to require Parliamentary ratification – a lengthy and uncertain procedure. A British declaration of such a conditional character was clearly not capable of serving as a *quid pro quo* for French concessions on naval figures, and hence the conversations on security were brought to an end by mutual consent.

On 10 April the diplomats turned desperately to the other possible avenue for placating the French, namely concessions from Italy. France had made it clear that in a formal agreement with Italy she 'could not go below a disparity of 240,000'.[5] The Italians, on the other hand, had from the outset insisted on complete theoretical parity and they now adhered

---

[1] For the full text, see *B.D.*, 2/1, no. 181, appendix. The implications of the French proposal were the subject of a detailed discussion by the British delegates on 30 March: I.C., Cab. 29/128.

[2] *B.D.*, 2/1, no. 181 (notes of a meeting between British and French representatives, 8 Apr 1930).   [3] Ibid.

[4] MacDonald's statement appeared in *The Times*, 31 Mar 1930. It is summarised in *F.R.*, 1930, I 98 n.

[5] *B.D.*, 2/1, no. 182 (notes of a meeting between British and French representatives, 9 Apr 1930).

to this position with a tenacity which did not invite further pressure upon them.[1]

In these circumstances the various delegations decided to suspend the negotiations and sign a treaty embodying the points on which they were agreed. All five powers were willing to accept those parts of the treaty which referred to a battleship holiday, to the scrapping of a small number of capital ships and to laws for humanising submarine warfare. But only the British, Americans and Japanese were prepared to adhere to Part III, which dealt with the auxiliary categories. An accelerator clause was accordingly included in this section of the treaty in order to safeguard British interests vis-à-vis the Mediterranean powers, in the event of the latter engaging in a naval race.

The final ceremonies and the actual signing of the treaty took place on 22 April.[2] The partial failure of the conference was mitigated by the fact that there had been no spectacular breakdown or withdrawal. The Mediterranean powers were induced to put up an appearance of amity, and agreed to continue separate negotiations on the outstanding questions. This way of handling the situation was probably of great psychological importance in soothing British public opinion. Indeed, if the French had left the conference in anger, the problem of securing British ratification might have proved insuperable. As it was, the treaty was accepted with little opposition on 24 July.[3]

In retrospect it would seem that the British efforts to meet French requirements on security had been wholly inadequate. Yet even if Henderson's policy had prevailed over MacDonald's, the French might even then have been reluctant to offer really substantial concessions on disarmament; for the French needed not only to obtain written commitments from the British but also to be shown that a collectivist outlook prevailed throughout the Foreign Office and in all three political parties.

The conclusion of the London Naval Conference of 1930 had been arranged in such a way that the failure of the Italians and the French to

---

[1] B.D., 2/1, no. 184 (notes of a meeting between British, Italian and French representatives, 10 Apr 1930).

[2] The final text is in B.D., 2/1, appendix 1, pp. 589–97. It is interesting to note that the treaty contained no reference to impartial verification or to measures for the enforcement of its terms.

[3] For details of the insignificant anti-treaty agitation in Great Britain and for the more powerful opposition elsewhere, see O'Connor, Perilous Equilibrium, chap. 10.

resolve their differences did not prevent the other three naval powers from securing the ratification of the treaty. This did not mean, however, that the prospect of a Mediterranean naval race was thereafter to be a matter of indifference to the other powers, least of all to Great Britain, since Admiralty pressure for the application of the treaty's accelerator clause would inevitably have followed any considerable expansion in the French and Italian fleets. In order to prevent a long-term undermining of the three-power arrangement, Henderson accordingly took it upon himself to attempt to bridge the gap between Paris and Rome. His efforts were painstaking and generally unspectacular, but came within an ace of success in March 1931. The Foreign Secretary had what amounted to a free hand in the negotiations, since MacDonald tended to lose interest in the naval disarmament question once his chairmanship of the Naval Conference was at an end.[1]

The British attempt to promote an agreement between the Italians and the French took a rather different form after the end of the London Conference, the principal change being that the British ceased entirely to offer security formulae to the French as a *quid pro quo* for concessions to Rome. The British in fact became pure mediators rather than partial participants in the bargaining which followed the dissolution of the conference. A second difference, for a time at least, lay in the Italians' attempt to link a settlement of the naval differences to a solution of certain outstanding issues between them and the French in North Africa.

Henderson's first task was to try to secure an agreed moratorium on naval construction for the duration of the negotiations, or, failing that, for as long as possible. In this respect the Italians showed themselves to be considerably more helpful and honest than the French. On 14 April, even before the signing of the London Naval Treaty, Dino Grandi, the Italian Foreign Minister, had given a verbal promise to MacDonald to recommend to Rome the acceptance of a truce for as long as the negotiations lasted, if the French would do likewise.[2] He repeated his offer more formally on 11 May in a letter to Sir Ronald Graham, the British

[1] At one stage, with Henderson abroad, MacDonald signed some Foreign Office telegrams on this subject but minuted specifically that he took no responsibility 'for the precise contents': *B.D.*, 2/11, no. 326 n. It is difficult to believe that the Prime Minister had ever been so out of touch with detail before or during the London Conference.

[2] *B.D.*, 2/1, no. 223 (enclosure in Graham to Henderson, 28 June 1930).

ambassador in Rome.[1] Henderson, while in Geneva for a meeting of the League Council, put the proposition to Briand and received an encouraging reply to the effect that the French Government would be recommended to agree.[2] But Briand was clearly temporising, for no reply from Paris was forthcoming and Henderson had to repeat his proposal in a formal communication on 2 July suggesting that 'a decision should be made not to lay down any part of the new programme before the meeting of the Preparatory Commission in November next'.[3] Briand eventually replied after a week's delay in terms that led Henderson to suppose that his proposal had been accepted both in the spirit and in the letter.[4] It turned out, however, that the French meant to evade the intention of Henderson's suggestion by laying down the whole of their original construction programme for 1930 in December.[5] This manœuvre was characteristic of much that was to follow in French naval policy.

The atmosphere in the naval negotiations for the remaining months of 1930 was clearly affected by the French attitude to the construction truce. Nor were prospects of agreement improved by Grandi's attempt to entangle Briand in simultaneous negotiations on colonial questions. At a meeting with Grandi during the League Council session in May 1930, Briand turned down a suggestion that the differences between the two countries concerning Tunisia and Libya should be dealt with in high-level conversations rather than through the normal diplomatic channels, which had not thus far proved adequate for reaching accommodation. Yet he also suggested that the naval negotiations ought to be postponed until progress had been made on the outstanding North African issues.[6] Given this attitude, it was not surprising that no advance proved possible on either subject for some months. Nor was France alone to blame for the deteriorating relationship, for on 17 May Mussolini had chosen to make a speech at Florence containing the following bellicose passage:

Words are very fine things; but rifles, machine-guns, warships, aeroplanes and cannons are still finer things. They are finer, Blackshirts,

[1] B.D., 2/I, no. 208 (enclosure in Graham to Henderson, 16 May 1930).
[2] B.D., 2/I, no. 209 (Henderson to Tyrrell, 23 May 1930).
[3] B.D., 2/I, no. 224 (Henderson to Briand and Grandi, 2 July 1930).
[4] B.D., 2/I, no. 225 (Briand to Henderson, 9 July 1930). Henderson was so pleased that he asked Tyrrell to convey his congratulations to Briand. See B.D., 2/I, no. 226 (Henderson to Tyrrell, 10 July 1930).
[5] B.D., 2/I, no. 231 (Tyrrell to Henderson, 15 July 1930).
[6] B.D., 2/I, nos 206 and 207 (Henderson to Vansittart, 14 and 15 May 1930).

because right unaccompanied by might is an empty word. . . . Fascist Italy, powerfully armed, will offer . . . two simple alternatives: a precious friendship or an adamantine hostility.[1]

It was thus in a somewhat strained atmosphere that the first serious naval talks between Italy and France began in Paris on 21 August. Moreover, from the outset the negotiations were, as a British diplomatist put it,

> overshadowed by the parity difficulty. What in reality M. Massigli and Signor Rosso were endeavouring to do, and in what they failed, was to find some formula which would enable Italy to show that she had obtained parity, and France to show that she had not accorded it. As might be expected, this task was too much for them.[2]

The opening gambit of Augusto Rosso, the Italian representative, was to propose an agreement which would provide for parity in theory but for a substantial French tonnage superiority in practice. On paper both countries would be limited to an identical number of units and of overall tonnage in each category. The Italians hopefully suggested that since France was in the habit of building larger cruisers than Italy, such an agreement would virtually guarantee the reality of disparity until 1936. René Massigli, the head of the League of Nations Section at the Quai d'Orsay, rejected this plan for the same reason that the Italians had advanced it: the acceptance of theoretical parity would prejudice the French negotiating position at the projected naval conference of 1935. France was, however, quite prepared to agree to parity in the number of units held by the two countries, provided the Italians abandoned their claim to theoretical parity in total tonnage. It came as no surprise when this transparent counter-proposal was rejected by the Italians.[3]

Efforts at mediation by Alexander in unofficial visits to Paris and Rome early in September failed to achieve any solution, and accordingly the Rosso–Massigli conversations were broken off. Nor was Henderson able to overcome the impasse despite a personal talk with Briand at the 1930 League Assembly in Geneva.[4]

---

[1] Toynbee et al., Survey of International Affairs, 1931, pp. 261–2. Further extracts from the Duce's speech appear in B.D., 2/1, no. 210, n. 3.

[2] B.D., 2/1, no. 233 (R. H. Campbell (Paris) to Henderson, 16 Sep 1930).

[3] On the Rosso–Massigli conversations, see B.D., 2/1, no. 234 (memorandum by Craigie, 20 Sep 1930).

[4] B.D., 2/1, no. 235 (Henderson to Tyrrell, 1 Oct 1930).

The next initiative came from Washington, where Gibson's influence was much in evidence. Two compromise solutions suggested themselves to the Americans. One possibility was that Italy and France should be invited, after consultations with a mediator, to make unilateral declarations of construction intention, thereby avoiding the creation of any precedent for the 1935 conference. Alternatively France alone should be persuaded to enter into negotiations, principally with Great Britain, as a preliminary to accession to Part III of the London Naval Treaty, leaving Italy temporarily free from formal commitments. With a proper concern for Italian susceptibilities, Gibson initially decided to concentrate his attention upon the first of these possible solutions. His first move was to visit Paris, where on 27 October he secured Tardieu's general assent to his scheme for unilateral declarations.[1] He then proceeded to Rome and had a meeting with Grandi. Since they appeared in essence to deny theoretical parity to the Italians while confirming actual French superiority, the American proposals were accorded an unenthusiastic welcome. Grandi was, moreover, reluctant even to discuss the American plan with Mussolini for fear of provoking the latter's annoyance – a not unusual problem for servants in dictatorships.[2]

His first efforts at a solution having broken down, Gibson next decided to sound out the French about the possibility of their converting the London Naval Treaty into a four-power agreement without Italy. The British reaction to this move was cautious but not unsympathetic. Henderson wrote of it:

We are very interested in the idea that France should now endeavour to reach an agreement with us to enable her to accede to Part III of the Treaty. What of course we have always desired is a Five-Power Treaty, but so great have the difficulties proved to be between France and Italy that we should not be averse from discussing the question of accession of France, provided that, as we are inclined to think possible, a way can be devised which will not militate against an eventual Italian accession or acquiescence; and provided also that we can be sure the present French proposal is really sincere and not merely an attempt to put Italy in a corner, and so perhaps render the situation still more embarrassing without any gain in the cause of disarmament.[3]

[1] *F.R.*, 1930, I 153–5 (Norman Armour (Paris) to Stimson, 27 Oct 1930).
[2] *F.R.*, 1930, I 163–4 (John Garrett (Rome) to Stimson, 30 Oct 1930); *B.D.*, 2/I, no. 257 (Graham to Henderson, 1 Nov 1930).
[3] *B.D.*, 2/I, no. 262 (Henderson to Tyrrell, 4 Nov 1930).

When it became known that the French and Italian Governments were to send naval experts to Geneva for the resumed meeting of the Preparatory Commission later in November, the United States and Great Britain decided that their respective naval experts, Gibson and Craigie, should also attend and endeavour to clarify the situation further. On arrival at Geneva, Craigie sought first to discover whether progress could be looked for on the lines of Gibson's plan for unilateral declarations. He learnt that Rosso, in a conversation with Massigli, had expressed 'readiness to discuss this proposal' but had warned that 'any programme figures which Italy would insert in the declaration must necessarily be the same as those proposed by France'.[1] If the Italian attitude was unhelpful, that of the French was no better. Massigli's initial position, as expressed to Craigie, was to demand 'as a prerequisite to further negotiations' that Great Britain accept 'the principle of a 642,000-ton French fleet'. In addition, he wanted what amounted to an Italian agreement to a French overall superiority of 240,000 tons.[2] Neither Great Britain nor Italy showed any willingness to fall in with such extreme requirements. Craigie, however, did not abandon hope and began instead to canvass a compromise scheme.[3]

The Geneva conversations ended with no concrete concessions from either France or Italy, but by 15 December the Italian Government expressed a desire to embark upon further consultations with Craigie on his compromise proposals. The latter accordingly hastened to Rome where on 20 December Grandi indicated that he was prepared to accept the broad lines of the suggested settlement provided the French would do so too.[4] Italy for the first time was willing to leave the question of theoretical parity in abeyance – signifying a clear victory for the Italian moderates in their struggle with the extremists for Mussolini's support. In the light of subsequent developments, Craigie's comment at the time makes interesting reading:

> There is no doubt in my mind that Signor Grandi, Signor Rosso and the moderate elements in Rome sincerely desire a settlement of the

[1] B.D., 2/1, no. 271 (memorandum by Craigie, 1 Jan 1931).   [2] Ibid.

[3] For details, see ibid. MacDonald was not at this time disposed to encourage further efforts to secure a compromise. He minuted: 'If we continue these negotiations now are they not bound to end in failure? If that is so, would not the best policy be to let them die away without any issue?': MacDonald minute, 10 Dec 1930, MacDonald Papers.

[4] B.D., 2/1, no. 271 (memorandum by Craigie, 1 Jan 1931).

naval question with France, not only on technical and financial grounds, but on account of the political *détente* which may be expected to follow and of their preference for working in cordial co-operation with the Naval Treaty Powers rather than with what may be termed the malcontent group of Powers. So far, the influence of these moderate elements prevails with Signor Mussolini, who, however, has his own ideas as to the correct method of bringing about good relations with France. But the Duce is naturally in close touch with representatives of the more extreme Fascist elements, who favour other and more adventurous courses. I hardly think it is an exaggeration to say that the success or failure of the present efforts to bring about a settlement of the naval question (at all events, up to 1936) will have a profound effect upon the future course of Italy's foreign policy.[1]

On 22 December Craigie went on to Paris, but to his disappointment 'perceived a distinct hardening in Massigli's attitude'. Far from expressing a willingness to match Italian conciliatory conduct, the French naval experts blatantly called attention to the fact that Italy was known to be in economic difficulties and that in consequence France intended to exploit this situation to secure even more concessions on disarmament. Massigli told Craigie that 'France had only to wait a little and Italy would come on hands and knees and beg France for a loan at almost any price'.[2]

No further progress was possible until it had been demonstrated to the French that their estimate of Italian economic difficulties was exaggerated. As late as 13 January Berthelot of the Quai d'Orsay told Tyrrell that 'the French Government thought that a solution would ultimately be found if only because of the increasingly serious economic situation in Italy'.[3] By 25 January, however, the French attitude had evidently been revised, for Briand indicated to Henderson in a personal meeting following a session of the League Council that the Massigli–Craigie–Rosso talks might usefully be resumed.[4] On 8 February Craigie accordingly returned to Paris, and by the 18th had negotiated *ad referendum* a

[1] Ibid.

[2] Ibid. Here incidentally is clear evidence of French willingness to utilise her financial strength to gain her ends.

[3] *B.D.*, 2/1, no. 279 (Tyrrell to Henderson, 13 Jan 1931). Vansittart's view was that the French expectation was 'idiocy'. 'As Mussolini has said,' he added, '"Italy will eat grass in order to build ships"': Vansittart to Tyrrell, 26 Jan 1931, MacDonald Papers.

[4] *B.D.*, 2/1, no. 281 (Henderson to Graham, 6 Feb 1931).

formula with the French.[1] Reaction in London was, however, unfavour-able, the French figures being judged too high.[2] Since the size of the joint Italian and French fleets would have been larger than the British fleet, the Admiralty, with its concern to maintain a European two-power standard, would have insisted upon Great Britain having recourse to the escalator clause in Article 21 of the London Naval Treaty.

Disappointment at this news in Paris was intense, and Briand decided to send a personal letter to Henderson appealing for a modification of the British attitude.[3] In addition, Tyrrell took up the French case with surprising forcefulness, telegraphing to his Secretary of State:

> So far M. Briand's confidence in you has been perfect; but I am bound to point out to you that if you fail to ratify this agreement it will not only mean that you have differed in opinion from him; it will mean that you will be thought to have allowed negotiations to be prolonged until you have got the last drop out of the French, and, having done so, to have decided that the last drop is not enough and that you must appeal to public opinion of the world to have the last say. If that were possible on the Continent, I should not hesitate to encourage you to attempt that test; but as far as this country is concerned in the matter of disarmament you will achieve more by co-operation with Briand than you will by any appeal to Caesar, or in other words, public opinion.[4]

These appeals struck a responsive chord in Henderson, who decided to go to Paris in person, along with Alexander, in an effort to reconcile the conflicting demands of the British Admiralty and the Quai d'Orsay.

After spending only a day in Paris, Henderson and Alexander were able to reach a tentative agreement with the French, largely as a result of the Foreign Secretary's willingness to abandon, temporarily at least, the two-power standard. The British statesmen also reluctantly gave way to the French insistence on a submarine tonnage of 81,989, while to placate their own Admiralty they put forward the following some-what inadequate formula:

> His Majesty's Government maintain that this figure [the French sub-marine figure] is too high in relation to British destroyer figure of 150,000 tons under London naval treaty but they agree to notify other

[1] For details see ibid., n.
[2] Henderson to Tyrrell, 19 Feb 1931, Henderson Papers, F.O. 800/283.
[3] B.D., 2/I, no. 284 (Briand to Henderson, 21 Feb 1931).
[4] B.D., 2/I, no. 283 (Tyrrell to Henderson, 20 Feb 1931).

Powers under part III of Naval Treaty that they will not have re-course to Articles [sic] 21 of that treaty pending general revision of naval question mentioned above. Should it not be possible at 1932 Conference to arrive at a more satisfactory equilibrium between French submarine tonnage and British destroyer tonnage His Majesty's Government will retain their right to make such increase as they may judge necessary in British destroyers figure of 150,000 tons.[1]

The two British Ministers then went on to Rome in order to complete the triangle. A revealing account of what occurred was recorded by Dalton:

> Sir Ronald Graham ... told Ruth [Dalton] that, when Arthur Hender-son ... came to Rome in 1930 with Albert Alexander to discuss the limitation of Naval Armaments, Mussolini had refused, twenty-four hours before their arrival, to see Henderson because, at an Inter-national Socialist Conference, Henderson had called him a murderer.
>
> It had taken all Graham's skill to talk Mussolini round and he had had to tell Henderson that the whole success of the negotiations depended on what impression he could make on Mussolini. But Henderson, Graham said, had played up very well, and it was largely due to him that the negotiations had succeeded in spite of the opposi-tion of the Italian Admiralty.[2]

After completing their delicate diplomatic task in Italy, Henderson and Alexander returned to Paris and on 1 March the news was formally announced that agreement had been reached subject to minor drafting amendments.[3] Japan and the United States did not appear likely to cause difficulty, since neither power had been particularly concerned about the size of the Mediterranean powers' fleets except in so far as Great Britain was likely to invoke Article 21 of the London Treaty. The British undertaking not to construct more destroyers to compensate for the large French submarine programme, at least until after the 1932

[1] B.D., 2/1, no. 285 (Tyrrell to Vansittart, 24 Feb 1931). This telegram was a repeat of a message sent directly by Henderson to Washington and Tokyo.

[2] Hugh Dalton, The Fateful Years: Memoirs, 1931–1945 (London, 1957) pp. 32–3. For a formal and detailed account of the British Ministers' negotia-tions in Rome, see C.P., no. 64(31) by Henderson and Alexander, n.d., Cab. 24/220.

[3] The Bases of Agreement, as they were known, were published in Great Britain on 11 March as Cmd. 3812 of 1930–1. They are reprinted in B.D., 2/1, no. 299, annex.

World Disarmament Conference, served to calm fears in Washington and Tokyo. It was further agreed that, in order to obviate any necessity for a renewal of the ratification debates elsewhere, Italy and France would not formally adhere to Article III of the London Treaty.

No sooner had the Labour Government ceased congratulating themselves on this outstanding diplomatic achievement than the realisation dawned on them that the French placed an unexpected interpretation upon the terms of the agreement. In essence, the issue turned upon whether or not France was entitled before the end of 1936 to lay down (as distinct from complete) the construction of vessels not specifically provided for in the Bases of Agreement. The British and Italians strongly dissented from the view that the French could lay down cruisers in 1935 and 1936 which would not actually put to sea until 1937, 1938 or 1939. Sir Ronald Graham described reaction in Rome as follows:

> Italian Government went to extreme limit of concession to secure agreement believing that general political considerations urged by you justified them in overriding advice of their technical experts. Actual agreement reached offered only one substantial advantage viz. stabilisation of naval construction till 1936. Now owing to French interpretation to which British experts are described as taking strong exception, bottom has been knocked out of agreement and formulas do little to mend matters.[1]

It seems improbable that the French had from the outset intended to place such an interpretation on the Bases of Agreement, since according to Henderson and Alexander 'it was certainly not put to us in either of our visits to Paris'.[2] On the contrary, the suspicion must be that French policy was deliberately reversed, particularly when it is appreciated that the unacceptable interpretation was only made clear to the British and the Italians after the existence of the Austro-German Plan for a Customs Union had become known in Paris.[3]

[1] *B.D.*, 2/II, no. 332 (Graham to Henderson, 27 Mar 1931).
[2] C.P., no. 64(31) by Henderson and Alexander, n.d., Cab. 24/220.
[3] A partisan and undocumented defence of the French position appears in Espagnac de Ravay, *Vingt ans de politique navale (1919–1939)* (Grenoble, 1941) pp. 88–90. Memoranda which present the French and British views of the misunderstanding – if such it was – appear in *B.D.*, 2/II, nos 345 and 346 (20 and 25 Apr 1931). One writer has placed the prime responsibility for the alleged reversal of French policy upon Pierre Laval. See Arthur H. Furnia, *The Diplomacy of Appeasement: Anglo-French Relations and the Prelude to World War II, 1931–1938* (Washington, D.C., 1960) p. 27. In support of his contention, Furnia

Whether or not it was the result of a policy reversal, the controversial French interpretation of the Bases of Agreement put an end to the chances of any immediate settlement. Throughout April the British Foreign Secretary vainly sought to save the situation at meetings of a formal drafting committee, assembled in London. But on 7 May the committee finally abandoned its efforts and thereafter no further progress was made during the lifetime of the Labour Government; and although serious negotiations were to be revived after the National Government came into office, final success was in fact never to be attained. For Henderson this outcome was naturally a severe disappointment. But he had no doubt where the principal blame lay, as is made evident in Beatrice Webb's diary:

Henderson was perturbed about the breakdown of the French–Italian negotiations owing to the intolerable untrustworthiness and greed for armaments of the French Parliamentary Committee – (how hateful the French Government is) – 'the Italians had been as good as gold'.[1]

---

cited *B.D.* 2/II no. 236 [*sic*] pp. 385–7. The document in question, however, makes no reference to the personal role of Laval.

[1] Cole (ed.), *Beatrice Webb's Diaries, 1924–1932*, p. 270.

RELATIONS between the Soviet Union and Great Britain between the two world wars were marred by a complete lack of mutual trust and understanding. The ill-feeling occasioned by Russia's withdrawal from the war and the consequent allied intervention was not in itself sufficient to account for the enduring estrangement; and even the difference in social and economic systems was of only marginal importance. Although the so-called Conservative die-hards may have been filled with horror at the Socialist experiments, the more practical men of affairs in control of British foreign policy throughout the inter-war years must have had other, more compelling motives for rejecting the pragmatic course of normal relations with a *de facto* regime. In essence, the cause of the difficulties lay in the unique attitude of the Soviet leaders to other foreign powers. They were committed to an internationalist philosophy which, if carried to its logical conclusions, was bound to lead them to pursue interventionist policies and to foment revolutions wherever practical. The rule of law, conventions of international practice concerning non-intervention in the affairs of other states, the sanctity of bilateral and multilateral treaties and obligations, all have no secure place in the outlook of an adherent of Marx and Lenin. If lip-service is paid to any of these things, it is, as almost all the architects of British foreign policy have readily perceived, no more than a tactical manœuvre on the part of the Soviet Union. From time to time most statesmen are driven by circumstances to practise deceit and to endorse actions inconsistent with rudimentary international law, but the Communist statesman differs from the majority in that he sets out embracing a philosophy in which such conduct is both justified and demanded on a systematic basis. Any politician who calls himself a Communist *ipso facto* advertises the fact that he believes in the morality of the necessary lie and that he is an opportunist in the name of high principle. The introduction of men of this ilk into the world of international affairs has indeed provided many problems for the older type of diplomatist.[1] The latter is used to a world of genuine compromises, of truth mixed with dissimulation, of the relatively restrained pursuit of legitimate national interests combined with a degree of benevolence towards the world at large; he knows that the rules of the game are in certain respects obscure, but he seeks by and large to play according to them and expects his opposite numbers to do the same. When such a man is suddenly faced with fanatics – and fanatics committed to ruthless opportunism – he is usually at a loss to know how to deal with them. If he cannot easily drive his tormentor off the stage, he may be tempted to embark on one of two inadequate courses: he may conclude that it is impossible to do business with such a rival, and in effect follow Trotsky's example of trying 'to shut up shop'; or he may delude himself into thinking that kindly words and a benevolent attitude will somehow lead to a withering away of an opponent's fanaticism.[2] Between the two world wars, British statesmen – Conservatives especially – tended to follow the former course in respect to the Soviet Union and the latter vis-à-vis National Socialist Germany and Mussolini's Italy.

In Great Britain as a whole during these years there were in fact four broad segments of opinion concerning the Soviet Union, though only two of these succeeded in finding expression in governmental policy after 1920. On the far Left there was to be found a romantic attachment to the so-called Workers' State and a total lack of awareness of the difficulties involved in maintaining normal relations with Moscow. On the far Right, by contrast, there were elements which were not only opposed to the Soviet Union's world strategy but sympathised with the émigrés and doubtless would have welcomed intervention from the 'civilised world' to put an end to Socialism, tyranny, slave camps and religious persecution. This attitude, of course, in its interventionist

[1] For the views of one who had a deeper insight than most, see Lord Vansittart, 'The Decline of Diplomacy', *Foreign Affairs*, xxviii (1949–50) 177–88.

[2] The most extreme exponent of the policy of non-recognition was the United States during the years prior to the advent of F. D. Roosevelt. Secretary of State F. B. Kellogg defined his country's attitude with complete frankness in February 1928 in these words: 'No result beneficial to the people of the United States, or, indeed to the people of Russia would be attained by entering into relations with the present regime in Russia so long as the present rulers of Russia have not abandoned those avowed aims and known practices which are inconsistent with international friendship'. Cited in Sir Bernard Pares, 'Anglo-Russian Relations', *Journal of the Royal Institute of International Affairs*, viii (1929) 490.

nature was analogous to that of the Communists. It was not a position shared by the other two major sections of British opinion concerned with the Russian problem. These two groups – the moderate Conservatives and the bulk of the Labour Party leadership – had in fact a good deal more in common than they cared to tell their wilder supporters. Both front benches tended to accept after 1920 that the Soviet Government could not and should not be overthrown from without; both took a strong line about Communist propaganda and revolutionary activities directed from Moscow; and neither had any real sympathy or enthusiasm for the extremist experiments being undertaken in the Soviet Union. The one major difference between the *official* attitudes of the two large parties concerned the utility of recognising and establishing formal diplomatic relations with the Soviet Union. The Conservatives and their coalition allies were at no time optimistic as to the possibility of a good relationship with Moscow. They made no move to recognise the new republic between 1917 and 1924; they dropped a draft treaty negotiated by the first Labour Government; they expelled the Soviet trading mission in 1927 following the revelations produced by the Arcos Raid; and in the 1930s they attached little importance to the Soviet Union as a potential ally against the Fascist powers. The Labour Party leaders were, by contrast, convinced that whatever the shortcomings of the Soviet Government, no useful purpose could be served by a policy of boycott. They believed that any relations – however strained – were better than none and hoped that in time Moscow would moderate its conduct as a result of being brought into communion with the rest of the world. Moreover, Labour opinion attached great importance to trade with the Soviet Union as a means of reducing unemployment; and they correctly argued that improved relations on a diplomatic level would tend to stimulate commercial intercourse. What no Labour leader appears to have appreciated fully prior to 1929 was that where trade is a state monopoly, the government concerned can pursue purely political aims by such practices as dumping or the withholding of supplies at critical junctures.

It may be concluded, therefore, that the differences between the major British parties on the Russian question were made to appear greater than they actually were because of the pressures of back-bench extremists and the sensational coverage given to the utterances of the latter by Fleet Street. The events of 1924 with regard to the Campbell Case and the so-called Zinoviev Letter also assumed quite disproportionate significance as a result of Conservative electioneering tactics. All the same, the one genuine bone of contention between the front benches – on the value of formal relations – was of sufficient importance to become an election issue of some significance in 1929. In *Labour and the Nation* (1928) and again in its 1929 election manifesto, *Labour's Appeal to the Nation*, the Labour Party pledged itself to establish diplomatic and commercial relations with the Russian Government and to encourage a revival of trade with Soviet Russia. The Liberals expressed a similar intention, albeit on the basis of safeguards concerning non-interference in internal affairs. The Conservatives, by contrast, made no reference to the possibility of resuming relations.[1]

Once in office, MacDonald and Henderson proceeded with far less enthusiasm concerning the Soviet Union than most of their followers desired or even expected. They did not attempt to evade their mandate but sought stringent assurances on propaganda and as many other concessions from Moscow as could be obtained without a complete breakdown in the negotiations. The whole course of Anglo-Russian discussions, culminating in an exchange of ambassadors more than six months after the advent of the Labour Government, was accompanied by misunderstandings and much mutual mistrust. Throughout there were striking displays of irritability by Henderson[2] and some tenacious obstinacy from the Russian representative over minor points of disagreement. Certainly it cannot be said that the actual process of resuming relations did anything to strengthen friendly ties or to break down old suspicions between the two governments.

From the very beginning, the Labour Government indicated that they intended to take a more cautious line in regard to the Soviet Union than had been the case in 1924.[3] The relevant section of the King's Speech stated:

My Government are examining the conditions under which diplomatic relations with the Government of the Union of Soviet Socialist

[1] W. P. and Z. K. Coates, *A History of Anglo-Soviet Relations* (London, 1944) p. 320.

[2] Henderson was nevertheless too conciliatory towards the Soviet Union to meet with the approval of Vansittart. See *The Mist Procession*, p. 398.

[3] For the events of 1924, see Stephen Richard Graubard, *British Labour and the Russian Revolution, 1917–1924* (Cambridge, Mass., 1956) chap. 13; Lyman, *The First Labour Government*, esp. chaps. 11 and 14; and Lewis Carter et al., *The Zinoviev Letter* (London, 1967).

Republics may be resumed and are in communication with My Governments in the Dominions and the Government of India on the subject.[1]

MacDonald went a stage further in replying to a question from Baldwin:

> *Baldwin*: ... I should like to know whether the Prime Minister adheres to the statement of principle as to relations with Russia which he laid down in his Note on the Zinovieff Letter.
> *MacDonald*: Those conditions are laid down in a published despatch. Everyone ... knows what they are. ... We stand by them; of course we do.[2]

The pained reaction of the Soviet Union to this pronouncement was voiced by *Izvestia*:

> The Labour Government is deeply mistaken if it thinks the Soviet Union will enter a preliminary discussion on conditions. The settlement of disputed questions must come not before but after the unconditional restoration of normal diplomatic relations.[3]

Soviet feelings of indignation on this point were naturally shared by pro-Communist elements in the Labour Party but not apparently by the bulk of Labour Members of Parliament. The latter were stirred to making vigorous protests, however, when the Prime Minister gave an undertaking on 15 July that the Government would not allow the exchange of ambassadors with the Soviet Union to take place without Parliamentary approval.[4] Lloyd George indicated that this would mean in practice that nothing would be done until the next Parliamentary session in October, a three-month delay which most Labour and Liberal Members regarded as unnecessary.[5] This view was also taken by Henderson and Dalton, both of whom were especially annoyed that the Prime Minister had committed the Government without prior consultation with either the Cabinet or the Foreign Office. The Foreign Secretary, according to Dalton, protested to the Cabinet but recognised that the Government could not now reverse the position without risking a Press outcry and a possible repetition of the events of 1924. 'Russia has brought us down once,' he told Dalton, 'We can't afford to let it

---

[1] *H.C. Deb.*, ccxxix, col. 48, 2 July 1929.
[2] *H.C. Deb.*, ccxxix, cols 59, 68–9, 2 July 1929.
[3] Cited in W. P. and Z. K. Coates, *Anglo-Soviet Relations*, p. 322.
[4] *H.C. Deb.*, ccxxx, col. 18, 15 July 1929.
[5] *H.C. Deb.*, ccxxx, cols 18–19, 15 July 1929.

happen twice.'[1] Henderson adopted the same attitude at a stormy meeting of the Parliamentary Labour Party, arguing that Russia was 'not the only pebble on the beach' and that the Government was 'not going out tomorrow'.[2] By contrast, MacDonald's conduct in the whole affair appears to have been somewhat inept. First came his provocative undertaking, given without consultation and based apparently on a misconception of the Liberal Party's attitude; secondly, according to Dalton,

There was an old man who said, 'Where
Can impressions be made on this Bear?
I will sit on this stile
And continue to smile,
Which may soften the heart of this Bear.'

(*Lines and picture after Edward Lear*)

'I AM ALWAYS TRYING TO IMPRESS THE SOVIET
GOVERNMENT WITH ONE THING OR ANOTHER.'—
MR. ARTHUR HENDERSON.

[1] Dalton, *Call Back Yesterday*, p. 231. No record of a formal protest by Henderson appears in the Cabinet Minutes for this period.

[2] Hamilton, *Arthur Henderson*, p. 311.

he handled a deputation of Labour M.P.s 'like a vain fractious child';[1] next, he proposed to change course by means of an early motion in Parliament granting prospective authorisation for an exchange of ambassadors; and finally, under pressure from Henderson, he reverted to his original position.[2]

However unpopular the Prime Minister's commitment may have been within his own party, it may have had a salutary effect in bringing about a more realistic attitude in Moscow, where it had originally been hoped that a Labour Government would resume relations immediately and unconditionally.[3] The Soviet leaders were forced to realise that some negotiations and even concessions would be necessary prior to the restoration of full relations; Great Britain tried to maximise these, the Soviet Union to minimise them. Henderson, who took charge of the British side of the negotiations, was no less firm than MacDonald and had earlier indicated his conviction that a Soviet propaganda guarantee was a *sine qua non* for an exchange of ambassadors.[4]

On 17 July the first official overture to the Soviet Union was made through the good offices of the Norwegian Government. A Soviet representative was invited to visit London 'in order to discuss with the Foreign Secretary direct the most expeditious procedure for reaching as rapidly as possible a friendly and mutually satisfactory settlement of the outstanding questions between the two countries including those relating to propaganda and debts'.[5] The Soviet reply, dated 23 July, accepted the invitation 'in view of the fact that the note from British Government aims at preliminary exchange of views exclusively regarding procedure to be followed in subsequent discussion of disputed questions and not at an actual discussion of these questions'.[6]

The outcome was that Valerian Dovgalevsky, the Soviet ambassador in Paris, travelled to London and first met Henderson on 29 July at the Foreign Office. The first meeting was not very successful and indeed

---

[1] Dalton, *Call Back Yesterday*, p. 230.　　　　[2] Ibid., pp. 230–1.

[3] See Litvinov's Report to the Soviet Central Executive Committee quoted in Jane Degras (ed.), *Soviet Documents on Foreign Policy*, 3 vols (London, 1951–3) II 420.

[4] *H.C. Deb.*, ccxxix, col. 420, 5 July 1929. It was in this speech that Henderson revealed that the question of renewed recognition of the Soviet Union was not involved – it had never in fact been withdrawn: ibid., col. 421.

[5] *B.D.*, 2/VII, no. 3 (Henderson to Sir Francis Lindley (Oslo), 15 July 1929).

[6] *B.D.*, 2/VII, no. 5 (Lindley to Henderson, 24 July 1929).

was the cause of a serious breakdown in negotiations. The Foreign Secretary, according to his own account, explained that the actual resumption of relations could not take place until a report had been made to Parliament in the autumn, but that 'in the meantime there was plenty of work to be done, and the interval could usefully be occupied in defining clearly the principles to be observed for the settlement of outstanding questions; it might even be possible to make some concrete advance in certain of the questions for discussion'.[1] Dovgalevsky insisted upon seeking new instructions from Moscow and in his report must have represented Henderson's position in a somewhat different way from that given in the latter's account. The Soviet authorities apparently gathered the impression that Great Britain was now insisting on a settlement of the *substance* of the outstanding questions prior to a resumption of formal relations. Dovgalevsky was consequently instructed to return to Paris after informing Henderson that the matter would have to be referred to the Praesidium of the Central Executive.[2] The Russian representative conveyed this information to the Foreign Secretary on 31 July and showed him a communication from Moscow in which it was alleged that the British Government did not wish to resume relations, since 'si tel n'était pas le cas, le Gouvernement britannique n'aurait pas proposé, comme condition préalable au rétablissement des relations normales, la solution de questions aussi compliquées et litigieuses que le sont les prétentions et contre-prétentions mutuelles'.[3] Certainly if Henderson had made such a demand it was a clear departure from the terms upon which a Soviet representative had been invited. It does not seem at all likely that he did in fact act in this way, especially as his Foreign Office advisers had pointed out in a memorandum that 'if . . . it is decided that an early resumption of relations would be advantageous, the conditions laid down should not include any reference to claims or confiscated properties, on which agreement cannot be looked for'.[4] Moreover, Henderson himself recorded that at the second

---

[1] *B.D.*, 2/VII, no. 10 (record of a conversation between Henderson and Dovgalevsky, 1 Aug 1929).

[2] Litvinov believed – or affected to believe – that this action was of great significance in that it forced Henderson to have second thoughts. See his report to the Soviet Central Executive Committee quoted in Degras (ed.), *Soviet Documents*, II 420.

[3] *B.D.*, 2/VII, no. 11, annex.

[4] *B.D.*, 2/VII, no. 1 (Foreign Office memorandum, 18 June 1929).

meeting with the Russian representative he 'took exception to the interpretation of the attitude of His Majesty's Government which was expressed in M. Dovgalevsky's communications'.[1]

Apart from tentative feelers put out in August by Dalton and by Frank Wise, no further steps were taken to clear up the misunderstanding – if such it was – until 4 September, when Henderson made a statement in Geneva, stressing that although the resumption of relations with the Soviet Union could not take place until Parliament had approved it, he would welcome a Soviet representative in London to discuss 'the most expeditious procedure'.[2] He made no mention of conditions and did not on this occasion even express the aspiration that there might in the meantime be some advance on some of the questions at issue. Litvinov's reaction was swift: he once again accepted the invitation 'if the declaration of the British Foreign Secretary is to be understood in the sense that he desires again to meet a representative of the Soviet Government to discuss only procedure into which will naturally enter formation of agenda of future negotiations'.[3]

Dovgalevsky presently returned to London and resumed his talks with Henderson on 24 September. The first session went over the old ground about procedure: 'The Secretary of State pointed out the great advantage of carrying matters as far as possible at the present stage', while the

---

[1] B.D., 2/VII, no. 11 (record of a conversation between Henderson and Dovgalevsky, 1 Aug 1929).

[2] Cmd. 3418 of 1929–30. On Dalton's feeler, which evoked no response from Moscow, see Donald N. Lammers, 'The Second Labour Government and the Restoration of Relations with Soviet Russia (1929)', *Bulletin of the Institute of Historical Research*, XXXVII (1964) 68–9. Frank Wise, a pro-Soviet Labour M.P., went to Moscow after an interview with Henderson at The Hague. MacDonald's view of Wise and his friends was that they 'have taken Moscow under their wing and . . . think it can do no wrong and that we should play with themselves in an orchestra, under Moscow conductorship'. He told Dalton that there was 'no reason why you should not use them, being careful lest they give you away if you show them any confidence and give them anything but what the Office is prepared to have published': MacDonald to Dalton, 3 Aug 1929, Henderson Papers, F.O. 800/280. Henderson wrote of his interview with Wise: 'though I was friendly, I adhered firmly to the position I had taken up with Dovgalevsky and told him that, in my opinion, he was not likely to help in securing the object he had in view if he gave the Russians the impression that we were always ready to modify our attitude whenever they presented a difficulty real or unreal': Henderson to Dalton, 17 Aug 1929, ibid.

[3] Cmd. 3418 of 1929–30.

Russian representatives stressed 'the difficulty of deciding details at this stage'.[1] Henderson had prepared a list of six issues for consideration as to procedure and these were presented to Dovgalevsky for his perusal. On the following day the Foreign Secretary produced a memorandum amplifying the British position in relation to the six points. These may be summarised as follows:

1. *Propaganda*
Great Britain called for an exchange of pledges in regard to propaganda on the lines of Article 16 of the draft General Treaty of 1924, and these were to be given 'at the moment of the actual exchange of ambassadors'.

2. *Diplomatic Missions and Consular Posts*
It was suggested that after relations had been restored, discussions should take place about the establishment of consular missions in important centres. In addition, Great Britain called upon the Soviet Union to release 'certain Soviet citizens formerly employed at the British mission in Moscow' who had apparently been exiled or imprisoned solely because of this.

3. *Debts*
All claims and counter-claims, in the British view, should be considered after the exchange of ambassadors by a joint committee of nominated representatives.

4. *Fisheries*
Until nominated representatives could negotiate a permanent treaty on the subject, Great Britain called for a revival of the provisional agreement of 1923 regarding the three-mile limit. Significantly, the British suggested that the temporary arrangement should be reaffirmed 'simultaneously with the re-establishment of diplomatic relations'.

5. *Commercial Treaties and Allied Questions*

6. *Application of Previous Treaties and Covenants*

Discussion of both these subjects was to be left until after the exchange of ambassadors.[2]

When the conversations were resumed on 26 September, Dovgalevsky

[1] *B.D.*, 2/VII, no. 18 (record of a conversation between Henderson and Dovgalevsky, 24 Sep 1929).
[2] The full text of the British memorandum is given in *B.D.*, 2/VII, no. 19, annex.

proposed a number of alterations to the British suggested list. Propaganda, he averred, should be relegated to fifth place and replaced at the top by the question of 'The Attitude of both Governments towards the Treaties of 1924'; and the item regarding diplomatic missions and consular posts ought to be omitted altogether. A lengthy wrangle ensued in which Henderson was especially insistent that the propaganda guarantees would have to be given at the time of the exchange of ambassadors. After an adjournment, he produced a 'Revised List of Questions' divided into two parts, covering firstly, those matters to be dealt with at the time of the resumption of relations and, secondly, those to be considered subsequently. In the former category came the questions of propaganda, of diplomatic missions and of the revival of the fisheries arrangement of 1923. List B contained all the other points dealt with in the original British proposals with, in addition, in first place, the Soviet demand for 'a definition of the attitude of both Governments towards the treaties of 1924'. Dovgalevsky accepted List B but stated that he could not agree to List A. He was prepared to discuss an arrangement with regard to propaganda at a later stage, but he contended that any consideration of diplomatic missions and of fisheries would almost certainly have to be left until after relations had been re-established.[1] This was in fact the point at which the talks came nearest to a complete impasse. Henderson, however, appears to have realised that the Russians were likely to prove obdurate and in consequence he decided to back down.[2] On September he abandoned the attempt to force an immediate settlement on any issue except that of propaganda. This was clearly the irreducible minimum so far as the British Government was concerned. Recognising this, Dovgalevsky eventually accepted the proposal that undertakings along the lines of the 1924 agreement would be given at the time of the exchange of ambassadors – a major Soviet concession.[3]

---

[1] For a record of the discussions of 26 September, see *B.D.*, 2/VII, no. 20.

[2] The speed with which Henderson reached this decision may not have been unconnected with the proximity of the Labour Party Annual Conference.

[3] *B.D.*, 2/VII, no. 21 (record of a conversation between Henderson and Dovgalevsky, 27 Sep 1929). This decision in fact marked a considerable retreat on the part of the Soviet Union. It had been thought in many circles that the Russians' concern for their *amour-propre* would prevent them agreeing to the prior propaganda guarantee – a humiliating demand never previously made to any sovereign state. The Soviet leaders, however, not only found adequate reasons for accepting the demand but also claimed, presumably for domestic

On 1 October the final session of Anglo-Russian conversations took place at the White Hart Inn, Lewes, where Henderson was staying for the duration of the Labour Party Annual Conference, then taking place at Brighton. All that remained to be completed was the drawing up of a formal protocol, and this was achieved without very much difficulty. It was eventually signed by the two negotiators on 3 October.[1] While at the White Hart, Henderson on 1 October took the opportunity to inform the Soviet representative that he interpreted the propaganda guarantee of the Soviet Union as covering the activities of the Third International and that Great Britain would act upon that interpretation.[2] Dovgalevsky made no comment on this point, though he must have known that the Soviet Government had consistently denied its responsibility in this connection.[3] It was doubtless because he knew that this was the Soviets' stand, and that they could not be expected to change it, that Henderson avoided insisting on a specific reference to the Third International in the terms of the protocol.[4] It was hoped, however, that a clear and firm statement that Great Britain would hold the Soviet Government responsible for the activities of the International might have the effect of deterring the latter from extremist conduct. True, neither the Foreign Secretary nor his advisers were particularly sanguine about the prospects of propaganda ceasing, but they had done all that was feasible, if it was seriously intended that relations should be resumed at all.[5]

Henderson made great play of the successful outcome of the talks in his address to the Labour Party conference on 3 October which appears

---

purposes, that Great Britain had in effect capitulated to them. They had followed much the same course in 1924 on the contentious issue of a British loan. See Lyman, *The First Labour Government*, pp. 198–9.

[1] For the full text of the Anglo-Soviet Protocol, see *B.D.*, 2/VII, no. 24.

[2] *B.D.*, 2/VII, no. 22 (record of a conversation between Henderson and Dovgalevsky, 1 Oct 1929).

[3] The Soviet position was reaffirmed in *Izvestia* on 10 Nov 1929. Cited in *B.D.*, 2/VII, no. 32 (A. D. F. Gascoigne (Oslo) to Henderson, 13 Nov 1929).

[4] The Cabinet decided on 7 Oct that 'it was unnecessary for the Secretary of State to insist on an explicit statement by the Russian Soviet Government that they regarded Clause 7 of the Protocol, relating to propaganda, as applicable to abstention from propaganda by the Third International . . .': Cabinet Minutes, Cab. 23/62, 36(29)1, 7 Oct 1929.

[5] For the Foreign Office view, see the memorandum in *B.D.*, 2/VII, no. 9.

to have been very well received by the majority of delegates.[1] The
Foreign Secretary's settlement with the Soviet Union was accorded
rather less support in the Press and in Parliament: he was widely
accused in Opposition circles of having capitulated to the Russians and
of having obtained no counter-concessions.[2] The opportunist Soviet
spokesmen claimed to have scored a startling triumph,[3] and there were
many in Great Britain eager to believe them. In reply to his critics,
Henderson, in a House of Commons debate held on 5 November 1929,
maintained that the propaganda guarantee, to which the Government
had been committed from the first, had in fact been obtained and that
the Opposition's protests were therefore unjustified.[4] With the support
of the Liberals, the Government's position was endorsed by the Commons and a mandate for an exchange of ambassadors was given by 324
votes to 199. The House of Lords was later to dissent from the decision
by 43 votes to 21, but as no legislation was necessary the Government
could afford to ignore the inconvenient sentiments of the peers.[5] The
Conservatives in fact received only one crumb of comfort in the affair,
namely when Henderson, in his major speech in the Commons, gave an
undertaking to refrain from granting any Government-guaranteed loan
to the Soviet Union. This decision, for which Dalton was later to claim
a primary responsibility,[6] was most unwelcome in Moscow and doubtless
accounted for the failure of all subsequent attempts to solve the outstanding problems with regard to debts and claims.

Henderson's next task in connection with the Soviet Union was that
of selecting an ambassador to go to Moscow. In the end he opted for Sir
Esmond Ovey, whose only outstanding qualification appears to have

[1] For Henderson's speech, see *Labour Party Annual Conference Report, 1929*,
pp. 206–10. For a somewhat partisan description, see Hamilton, *Arthur Henderson*, pp. 332–5.
[2] See, for example, a speech by Baldwin, *H.C. Deb.*, ccxxxi, cols 904–13,
5 Nov 1929. The King was also a critic, arguing that 'the British Government
had been outwitted by the Russian in the recent discussion between Mr Henderson and Mr Dovgalevsky': Stamfordham memorandum of a conversation with
Selby, 12 Oct 1929, R.A. GV, M 2229/38.
[3] Cited by Baldwin, *H.C. Deb.*, ccxxxi, col. 907, 5 Nov 1929.
[4] For the text of Henderson's speech, see *H.C. Deb.*, ccxxxi, cols 895–904,
5 Nov 1929.
[5] For the debate see *House of Lords Debates* (hereafter abbreviated to *H.L.
Deb.*), lxxv, cols 867–922, 4 Dec 1929.
[6] See Dalton, *Call Back Yesterday*, pp. 232–3.

been that he spoke Russian. Despite representations, the Foreign Secretary refused to recommend any Labour Member of Parliament for the post.[1] The Russians, on their side, chose Gregory Sokolnikov to be accredited to St James's. The new ambassador was duly received on 20 December by the Prince of Wales, the King having refused to shake hands with any of the murderers of his 'favourite first cousin', the late Tsar.[2] Thus at last, twelve years after the Bolshevik Revolution, a Russian ambassador once more took his place in London society. Beatrice Webb expected him 'at first at any rate' to be 'a nonentity' and he seems to have been so.[3]

The exchange of envoys did nothing to create a better feeling between the two countries; on the contrary, the existence of official channels only served to facilitate the speedy expression of discontents on either side. The thesis that a clearer understanding of an opponent's viewpoint would lead to a more sympathetic relationship was thus exposed as a dangerous fallacy. The more Henderson dealt with the Russians, the less he cared for them. In particular, he was angered by the fact that

[1] According to Dalton, Arthur Ponsonby, Parliamentary Under-Secretary for the Dominions, made a personal application to Henderson but to no avail: Dalton Diary, entry for 31 Oct 1929. Another unsuccessful applicant was Sir Daniel Stevenson, formerly a leading figure in the Union of Democratic Control: Henderson to Stevenson, 1 July 1929, Henderson Papers, F.O. 800/280. By refusing to appoint other than career diplomats to British missions, the Labour leaders made it clear that, despite much fierce oratory in Opposition against the class character of the diplomatic service, they were not prepared in practice to challenge the traditional system. For an exposition of the Left-wing point of view, see Robert T. Nightingale, *The Personnel of the British Foreign Service and Diplomatic Service*, Fabian Tract, no. 32 (London, 1930). His concluding words were: 'a Foreign Service manned by those drawn from the privileged classes will remain antipathetic to the new internationalist ideals'.

[2] See Dalton, *Call Back Yesterday*, p. 233, and Nicolson, *King George the Fifth*, p. 331 n. In March 1930, however, the King was compelled, under pressure from Henderson, to receive Sokolnikov at a Palace levée: ibid. Fearing such an abhorrent eventuality, the King had at an earlier stage claimed 'that, when he saw Mr Ramsay MacDonald on the latter's becoming Prime Minister, he accepted the King's condition that on the re-establishment of relations with Russia, her representative in London should be a Chargé d'Affaires': Stamfordham memorandum of a conversation with Lindsay, 10 Aug 1929, R.A. GV, M 2229/10. Henderson, however, had refused to take this idea seriously and MacDonald appears to have made no attempt to stand by his pledge to the King.

[3] Beatrice Webb Diary, entry for 20 Feb 1930. The Webbs treated him as a kind of pet and he in turn seems to have played some part in turning them into admirers of the Soviet system.

anti-British propaganda became strident and troublesome in 1930 – more so than it had been for some years. The result was that the Foreign Secretary wrote to Ovey in a rather plaintive fashion:

> I can claim to have done more than any other to bring about resumption of relations with the Soviet Government in the teeth of strong and formidable opposition, and my desire to develop and improve those relations continues; nevertheless my difficulties have been immensely increased by reason of the fact that far from campaign of propaganda and abuse undergoing some diminution as a result of action of His Majesty's Government in exchanging Ambassadors, campaign would seem to all appearances to have been increased in intensity since exchange has taken place.[1]

The well-intentioned 'Uncle Arthur' had one great failing: as Vansittart put it, 'he believed in all that we wish to hold without evidence – brotherhood, peace and goodwill . . . he thought too well of the Soviets . . . and I could only diminish his optimism by fractions'.[2] He found it difficult to believe that other people could be totally unresponsive to an appeal for 'fair play'. That he was both hurt and surprised by the Soviet attitude is a sign of a certain naïveté in his outlook. The true Soviet approach to British Labour was clearly explained to Ovey by President M. I. Kalinin at the very start of his mission. The uncomprehending British diplomat reported that Kalinin 'talked quite frankly and even went so far as to state à propos of His Majesty's Government that the Bolsheviks naturally disliked most of all those people whose policy was nearer to theirs than that of the reactionaries and therefore more dangerous'.[3]

The propaganda of which Henderson complained was disseminated mainly, though not exclusively, under Comintern auspices, and this raised rather special difficulties because of the Soviet Government's refusal to accept any responsibility for the former's outpourings. The MacDonald administration, both publicly and in diplomatic exchanges, took the opposite view, but pressure on Moscow proved fruitless. Parmoor, the Lord President of the Council, took an unusually strong line in the House of Lords on 20 February 1930,[4] but this brought no

---

[1] *B.D.*, 2/VII, no. 69 (Henderson to Ovey, 26 Feb 1930).

[2] Vansittart, *The Mist Procession*, p. 398.

[3] *B.D.*, 2/VII, no. 49 (Ovey to Henderson, 24 Dec 1929). Ovey found the remark 'somewhat curious': ibid.

[4] *H.L. Deb.*, lxxvi, cols 651–61, 20 Feb 1930.

more than a slight response from Moscow. In a talk with Ovey, Litvinov was critical of the Third International's activities and even suggested it might move to London, but continued to deny the Soviet Union's responsibility. The latter point was one on which Ovey concluded that 'much as Litvinov may even personally deprecate the activities of the Third International no concession is possible'.[1]

Since the British could obtain no satisfaction from Moscow on the increasing Comintern activity, they had simply to choose between agreeing to differ and breaking off diplomatic relations. The Labour Government opted for the former course.[2] Henderson's initial instincts had therefore been correct when he had telegraphed to Ovey: 'There appears to be no prospect of reconciling divergent views of His Majesty's Government and Soviet Government on propaganda issue and I think it unnecessary for Your Excellency to initiate any discussions on the subject at present.'[3] That further protests were made was probably occasioned less by any expectation of progress than by a need to appease the Opposition and various pressure groups, which unfortunately for the Government were not prepared to endorse the *New Statesman*'s view about what it called the Comintern's 'nursery chatter', namely that 'the vast majority of the British people, at any rate, are neither interested in nor afraid of this twaddle'.[4]

Towards the end of 1930 the British Government had a direct clash with the Soviet Government, as opposed to the Comintern, on the

[1] *B.D.*, 2/VII, nos 66 and 68 (Ovey to Henderson, 22 and 25 Feb 1930). See also Ovey to Henderson, telegram no. 335, 7 June 1930, F.O., 418/72. Whether the Comintern was at this time to any degree independent of Stalin's will – as it had certainly been earlier – seems extremely doubtful. On the Comintern's curious history, see Günther Nollau, *International Communism and World Revolution: History and Methods* (London, 1961); Jane Degras (ed.), *The Communist International, 1919–1943: Documents*, 3 vols (London, 1956–65); and Milorad M. Drascovic and Branko Lazitch (eds.), *The Comintern: Historical Highlights: Essays, Recollections, Documents* (New York, 1966).

[2] A Cabinet Committee, chaired by Lord Sankey, the Lord Chancellor, reported to the Cabinet in October 1930 that it was 'of opinion that the Soviet Government has not fulfilled the terms of its obligation', but added that it did 'not recommend that the subject matter revealed by our investigations should now lead His Majesty's Government to consider the advisability of a diplomatic rupture': Cabinet Minutes, Cab. 23/65, 64(30)1, 28 Oct 1930. For the full text of the Cabinet Committee's report, see C.P., no. 349(30), 20 Oct. 1930, Cab. 24/215.   [3] *B.D.*, 2/VII, no. 54 (Henderson to Ovey, 7 Jan 1930).

[4] *New Statesman*, 9 Nov 1929.

matter of propaganda. In a well-publicised trial, various Soviet officials were indicted for sabotage and counter-revolutionary activities. They all 'confessed' to the most unlikely crimes and naturally admitted to having connections with 'Imperialist' Governments and agencies. The British and French Governments were given special mention in this connection at the trial. The remarks of the Public Prosecutor together with provocative pamphleteering and broadcasting by Maxim Gorky led to British and French *démarches*.[1] The Soviets offered no apology or even explanation, and Ovey was left only with the hopeful consolation 'that strength of protest cannot fail to produce effect'.[2]

Meanwhile in Great Britain various anti-Soviet campaigns continued to flourish. In particular, attention centred upon the materialists' alleged persecution of the religious and on the alleged use of slave labour in Russian timber camps. Much of the factual information garnered by the British protest movement was of a highly dubious character, and the reports in the Press on the real situation in the Soviet Union were equally unreliable, since most foreign correspondents got no nearer to that country than Riga.[3] However, the extent of Opposition pressure was such that the British Government gave the appearance of making representations at Moscow on both religious persecution and slave labour. In practice, however, care was taken not to offend Soviet susceptibilities. For example, Henderson mentioned the matter of slave labour to

---

[1] The course of the trials and their diplomatic repercussions may be followed in a series of telegrams between Henderson and Ovey. See *B.D.*, 2/VII, nos 105 to 134.   [2] *B.D.*, 2/VII, no. 120 (Ovey to Henderson, 5 Dec 1930).

[3] The Foreign Secretary was in possession of more authoritative information, but did not choose to convey it to the general public. For example, Ovey, in the course of a lengthy report on the religious situation, stated: 'I have no evidence of any general shootings of priests as priests, or massacres of religious congregations. There has been no return to the thumbscrew-and-rack period of religious persecution.' Ovey to Henderson, telegram no. 128, 24 Feb 1930, F.O., 371/14842. On Ovey's advice, Henderson suggested to the Cabinet that the report should not be made public. 'If it is laid,' the Foreign Secretary minuted, 'there is always a possibility of the Soviet Government stating that . . . Ovey is no longer *persona grata* to them for having reported on a subject which, in their opinion, is one of internal concern. In that case they would be furnished with the whip-hand for breaking off relations.' The Cabinet accepted this advice: Cabinet Minutes, Cab. 23/63, 13(30)2, 5 Mar 1930; and C.P., no. 74(30) by Henderson, 3 Mar 1930, Cab. 24/210. The King was for once in agreement with what Henderson recommended: Stamfordham to Vansittart, 4 Mar 1930, R.A. GV, M 2229/70. Ovey's report was surprisingly omitted from the relevant volume of published British documents.

Sokolnikov in 1931, but he carefully avoided any suggestion that he was interfering in the internal affairs of the Soviet Union, as he made clear in a message to Ovey:

> After reminding His Excellency of the numerous questions which had been asked in Parliament on the subject of labour conditions in the Russian timber trade, I impressed upon him that this agitation was growing more serious and was producing real feeling both in political and non-political circles. The Soviet Government had indicated that they would not permit actual conditions to be investigated by an out-side enquiry. In taking this line *they were doubtless within their rights*, but His Excellency must realise that the attitude of his Government made it impossible to deal with the accusations in an authoritative manner.[1]

The following passage from Dalton's diary also suggests that Henderson was disinclined to break a lance on behalf of either the Soviets or their opponents:

> 'Religious persecution' stunt is worrying Uncle a great deal. Ovey and his Officials want us to do nothing. But the Wesleyan and the politician combine to make him try to do something. In the last resort he and I agree we may have to choose between sending Sokolnikoff away or see the Government go down. If that wretched choice comes, we shan't willingly choose the latter. But we aren't there yet![2]

The only relatively cheerful aspect of Anglo-Soviet relations during the second Labour Government's term lay in the field of international trade, though even this expanded less than initially expected, for, while trade had certainly increased by 1931, it was still, on Henderson's calculation, below that existing between 1925 and 1927.[3] But with the Labour Government facing an ever worsening world depression, any expansion was welcome and probably compensated for all the other irritations. At first it seemed that the Soviets would insist on linking increased trading facilities to a settlement of the vexed question of past claims and counter-claims;[4] but they eventually fell in with Henderson's

[1] *B.D.*, 2/VII, no. 135 (Henderson to Ovey, 24 Feb 1931). Italics added.

[2] Dalton Diary, entry for 18 Feb 1930.

[3] *B.D.*, 2/VII, no. 135 (Henderson to Ovey, 24 Feb 1931). This fact occasioned Henderson 'great disappointment': ibid.

[4] Throughout the period of the second Labour Government's tenure of office protracted negotiations took place to seek agreement on this matter of claims and debts, but it was obviously a hopeless quest. For details, see numerous

F

desire for temporary commercial and fisheries agreements. These were duly signed on 16 April and 22 May 1930 respectively.[1]

The resultant increased trade with the Soviet Union was generally welcome in Great Britain, although certain vested interests took exception to it. In particular, there was a short Press campaign on the subject of Soviet wheat, which, it was alleged, was knocking the bottom out of the world market. Certainly wheat prices fell noticeably at this time, but this was part of a trend that had commenced several years earlier.[2] In this case at least, allegations of deliberate Soviet 'dumpings' in order to undermine 'capitalism' appear to have had little foundation, although the danger that the Soviets might one day embark upon such a course remained a possibility to be reckoned with.

For the Labour Government, then, the experience of 'Left speaking to Left' was far from encouraging. As Foreign Secretary, Henderson had to bear the brunt of dealing with most of the difficulties; it had been calculated, for example, that he had to answer almost seven hundred Parliamentary Questions on the subject.[3] He gave vent to his irritation at the end of 1930 when he told Ovey: 'For my own part, I am bitterly disappointed at the results of one year's experience of renewed relations with the Soviet Government whose actions seem designed deliberately to play into the hands of the opponents of continued Anglo-Russian relations.'[4] Nor was Dalton able to summon up any enthusiasm when he later came to analyse the achievements of Labour's foreign policy. All he could find to say was that 'at the lowest we succeeded in making Anglo-Soviet relations less unsatisfactory than they would otherwise have been'.[5]

---

telegrams and memoranda in F.O., 418/71, 72, 73, 74 and 75. Henderson's firm refusal in November 1929 even to consider permitting the Soviets a guaranteed loan meant that the Soviets lost all incentive to settle Tsarist debts.

[1] For the diplomatic exchanges leading to the Commercial Agreement, see B.D., 2/VII, nos 55, 58, 75 and 80 (Ovey to Henderson, 13 Jan 1930; Soviet memorandum, 25 Jan 1930; Henderson to Ovey, 25 Mar 1930; and Soviet memorandum, 8 Apr 1930). For the texts of the commercial and fisheries agreements, see Cmd. 3552 and Cmd. 3583 of 1929–30.

[2] On this, see W. P. and Z. K. Coates, *Anglo-Soviet Relations*, pp. 360–1. Their arguments are convincing on this particular question, but their work as a whole should be treated with the greatest caution and suspicion.

[3] Elaine Windrich, *British Labour's Foreign Policy* (Stanford, 1952) p. 73.

[4] B.D., 2/VII, no. 118 (Henderson to Ovey, 3 Dec 1930).

[5] Dalton, in *Political Quarterly*, II 499–500.

AFTER Disraeli's decision to purchase shares in the Suez Canal, the Egyptian question assumed a place of permanent importance for successive British Governments, since it presented problems which, like those associated with Ireland, appeared to defy all attempts at solution. The basic cause of the trouble lay in the total incompatibility of Egyptian and British aspirations in two significant respects. First, Great Britain came to regard the Suez Canal as of quite fundamental strategic importance and as the lifeline of her whole Empire. Secondly, an ideological conflict arose on the question of the Sudan, when the British after 1899 developed a missionary zeal for the separate development of this area while the Egyptians clung tenaciously to the view that the Nile Valley should become a single political unit.[1] An *Anschluss* between Cairo and Khartoum came to be as unacceptable to Great Britain, whether under Labour or Conservative rule, as that between Austria and Germany was to the victorious allies immediately after the First World War.

The first Labour Government of 1924 had fully accepted the basic tenets of the traditional British position. For example, on the Sudan, MacDonald had given a firm pledge: 'Since going there [the Sudan] they [the British Government] have contracted heavy moral responsibilities as a trust for the Sudan people; there can be no question of their abandoning the Sudan until their work is done.'[2] Again, it was MacDonald in 1924 who saw to the heart of the problem when he claimed that Egyptian aspirations 'do conflict too hopelessly with our irreducible requirements regarding the Sudan and the defence of the Canal.'[3]

---

[1] For a summary of the Egyptian reasons for demanding the unity of the Nile Valley, see L. A. Fabunmi, *The Sudan in Anglo-Egyptian Relations: A Case-Study in Power Politics, 1800–1956* (London, 1960) pp. 147–59.

[2] Cmd. 2269 of 1924.

[3] Cited in Fabunmi, *The Sudan in Anglo-Egyptian Relations*, p. 82.

The second Labour Government came into office with the Egyptian situation virtually unchanged, although relations were in a quiescent phase.[1] It was characteristic of Henderson that he should aspire to a more enduring settlement, and it was characteristic of the problem that he had to admit eventual defeat. He began with the best of intentions, but from the outset the odds were heavily stacked against him. He had to satisfy not only the Egyptian negotiators but also the masses that stood behind them, since a treaty lacking popular approval would have been of little value. On the other hand, he had to grapple at home with the frank hostility of the King and the scarcely veiled mistrust of MacDonald, both of whom had vivid memories of the dramatic events of 1924 involving the Sudan and the murder of the Governor-General, Sir Lee Stack. Henderson was, moreover, fully aware of the difficulties facing a minority Government dependent on fickle Liberal support. He had to weigh the importance of Egyptian relations against other more immediately vital world issues. It is not surprising, therefore, that he treated the subject as being of a less than essential character, just as for him the Far East and even the resumption of Anglo-Soviet relations were not issues on which to break a lance and thereby risk the fall of the administration.

It must now be asked what Henderson, within these self-imposed limitations, was really seeking with regard to Egypt. First, it may be confidently asserted that he showed no sympathy for a doctrinaire left-wing approach. He did not see Great Britain's previous relations with Egypt simply as a form of disguised imperialism, and hence he did not seek to repudiate his predecessor's position. On the contrary, he spoke of it having been 'a conspicuous part of the policy of each Government, including the Labour Government of 1924, to raise the relationship between Egypt and this country above party. . . .'[2] He favoured the continued presence of British troops in the neighbourhood of Suez–'located there for the purpose of ensuring the defence of that vital artery of British Imperial communications'.[3] On the Sudan, he made it clear that the Government 'were most unwilling to agree to anything which

---

[1] For an outline of earlier developments, see Arnold J. Toynbee *et al.*, *Survey of International Affairs, 1925*, 2 vols (London, 1927–8) I 189–269, and Arnold J. Toynbee, *Survey of International Affairs, 1928* (London, 1929) pp. 235–83.   [2] *H.C. Deb.*, ccxxx, col. 1638, 26 July 1929.
[3] *H.C. Deb.*, ccxxxiii, col. 1973, 23 Dec 1929.

might in the slightest degree create a danger, however remote, of a re-
currence of the deplorable events of 1924'.[1] Basically, he seems to have
believed that the Egyptians would be prepared to reconcile themselves
to the British minimum demands and indeed provide valuable assistance in implementing them, provided only that they were approached
in the right way. He wanted to win this support by a greater degree of
conciliation than had previously been contemplated; but his concessions
were limited to questions of marginal significance to Great Britain and
he never came near to surrendering to the Egyptians on the basic issues
of Sudan and the Suez Canal. Hence Henderson must, on the Egyptian
question at least, be described as an 'enlightened patriot' rather than as
an internationalist idealist in the I.L.P. tradition. If he appeared at the
time to be a Left-winger, this was mainly because most of the opposition
to his policy came from the extreme Right, which rejected his tactical
concessions to Egyptian aspirations and which consisted in the main of
Conservatives, the Court, and his own Prime Minister.[2]

When the Labour Government took office, the Egyptian Prime
Minister was Mohammed Mahmud Pasha, one of the so-called 'King's
friends'. He was a relatively moderate man who was clinging to office in
defiance of the popular majority party, the Wafd. The British had found
him a good deal easier to do business with than such Wafd leaders as
Zaglul Pasha and Nahas Pasha; and indeed it had proved possible in the
early months of 1929 to reach agreements on two unsolved problems. A
financial settlement was initialled on 17 March, and this was followed by
a series of conversations leading up to the signing, on 1 May, of the Nile
Waters Agreement.[3] Early in June, Mahmud and a delegation of
Egyptian leaders came to London to pursue some further minor aspects
of the financial agreement and found to their gratification that Henderson had become Foreign Secretary. The Egyptians immediately asked
for the basis of the talks to be widened in the hope that a Socialist
Government would make more generous concessions. The negotiations
continued sporadically until 6 August, when a set of draft proposals was
published. But before turning to the details of this agreement, it will be

[1] *H.C. Deb.*, ccxxxiii, col. 1975, 23 Dec 1929.
[2] Selby said of MacDonald's attitude, 'On Egypt the P.M. has a diehard
streak': Dalton, *Call Back Yesterday*, p. 227.
[3] For the texts of these two agreements, see Cmd. 3305 of 1928–9 and Cmd.
3348 of 1929–30. See also Pierre Crabitès, 'The Nile Waters Agreement',
Foreign Affairs (New York), VIII (1929–30) 145–9.

convenient to consider an issue which engendered a far larger degree of public controversy, namely the dismissal of Lord Lloyd.

In considering the possibility of negotiations with Mahmud, the Foreign Secretary had been obliged to study the record of the outgoing Government in this field, and it soon became apparent to him that there had been marked differences in approach over a number of years between his predecessor, Austen Chamberlain, and the British High Commissioner in Cairo, Lord Lloyd. The latter had been a Conservative Member of Parliament prior to his appointment in Egypt, and he was not therefore a trained career diplomat.[1] This fact may have occasioned some resentment among the professionals in Whitehall. At all events, Henderson soon found himself being pressed by the Permanent Under-Secretary in the Foreign Office, Lindsay, to adopt the extreme course of outright dismissal. That Henderson was initially disinclined to agree to this but yielded to pressure is made clear in the following extract from a letter sent by Lindsay to Austen Chamberlain:

> Mr Henderson suggested that perhaps if spoken to when he came on leave Lord Lloyd might acquiesce in liberalism of policy in the spirit not less than in the letter and I expressed the view that Lord Lloyd's ideas were so ingrained in his character that he would not be able to change. I did not hide my own desire to see Lord Lloyd replaced by some other High Commissioner.[2]

Whether or not it was against Henderson's better judgement, there can be little doubt that Lloyd was rather brutally treated by the new Government. First, he appears to have been largely kept in the dark about the Anglo-Egyptian talks of June and July, although he was still Great Britain's accredited representative in Cairo.[3] Then, late in July, the Foreign Secretary finally decided to dismiss him. A blunt telegram in this sense was apparently countermanded by the Prime Minister on the advice of his Private Secretary, Vansittart.[4] Instead, Lloyd was invited to return home for discussions in a telegram which, in Henderson's words, 'was of such a character that . . . most people would have

---

[1] For a mediocre biography, see C. F. Adam, *Life of Lord Lloyd* (London, 1948).

[2] Lindsay to Chamberlain, 17 June 1929, Austen Chamberlain Papers.

[3] Churchill drew attention to this aspect of the ill-treatment of Lloyd in the House of Commons. See *H.C. Deb.*, ccxxxiii, cols 1994–5, 23 Dec 1929.

[4] See Vansittart, *The Mist Procession*, pp. 372–3.

accepted it as an invitation to terminate their position'.[1] Surprisingly, the High Commissioner tried to avert the inevitable. 'I can only say', he wrote to Henderson in acknowledgement of the telegram, 'I have every confidence that the differences of opinion which you apprehend do not really exist on any important point of policy. I feel sure our talks will convince you of this.'[2] The talks, however, resulted on 24 July in the submission of Lloyd's resignation.

Lloyd's departure caused a sensation in Parliament, with Right-wing Conservatives in a state of great indignation and Left-wing Socialists exultant at the fall of so prominent a proconsul of the British Empire. The result was a House of Commons debate on 26 July which provided Henderson with his first opportunity, as Foreign Secretary, to cross swords with the Opposition. He skilfully undermined the Opposition's case from the outset by drawing attention to the great differences of opinion that had existed between Chamberlain and Lloyd since 1926.[3] He proceeded to cite five outstanding incidents between the two men on which Cabinet adjudication had been necessary; and to forestall any possibility of denials, he challenged the Opposition to call for the laying of papers, a challenge they understandably evaded. According to Henderson, the position had been that Lloyd had taken the view that considerable intervention in Egyptian internal affairs and even harshly repressive measures were called for, while Chamberlain tended to favour a more conciliatory path, seeking as far as possible to heal the wounds opened up in 1924.[4] Having played upon the divisions in the ranks of the

[1] *H.C. Deb.*, ccxxx, col. 1301, 24 July 1929. The text of the telegram from Henderson to Lloyd, dated 3 July 1929, is given in Toynbee *et al.*, *Survey of International Affairs, 1930*, pp. 201–2. The Cabinet gave express authorisation for the despatch of this telegram: Cabinet Minutes, Cab. 23/61, 27(29)2, 3 July 1929. The King, however, complained that Lloyd had not been enabled to lay down his work with due self-respect: Nicolson, *King George the Fifth*, pp. 442–3.

[2] Lloyd to Henderson, 5 July 1929, Henderson Papers, F.O. 800/280. In public Lloyd was later to take a different line. 'I could not but concur with them [the Government]', he told the House of Lords, 'that I was not a suitable agent for the execution of their present policy in Egypt today': *H.L. Deb.*, vol. 75, col. 1133, 11 Dec 1929.

[3] For the full text of Henderson's speech, see *H.C. Deb.*, ccxxx, cols 1637–46, 26 July 1929.

[4] For details of the strained relationship between Chamberlain and Lloyd, see Sir Charles Petrie (ed.), *The Life and Letters of Sir Austen Chamberlain*, 2 vols (London, 1939–40) II 351–60. See also C.P., no. 181(29) by Henderson,

Conservative Party, the Foreign Secretary then summed up his reasons for calling upon Lloyd to resign. In brief, they rested upon one sentence in his original telegram to the High Commissioner: 'The success of my policy, which will certainly not be less liberal than that of my predecessor, will depend on the extent to which it may be interpreted with understanding and sympathy by His Majesty's representative.'[1]

Churchill came forward as Lloyd's principal defender and attempted to counter Henderson's arguments by suggesting that the High Commissioner had been the victim of a conspiracy: not only had there always been an element of prejudice against him in the Foreign Office, but the Foreign Secretary had now decided to dismiss him solely for holding certain sincere opinions. Lloyd, he stressed, had always obeyed his instructions loyally. Was he to be punished for having the courage to express his personal views in his dealings with London? Churchill added with perhaps pardonable exaggeration: 'The Foreign Secretary . . . has probably made it extremely difficult for our representatives in every part of the world to express their views with candour and with courage.'[2]

In spite of this gallant effort by Churchill on behalf of his friend, the outcome was never in doubt. Austen Chamberlain was conspicuous by his absence; and the Liberal Party early indicated its intention of supporting the Government. The Opposition accordingly did not choose to divide the House. The result was regarded as a great triumph for the new administration. The Foreign Secretary, it was rumoured, was greeted by the Cabinet with 'cries of see the conquering hero comes'.[3] Only the Prime Minister showed no pleasure in the achievement – but as Henderson remarked to Dalton, 'He has never thanked me for anything I have done these six and twenty years.'[4]

MacDonald was in fact out of sympathy with the whole tenor of Henderson's Egyptian policy. He rather found himself in agreement with the King, who had taken exception to some of the clauses which

---

13 June 1929, Cab. 24/204. For the High Commissioner's side of the story, see Lord Lloyd, *Egypt since Cromer*, 2 vols (London, 1933–4) II chaps. 17 and 18.

[1] Telegram from Henderson to Lloyd, cited in Toynbee *et al.*, *Survey of International Affairs, 1930*, p. 202.

[2] *H.C. Deb.*, ccxxx, col. 1652, 26 July 1929.

[3] Dalton, *Call Back Yesterday*, p. 226. Unfortunately this rumour finds no confirmation in the portentous Cabinet Minutes of the period.   [4] Ibid.

the Foreign Office and Mahmud were in the process of drawing up and, in particular, to the possibility of allowing even a token number of Egyptian troops to return to the Sudan.[1] The Prime Minister wrote to the Foreign Office expressing his alarm in what Dalton called 'a fussy letter', in which he characterised Mahmud as a 'drowning man' with whom it was scarcely worth doing business. Of Henderson's proposal to allow a token Egyptian force to return to the Sudan, MacDonald wrote:

In many conversations I had with Wafdist representatives when we were in Opposition, I told them that we really could not agree to a return of conditions in the Soudan which under Zaghloul had been so patently abused and which would inevitably lead, if re-established, to chaos in the administration of the Soudan. An Egyptian battalion was not a military co-operation but a political friction. . . .

Before I made up my mind what I should do in 1924 I studied with great care the whole problem of Egypt and the Soudan and only slowly and carefully came to my conclusions. A revision of those conclusions should be made only after the same care and forethought and the dominating considerations would be:
1. Is it essential to an understanding with Egypt?
2. Would it accord with the most liberal views regarding the interests and tranquillity of the Soudan itself?
So far as I am able to judge, and with the information at my disposal, I should answer both of those questions in the negative.[2]

Henderson replied without equivocation: 'my answers to the two questions you put would be these:—1) Is the return of an Egyptian unit essential to an agreement? *Yes.* 2) Would this affect the tranquillity of the country? *No.*'[3] Then, according to Dalton, he threatened to resign if he were 'pulled about much more'.[4] In the face of this determination

[1] Stamfordham to the Foreign Office, cited in Nicolson, *King George the Fifth*, p. 443. The King stated, 'It was British lives and British money that rescued the Sudan from tyranny and barbarism and surely we shall see to it that the sacrifice was not made in vain.': ibid.

[2] Dalton, *Call Back Yesterday*, p. 226; and MacDonald to Henderson, 27 July 1929, Henderson Papers, F.O. 800/280.

[3] Henderson to MacDonald, 30 July 1929, ibid.

[4] Dalton, *Call Back Yesterday*, p. 227. Mention has already been made of Shinwell's allegation to the effect that MacDonald inspired anonymous newspaper articles criticising his own Foreign Secretary's Egyptian policy (see above, p. 24). Perhaps Henderson had this in mind also when he spoke of being 'pulled about'.

F 2

MacDonald gave way, and hence Stamfordham had to report dolefully to the King:

> The impression given me by the Prime Minister was that he had been beaten by the Foreign Office and that the alternative would be the resignation of Mr Henderson, although he did not say this in so many words. . . . From all the Prime Minister told me, and from all I have heard, I am convinced that he is not happy at what has been done.[1]

Henderson, then, got his way. He succeeded in obtaining the support of both a Cabinet Committee and the Cabinet as a whole for the draft proposals eventually published on 6 August 1929.[2] Yet on examination the agreement must be judged to have been only slightly more favourable to the Egyptians than that offered by Chamberlain to Sarwat Pasha in 1928.[3] Basically, the Mahmud–Henderson draft provided for a return to the situation obtaining before the upheaval of 1924, with an end to the occupation of Cairo and Alexandria, the withdrawal of British troops to the immediate environs of the Suez Canal, and the liquidation of the now anachronistic Capitulations. The only concrete reference to the Sudan was innocuous enough in spite of the misgivings at Buckingham Palace: the British Government merely undertook to 'examine sympathetically a proposal for the return to the Sudan of an Egyptian battalion simultaneously with the withdrawal of the British forces from Cairo. . . .'[4] Indeed, so mild was this proposal that it even commended itself to the Governor-General of the Sudan, as is made apparent in these lines written by a secretary to the King, Major Alexander Hardinge:

> In conversation with Sir John Maffey I told him of the King's surprise at his concurrence in the proposed return of an Egyptian

---

[1] Cited in Nicolson, *King George the Fifth*, pp. 443–4. Of the King's attitude Sir John Maffey, the Governor-General of the Sudan, wrote: 'I know . . . how it irks him that he cannot sign the commissions of British Military officers serving in the Sudan, and how he is always hoping that the condominium is yielding to something more healthily red': Maffey to John Murray (British Foreign Office), 29 July 1929, Henderson Papers, F.O. 800/280.

[2] Cabinet Minutes, Cab. 23/61, 30(29)5, 24 July 1929. MacDonald withdrew from the Cabinet while this subject was under consideration. For the proceedings and report of the Cabinet Committee, see C.A.H.C., Cab. 27/387. On this committee Henderson successfully resisted the plea of Sir George Milne, the Chief of the Imperial General Staff, for a continued British military presence in the outskirts of Cairo.

[3] For a comparison of the two cases, see Toynbee *et al.*, *Survey of International Affairs, 1930*, pp. 188–90.   [4] For the full text, see Cmd. 3376 of 1929–30.

Battalion to the Sudan. He replied that he perfectly understood His Majesty's dislike of this reversal of the policy adopted in 1924, when the mutinous Egyptian troops were ejected from the Sudan. It is however his definite opinion that our position in the Sudan is infinitely stronger if based on the condominium with Egypt, than if we were in sole occupation of the country. Not only does the condominium provide us with the moral justification in the eyes of the world for our presence in the Sudan, but it also serves as a buffer against the hostile attitude which other countries, such as France and Italy, would sooner or later be likely to adopt towards us if we claimed the country for our own. . . . As long as Egypt is there with us, no other country will try to get us out. Egypt's share in the condominium is, in actual fact, purely nominal, and its only outward and visible sign will be this one Battalion, which from a Military point of view will be quite innocuous. In short his view is that, with the condominium, we are in the Sudan for ever, without it it is only a matter of time before world opinion drives us out.[1]

The agreement was, however, only tentative in character. If it was to become definitive, not only would it have to receive approval in the British Parliament but, largely as a result of pressure by Dalton, it was also deemed necessary for an Egyptian Assembly, elected on the basis of existing laws, to signify its support.[2] King Fuad and Mahmud might have been prepared to ratify the treaty without consulting the Assembly, but this possibility was rejected by the British as undesirable whether feasible or not. The outcome was that the Wafd once again came back into the picture. On 2 October Mahmud resigned and was succeeded by Adli Pasha, who headed a coalition administration. In elections held in December 1929 the Wafd, as usual, gained a clear victory despite their refusal to state their attitude to the Mahmud–Henderson Heads of Proposals.[3] Having been returned to power, however, the Wafd, under the leadership of Nahas Pasha, soon made it clear that they thought the draft inadequate. They sought and obtained a mandate from the Assembly to return to Westminster with a view to seeking improvements.

[1] Memorandum by Hardinge, 26 July 1929, R.A. GV, M 2226/17.

[2] On this, see a speech by Dalton to an I.L.P. summer school reported in the *Daily Herald*, 10 Aug 1929. Lindsay wrote to Dalton criticising the tactical wisdom of this speech. He did not wish to place Mahmud in an impossible position: Lindsay to Dalton, 14 Aug 1929, Dalton Papers. But Henderson appears to have agreed with Dalton's approach. See also Dalton, *Call Back Yesterday*, p. 229.

[3] For an account of the Egyptian elections, see *New Statesman*, 18 Jan 1930.

Nahas, together with several prominent Cabinet colleagues, accordingly came to London and on 31 March 1930 the talks recommenced. Over the ensuing days the British made further minor concessions, particularly with regard to the stationing of troops in the Suez area, but an impasse was reached on the Sudanese issue although as many as fourteen plenary meetings were held in an attempt to bridge the gap. On 17 April the negotiations were adjourned to enable Nahas to consult his colleagues in Cairo, and for a short time it appeared that a compromise might be reached. When, however, the talks were resumed, the situation was soon seen to be hopeless. Throughout the day and much of the night of 7-8 May the indefatigable Henderson vainly tried to save the talks.[1] A sceptical and unimpressed Vansittart, by now Permanent Under-Secretary, subsequently wrote of this affair in characteristic vein:

> When I mentioned that Nahas had once passed for barmy, he [Henderson] rejected such unaffable explanation and left the room patting him on the back. The experts smoked till Uncle returned. I often did not know what he was doing, but located him in the room which I had used as Curzon's Private Secretary. Dim shouts emerged from this distance, for unsophisticated Britons still think that they can make foreigners understand better by noise. . . .
>
> We broke as before on the Sudan, this time on a minor point of immigration, though the Egyptian aim was visibly to incorporate the whole country.[2]

In addition to the issue of unrestricted Egyptian immigration into the Sudan, there was a further bone of contention never finally overcome. This arose out of the Egyptian insistence that if admitted to the League of Nations they would reserve the right to raise the question of the legality of the Condominium Agreement of 1899 and might even seek leave to take Great Britain before the Permanent Court of International Justice. The Egyptians consequently refused to consider any form of wording in the projected treaty of 1930 that might prejudice their case, while the British naturally tried to trap them into this.[3]

---

[1] For an official description of these abortive negotiations, see Cmd. 3575 of 1929–30. The full minutes of the proceedings are in F.O., 407/211. For an entertaining blow-by-blow account, see Dalton Diary.

[2] Vansittart, *The Mist Procession*, p. 407.

[3] Henderson was under strong pressure from Maffey in Khartoum not to agree to any treaty with Egypt in which the Sudanese issue was not definitely settled on British terms: Maffey to Henderson, 7 May 1930, in Cabinet Minutes, Cab. 23/64, 25(30), appendix, 7 May 1930.

In spite of the breakdown, the Wafd leaders were not unappreciative of Henderson's efforts to reach an accommodation, and within the limits imposed by their domestic situation they sought to express their gratitude to him. For example, Nahas Pasha's verdict on the failure of the talks was singularly cheerful: 'We have lost a treaty of friendship with Great Britain, but we have won her actual friendship, which is all important.'[1]

The verdict on the Labour Government's Egyptian policy must therefore be that while no enduring settlement was obtained, the character of relations with Cairo showed a marked improvement. The dismissal of Lord Lloyd and his replacement by a moderate career diplomat, Sir Percy Loraine, did much to calm the atmosphere there, while the two major efforts of Henderson in London had some beneficial influence on the leading Egyptian statesmen. Looked at from the British Labour angle, the most apt conclusion must be some words from a detailed study of Anglo-Egyptian diplomacy:

in Britain, Governments come and go, but the objective remains essentially the same; British Labour Governments have always been as jealous and fully as capable of upholding British vital interests abroad as any other Government, Conservative or Liberal. The main difference lies in the general method of approach – Labour appears readier to obtain Britain's objectives through a degree of fraternisation.[2]

[1] Quoted in Toynbee et al., *Survey of International Affairs, 1930*, p. 190.
[2] Fabunmi, *The Sudan in Anglo-Egyptian Relations*, p. 83.

CHAPTER NINE

Anglo-Chinese Relations
1929–1931

THE second Labour Government, unlike both their predecessors and their successors, were fortunate in that throughout their period of office the perennial Chinese problem was in a relatively quiescent phase. In 1928, after several years of bitter civil war, China had again come under the nominal control of one administration, that of Chiang Kai-shek, and despite intermittent outbursts of unrest and disorder, she was to remain in a tolerably peaceful condition until September 1931, when the Japanese attack on Manchuria began. Henderson was therefore never under serious pressure to take military action in the Far East either to defend British lives and property from the effects of civil strife or to preserve the integrity of China from external aggression. On the other hand, the existence of a more tranquil situation was not an unmixed blessing for the British, since they no longer had any convincing excuse for refusing to negotiate the surrender of various extraterritorial privileges mostly accumulated and maintained as a result of the Chinese Government's inability to provide adequate protection for British traders.[1]

On 2 May 1929 the Chinese Chargé d'Affaires in London presented to the British Government a Note, originally dated 27 April, asking for negotiations with a view to the ultimate restoration of full sovereignty to China.[2] The Conservative Government went out of office without sending more than a formal acknowledgement, and hence the burden of drawing up a suitable reply fell upon Henderson, who in the event

[1] For the background to the extraterritoriality problem, see George Williams Keeton, *The Development of Extraterritoriality in China*, 2 vols (London, 1928), and Wesley R. Fishel, *The End of Extraterritoriality in China* (Berkeley, Cal., 1952).

[2] *B.D.*, 2/VIII, no. 3 (Chinese Chargé d'Affaires to Chamberlain, 2 May 1929). The Note was presented following the receipt in London of a telegram from Nanking dated 27 April. Five other powers (France, Norway, Brazil, the Netherlands and the United States) received similar formal requests at this period.

kept the Chinese waiting until 10 August. The ostensible reason for the delay was that the British Government wished to sound out the other extraterritorial powers which had received similar Notes from Nanking, in the vain hope that all would agree to send similar replies.[1]

Meanwhile, with the general issue of extraterritoriality under leisurely consideration in London, Anglo-Chinese negotiations centred for some months on a particular set of British privileges, those relating to Weihai-wei. In itself Weihaiwei, as the Marquess of Salisbury had foreseen in 1898, was of little intrinsic importance, but during 1929 and 1930 it acquired symbolic significance as a pointer to the state of Anglo-Chinese relations. It had been the subject of separate Anglo-Chinese discussions in the years following the Washington Treaty of 1922 when all other powers had relinquished their interests there. In 1924 'agreement in principle' had been reached that Great Britain would surrender her rights in Weihaiwei subject to three conditions, namely that the British Navy should retain limited harbouring privileges, that the rights of British property-owners should be safeguarded and that the Chinese Government should be in effective control of the unruly Shantung hinterland. But just as the agreement was about to be signed, a re-crudescence of civil war had invalidated the condition concerning Shantung and discussions had been broken off.

In May 1929, with the restoration of relative tranquillity, the two Governments had prepared to reopen the negotiations on the basis of the 1924 draft agreement, but a month later, at the time of the change of ministry in London, China's attitude underwent a dramatic volte-face. According to her Foreign Minister, Dr C. T. Wang, China had decided to develop Weihaiwei as a major naval base and therefore could no longer negotiate on the 1924 terms. The Chinese instead proposed that 'facilities of His Majesty's ships should be discontinued after a term of three years, that the place should be closed as a commercial port and no facilities given for foreign residents or trade'.[2] The British minister in China, Sir Miles Lampson, told Henderson that he regarded this move as 'a try on' obviously related to the fall of the Conservative Government.[3]

[1] On the failure of the interested powers to reach unanimity, see Fishel, *The End of Extraterritoriality*, pp. 162–3.
[2] *B.D.*, 2/viii, no. 1 (Foreign Office memorandum, 8 Jan 1930).
[3] *B.D.*, 2/viii, no. 47 (Lampson to Henderson, 21 June 1929).

If, as seems probable, Lampson was correct, the Chinese had gravely misread the situation in London, where Henderson was determined not to be rushed into ill-considered concessions. Indeed, on first receiving news of the changed Chinese attitude, the Foreign Secretary was tempted simply to break off discussions on the Weihaiwei question on the grounds that the Chinese themselves had chosen to tear up the 1924 draft agreement. At the same time, fearing an outburst of 'boycotts, agitation, etc.', he was doubtful of the 'expediency' of so extreme a course and he therefore sought Lampson's advice.[1] He also wondered rather naïvely whether it might be possible to obtain, in exchange for Weihaiwei and a money payment, the permanent possession of the Kowloon Leased Territories (opposite to Hong Kong) which were due to revert to China in 1997.[2] Lampson, in replying to the Foreign Secretary's surprisingly vigorous telegram, urged caution: on Weihaiwei he thought it 'premature to anticipate rupture of negotiations at present stage', and on Kowloon he held that the Chinese 'would never listen to such a proposed bargain' since 'their whole policy is to regain whatever territory was once Chinese soil'.[3]

Having received this advice, Henderson made no move to break off discussions on Weihaiwei or to fly his Kowloon kite. On the other hand, he was not initially prepared to fall in fully with Lampson's suggested concessions to the Chinese on Weihaiwei. The envoy wished to modify the 1924 draft treaty in two important respects. He proposed first to allow the Chinese to close completely Port Edward, where a small number of British subjects resided, in return for full compensation; and secondly, he was willing to concede that British naval facilities should be maintained for a period of only ten years.[4] On 7 August Henderson replied that he was in 'general agreement' with the first point, but on the naval aspect he wrote:

Climate of the British naval bases on the China station, Hong Kong and Singapore, during the summer months is extremely trying to northern Europeans. Present establishment at Weihaiwei, which allows the crews of war vessels to be landed for recuperation and recreation and also provides a small hospital in a healthy climate is therefore indispensable. I am not therefore prepared to adopt the

[1] B.D., 2/VIII, no. 61 (Henderson to Lampson, 2 July 1929).   [2] Ibid.
[3] B.D., 2/VIII, no. 63 (Lampson to Henderson, 8 July 1929).   [4] Ibid.

suggestion that tenure of these facilities should be limited to ten years.[1]

He was prepared to surrender Weihaiwei only on condition that satisfactory alternative arrangements were made; if not, the British Government could not 'depart from the provisions of the 1924 agreement for a ten year tenure with option of renewal'. Given this attitude, no further progress was made on the Weihaiwei issue during the remaining months of 1929, and negotiations were only resumed in 1930 when the British policy was suitably modified in the direction recommended by Lampson.

Meanwhile attention had switched to the general problem of extra-territorial rights following the delivery on 10 August of the British Government's considered reply to the Chinese Note of 27 April. After stressing the lack of and need for a wide acceptance of Western legal principles throughout China, the British Note ended with the following discouraging conclusions:

> So long as these conditions subsist there appears to be no practicable alternative to maintaining, though, perhaps, in a modified form, the treaty port system that has served for nearly a century to regulate the intercourse between China and the British subjects within her domain. Some system of extraterritoriality is the natural corollary to the maintenance, even in modified form, of the treaty port system, and the problem as it presents itself to His Majesty's Government at the present moment is to discover what further modifications in that system . . . it would be desirable and practicable to effect.

On the subject of possible modifications in existing arrangements, the British Note contained no concrete suggestion but merely invited the Chinese Government to put forward their proposals.[2]

The Chinese found the British Note most disappointing, since it was as conservative in tone as that of the French and much more so than that of the Americans. Accordingly, in their reply of 6 September the Chinese merely repeated their earlier request for negotiations on the total abolition of extraterritoriality and pointedly abstained from advancing any proposals for a modification in the existing arrangements, as that would have signified a willingness to enter discussions on the basis of

[1] *B.D.*, 2/VIII, no. 84 (Henderson to Lampson, 7 Aug 1929).
[2] *B.D.*, 2/VIII, no. 86 (Note presented to Chinese Government, 10 Aug 1929).

the British approach.[1] A further British Note, dated 1 November, after stating disingenuously that 'there would . . . appear to be a large measure of common ground between the two Governments in their mutual desire to enter into a discussion of the problem', gave no ground on the issue of principle.[2]

The deadlock was quickly broken, however, when Henderson realised that the Chinese were seriously intending to take unilateral action on 1 January 1930 to try to end extraterritoriality. Rumours to this effect had been heard throughout the summer of 1929, but these only received official confirmation from the Chinese Foreign Ministry on 7 November 1929.[3] Lampson suggested to Henderson that the British Government should issue 'a most serious warning to Chinese Minister in London against danger of unilateral denunciation'. He added: 'It could do no harm and might do much good; it might also prevent subsequent charge that we had had fair warning of what was coming and had taken no notice of it.'[4] But Henderson disagreed:

> Chinese Minister has already been seriously warned that unilateral denunciation would be very foolish and would only poison the atmo-sphere. I am reluctant to take a more solemn and formal step defiance of which would make us look foolish. . . .[5]

From this significant admission it may be inferred that the Foreign Secretary had virtually ruled out the use of force in the event of Chinese unilateral action and that his main concern at this stage was to avoid a humiliation for British diplomacy.[6] Accordingly, on 20 December he

[1] B.D., 2/VIII, nos 98 and 113 (Waichiaopu to Lampson, in Lampson to Henderson, 18 Sep 1929; Lampson to Henderson, 1 Nov 1929).

[2] B.D., 2/VIII, no. 119 (Lampson to Wang, in Lampson to Henderson, 6 Nov 1929).

[3] B.D., 2/VIII, no. 124 (Lampson to Henderson, 12 Nov 1929).   [4] Ibid.

[5] B.D., 2/VIII, no. 131 (Henderson to Lampson, 18 Nov 1929).

[6] Henderson's attitude to the use of force against China was in marked contrast to that adopted at this period by the Soviet Union. On 17 November 1929 Soviet forces invaded Chinese territory to put an end to Chinese claims in a dispute about the Chinese Eastern Railway. For details, see Peter Richards, 'British Policy in China, with special reference to the Problem of Extraterri-toriality, 1929–1931', unpublished London University M.Sc.(Econ.) thesis, 1967, pp. 99–103. The development of the Sino-Soviet quarrel, as seen through British eyes, may be traced in numerous despatches to and from Lampson in F.O., 405/262 and 263. The quarrel was of course of a much more fundamental character than that between the Labour Government and China.

handed to the Chinese Minister in London an *aide-mémoire* which re-presented a complete reversal of previous British policy on the disputed question of principle. The new British position was as follows:

> . . . His Majesty's Government are aware of official and semi-official declarations on the part of the Chinese Government which they interpret as indicating the earnest desire of the Chinese Government that substantial progress should be made before the 1st January, 1930, if not with the actual process of abolition of extraterritoriality, at any rate with serious negotiations having in view the initiation of that process, in the immediate future. . . . His Majesty's Government are therefore willing to agree that the 1st January, 1930, should be treated as the date from which the process of the gradual abolition of extra-territoriality should be regarded as having commenced in principle and would have no objection to any declaration conformable with that attitude which the Chinese Government may think it desirable to issue.[1]

On the same day Henderson instructed Lampson to open negotiations with the Chinese at an early opportunity and without conditions.[2]

Encouraged perhaps by the volte-face in London, the Chinese on 28 December issued a proclamation or a so-called 'Mandate' which concluded:

> For the purpose of restoring her inherent jurisdictional sovereignty it is hereby decided and declared that on and after the first day of the first month of the nineteenth year of the Republic (the 1st January, 1930), all foreign nationals in the territory of China who are now enjoying extraterritorial privileges shall abide by the laws, ordinances and regulations duly promulgated by the central and local Governments of China. The executive yuan and juridicial yuan are hereby ordered to instruct the Ministers concerned to prepare as soon as possible a plan for the execution of this mandate, and to submit it to the legislative yuan for examination and deliberation with a view to its promulgation and enforcement.[3]

[1] Cmd. 3480 of 1929–30.

[2] *B.D.*, 2/VIII, no. 174 (Henderson to Lampson, 20 Dec 1929). This policy decision was at variance with the advice tendered in three separate telegrams by Lampson, who did not wish to negotiate with the Chinese under duress and without first making a sustained attempt to agree on a common policy with France and the United States: *B.D.*, 2/VIII, nos 147, 153 and 167 (Lampson to Henderson, 1, 3, and 9 Dec 1929). Henderson did not rate highly the chances of persuading either the United States or France to act in concert with Great Britain, and was therefore disinclined to favour further delay on this count: *B.D.*, 2/VIII, no. 148 (Henderson to Lampson, 2 Dec 1930).

[3] Cmd. 3480 of 1929–30.

The British Government's reaction was to hand to the Chinese envoy in London a further *aide-mémoire*, which ranks as a model for deliberate obtuseness in international diplomacy. It began thus:

His Majesty's Government have had under consideration the mandate issued by the Chinese Government on the 28th December on the subject of extra-territoriality. His Majesty's Government assume that in issuing this mandate it was the intention of the Chinese Government to make a declaration of the character indicated in . . . the British aide-mémoire of the 20th December. They have, therefore, authorised His Majesty's Minister to accept the invitation extended to him by the Minister for Foreign Affairs to enter into detailed negotiations on the subject, and they understand that His Majesty's Minister is preparing to leave for Nanking on the 2nd January. . . .[1]

Discussions between Lampson and the Chinese began at once in Nanking and on 10 January a brief Chinese plan for ending extraterritoriality was produced. Under the plan no vestige of former privileges was to remain for British citizens, who were, however, in the event of arrest by the Chinese authorities, to be guaranteed speedy trials in modern courts.[2] To this proposal the British, conscious that they were fighting a rearguard action, made no formal counter-proposals until 11 September. Meanwhile they sought informally to convince the Chinese that privileges for British citizens could only be abandoned gradually. As early as 2 November 1929 Henderson had decided against a policy of ceding all legal privileges in successive geographical zones, and had favoured instead the method of yielding ground uniformly throughout China in the following three stages:

1. Civil cases
2. Criminal cases, and
3. Personal status matters.[3]

On 20 January Lampson was authorised to explain this programme to the Chinese; but no formal British draft treaty was advanced for a further nine months.[4] In the interim Henderson and Lampson

---

[1] Cmd. 3480 of 1929–30. The *aide-mémoire* went on to urge that existing privileges should continue until the negotiations for modification were concluded.
[2] *B.D.*, 2/VIII, no. 197 (Lampson to Henderson, 10 Jan 1930).
[3] *B.D.*, 2/VIII, no. 116 (Henderson to Lampson, 2 Nov 1929).
[4] *B.D.*, 2/VIII, nos 207 and 210 (Lampson to Henderson, 18 Jan 1930; Henderson to Charles Garstin (Shanghai), 20 Jan 1930).

sought to arrive at an agreement with the other interested powers, and especially the United States and Japan, on the approach to be adopted.[1]

Although no definite progress was made in the first half of 1930 on the legal aspects of extraterritoriality, Chinese impatience was kept within bounds largely as a result of timely British concessions with respect to Weihaiwei. On 11 January Lampson urged Henderson to allow him to negotiate with the Chinese on this issue on terms which involved a retreat by both parties from the position they had taken in 1929.[2] On 5 February Henderson telegraphed his concurrence, with the result that an agreement was quickly reached, being initialled on 18 April in Nanking and published on 5 May. The most important modification of the 1924 draft treaty was the abandonment by Great Britain of the option to renew its lease of naval facilities after an initial period of ten years. The formal rendition ceremony took place on 1 October.[3]

Meanwhile negotiations between Great Britain and other interested powers on the general question of extraterritoriality had culminated early in September in the separate submission to Nanking of a British and an American draft treaty. The British draft differed only in minor respects from the cautious programme formulated originally in November 1929 and communicated to the Chinese by Lampson in January 1930.[4] Wang's reaction was to say that the British proposals 'had come as a great disappointment to his Government'.[5] By 1 December he was ready with a counter-draft, which, though more detailed than previous

[1] For these complex and not wholly successful negotiations, see Akira Iriye, *After Imperialism: The Search for a New Order in the Far East, 1921–1931* (Cambridge, Mass., 1965) pp. 272–7, and Richards, unpublished London University thesis, chap. 5. In this connection Henderson told the Cabinet on 5 February 1930 that 'a not altogether helpful development had intervened as the United States Government had submitted a draft Agreement to the Nanking Government which made concessions considerably in excess of what His Majesty's Government, in existing circumstances, were prepared to make': Cabinet Minutes, Cab. 23/63, 8(30)1, 5 Feb 1930.

[2] *B.D.*, 2/VIII, nos 199 and 200 (both Lampson to Henderson, 11 Jan 1930).

[3] For details of the negotiations, see *B.D.*, 2/VIII, nos 216, 223, 250, 260, 264, 270 and 327. The text of the final Convention was published as Cmd. 3741 of 1930–1.

[4] For a summary of the text of the British draft treaty of 11 September 1930, see *B.D.*, 2/VIII, no. 320, enclosure no. 2.

[5] *B.D.*, 2/VIII, no. 322 (Lampson to Henderson, 19 Sep 1930).

efforts, was in substance a reiteration of China's demand for complete and early abolition of all significant extraterritorial privileges.[1]

At this stage, with deadlock apparently complete, the Chinese decided once again to have recourse to threats of unilateral action. A memorandum, handed to a British representative on 17 December, contained the following ominous sentence: 'The Chinese Government still believe that it is possible to settle once and for all the question of abolition of extra-territoriality by negotiation, and that it will not be necessary for the Chinese Government to take a different course of action towards that end.'[2] Four days later this threat was studiously underlined by Wang in verbal form.[3]

In the face of these warnings the British quickly perceived the dangers inherent in a policy of continued intransigence: they might be at any moment confronted with a choice between accepting a spectacular humiliation and consolidating their privileges in China by military force. Recognising that a Labour Government would have had the utmost difficulty in justifying to its supporters any recourse to physical intervention, Henderson again took fright and decided to offer far-reaching concessions. The substance of the new British negotiation position, as embodied in a telegram to the Dominions, was as follows:

we believe that it will be necessary to abandon some of the safeguards of the September 11 draft which it will be remembered included more than it was contemplated that the Chinese would be willing to accept. It is not proposed however to embody these concessions in any fresh draft or series of drafts but to authorise Lampson, when active negotiations are resumed, progressively to abandon so far as may be necessary certain demands contained in the draft of September 11 with a view to securing in return the assent of the Chinese Government to the retention of those safeguards which are regarded as really vital. . . .

We agree with Lampson's view that negotiations are unlikely to pursue a satisfactory course until the Chinese demand for the surrender of criminal jurisdiction is acceded to. . . .

We agree with Lampson's view that the most important interest at

[1] For the full text of the Chinese counter-draft, see *B.D.*, 2/VIII, no. 334, enclosure no. 2.

[2] Enclosure in Lampson to Henderson, telegram no. 745, 19 Dec 1930, F.O., 405/267.

[3] *B.D.*, 2/VIII, no. 341 (Lampson to Henderson, 22 Dec 1930). The United States was faced with a similar threat at this time. See Fishel, *The End of Extraterritoriality*, pp. 176–7.

stake is the exclusion of Shanghai. The exclusion of Tientsin, Canton and Hankow is not so vital and might possibly be abandoned in the last resort, but the exclusion of Shanghai even if the area excluded is limited to the International Settlement only would seem to be a vital necessity.

The Chinese would appear to be strongly opposed, for reasons of national prestige, to granting the powers of a co-judge to legal advisers employed by them. To insist on legal advisers being granted such powers might therefore give rise to friction and might jeopardise their utility in a purely advisory capacity. In order to avoid losing the benefit of a safeguard to which the greatest importance is attached it is proposed to authorise Lampson as a final concession to the Chinese Government to abandon the provision that the legal advisers shall act as co-judges. . . .[1]

Having finally resolved to abandon the substance of his earlier demands respecting criminal jurisdiction, Henderson's principal aim with regard to Chinese policy during the remainder of his period of office was to retain Great Britain's special position in the four reserved areas, Shanghai, Tientsin, Canton and Hankow.[2] At first the Chinese adopted an inflexible attitude regarding these areas and, doubtless encouraged by the previous British retreats, issued veiled threats of unilateral action which would be taken if no agreement had been reached by 5 May.[3] By 21 April Lampson was reconciled to yielding on both Hankow and Canton, believing that he had been authorised by Henderson to do so. On Shanghai and Tientsin, however, he was prepared rather than surrender to accept 'a break with all its risks'.[4] The Chinese, on the other hand, were prepared to offer only the exclusion of the Shanghai International Settlement for a period of three years. This was quite unacceptable to Henderson.[5] When therefore the critical day of 5 May

---

[1] B.D., 2/VIII, no. 358 (Henderson to Edward Ingram (Peking), 18 Feb 1931).

[2] B.D., 2/VIII, nos 380 and 384 (Lampson to Henderson, 30 Mar 1931; Henderson to Lampson, 2 Apr 1931).

[3] B.D., 2/VIII, nos 384 and 395 (Henderson to Lampson, 2 Apr 1931; Lampson to Henderson, 20 Apr 1931).

[4] B.D., 2/VIII, no. 397 (Lampson to Henderson, 21 Apr 1931). Doubts later arose about whether Lampson had in fact received permission to yield at this stage on Canton and Hankow. See B.D., 2/VIII, no. 460, para. 40 (Lampson to Henderson, 8 June 1931).

[5] B.D., 2/VIII, nos 405, 410 and 414 (Lampson to Henderson, 27 Apr 1931; Henderson to Lampson, 29 Apr 1931; Lampson to Henderson, 1 May 1931); and C.P. no. 109(31) by Henderson, 27 Apr 1931, Cab. 24/221.

arrived, the Chinese could not point to any advance in the negotiations as justifying the abandonment of their threatened unilateral action. Forced to choose between the risky policy of taking physical steps to end extraterritorial privileges and the humiliating course of issuing a further empty mandate, they opted for the latter. 1 January 1932 was named as the date on which it was claimed that firm unilateral action would be taken. The Mandate of 5 May 1931, like that of 1 January 1930, came as something of an anticlimax and had the effect of stiffening British resolve and inclination to procrastinate.

Although the text of a draft treaty was in every other respect completed by 6 June, no final agreement could be reached on the reserved areas, the British insisting on the exclusion of Shanghai and Tientsin for a longer period than the Chinese would accept. After Chinese concessions on Shanghai and Tientsin and a firm British decision to abandon claims with respect to Canton and Hankow, the remaining difference was indeed a small one, but both parties insisted that they could not retreat further.[1]

At this juncture negotiations were broken off by mutual consent for the duration of the summer. There appears to have been no serious doubt on either side that the outstanding problem would be overcome by a compromise in the autumn. In the event, however, the outbreak of Sino-Japanese hostilities in September 1931 brought about a total change in the situation, with the result that the British National Government, which had come into office in August, declined to renounce extraterritorial privileges by treaty.[2] Only on 11 January 1943, when both China and Great Britain were at war with Japan, was a formal treaty ending extraterritoriality finally signed.

[1] B.D., 2/VIII, nos 456 and 457 (Henderson to Lampson, 4 June 1931; Lampson to Henderson, 6 June 1931). For the full text of the agreed articles of the draft treaty, see B.D., 2/VIII, no. 458, enclosure no. 3. For a summary of the negotiations during May 1931, see B.D., 2/VIII, no. 460 (Lampson to Henderson, 8 June 1931).

[2] Richards, unpublished London University thesis, p. 207, concluded: 'It would seem that but for the Japanese military actions in the latter half of the year the draft agreement of June, 1931 . . . would have been implemented.'

CHAPTER TEN

The Austrian Crisis, 1931

IT has already been shown how the reparations issue haunted Europe in the decade after Versailles with disastrous consequences for stability in Germany and very few meaningful benefits for the victors. A further and still more tragic paradox arose out of the collapse of the Dual Monarchy. When, at the end of the First World War, the succession states emerged with Woodrow Wilson's blessing, a *grossdeutsch* solution suggested itself as the most reasonable way of dealing with the problem of the German-speaking rump of the former Hapsburg lands. But Germany had just lost a war, whose outbreak, moreover, was judged by the victors to be her responsibility. It was therefore unthinkable that she should be rewarded for her crime by an accession of new territory, whatever the wishes of the German-Austrians might be and notwithstanding Wilson's commitment to the principle of self-determination. The French and the British accordingly made efforts in the first years of peace to breathe life into the new and clearly somewhat artificial state of Austria. The inhabitants were not even allowed to call their country German-Austria as they would have preferred, and the most elaborate precautions were taken to ensure the permanent separation of Vienna and Berlin. Article 55 of the Treaty of St Germain of 1919 and the Geneva Protocol of 1922 both bound the new state to abstain 'from any act which might directly or indirectly compromise her independence'.[1] But any attempt by statesmen to bind their successors is a risky venture and cannot be guaranteed to succeed. The *Anschluss* could only have been permanently averted if the allies had maintained the will and the military superiority to prevent it, or if the Austrians themselves had developed a nationalism of their own and had repudiated any desire for

[1] For details, see Bennett, *Germany and the Diplomacy of the Financial Crisis*, p. 41, and Jürgen Gehl, *Austria, Germany, and the Anschluss, 1931–1938* (London, 1963) p. 8. Both these works are extremely useful for a study of the Austrian crisis of 1931 and the present account draws heavily upon them. By contrast, the German Foreign Minister's retrospective account is most misleading. See Julius Curtius, *Bemühung um Österreich: Das Scheitern des Zollunionsplans von 1931* (Heidelberg, 1947).

Anschluss. In the event neither condition was fulfilled, and hence the way was paved for the eventual triumph of Hitler in 1938.

It was the fate of the second Labour Government to hold office at the period when Berlin made its first serious move to test the will power of the allies on this question. The result was that, while some weakening in allied resolve became apparent, in the end sufficient strength still remained in Paris alone to scotch Berlin's plans for a time. The great tragedy of the affair from the British point of view was that relations between France and Germany deteriorated markedly at a time when London was still hoping to sponsor the further development of European pacification, disarmament and the peaceful and orderly revision of Versailles.

The first probe from Berlin took the form of an attempted Customs Union, which in theory is totally different from an *Anschluss*. No one, however, was deceived as to Berlin's purely political motives, since the Austrian finances were in such a parlous condition that there was clearly no economic advantage for Germany in the project. It was doubly ironic that the Austrians, who by contrast had some sound economic reasons for supporting a Customs Union, showed a greater willingness than the Germans to abandon the scheme in the international crisis which ensued.

The final initiative leading up to the crisis came when Curtius visited Austria on 3 March 1931.[1] During the next two days he negotiated with the Austrian Foreign Minister, Johannes Schober, the so-called Vienna Protocol, which contained a fairly complete plan for a Customs Union but which in order to avoid presenting other interested powers with a *fait accompli* did not go as far as a final agreement.[2] It has been suggested that the violent reaction in other states, even to the Vienna Protocol, came as a surprise to the Germans, and certainly this was the impression they attempted to convey at the time.[3] But that their real expectations

[1] The earlier feelers, over a period of a year, are described in Gehl, *Austria, Germany, and the Anschluss*, pp. 5–6. See also F. G. Stambrook, 'The German-Austrian Customs Union Project of 1931: A Study of German Methods and Motives', *Journal of Central European Affairs*, XXI (1961–2) 15–44.

[2] The text of the protocol is given in Jan Krulis-Randa, *Das Deutsch-Österreichische Zollunionsprojekt von 1931: Die Bemühung um eine wirtschaftliche Annäherung zwischen Deutschland und Österreich* (Zürich, 1955) pp. 88–92.

[3] See Bennett, *Germany and the Diplomacy of the Financial Crisis*, p. 59.

and feelings were rather different is apparent from a sentence in State Secretary Bernhard von Bülow's instructions to the German ambassadors in Paris and London: 'Under no circumstances must we show any sign whatsoever of a bad conscience during the discussions on this matter and during the outcry in the press which is to be anticipated.'[1]

The risks of premature leakage of the plan were considered to be so great that an early announcement was decided upon; and approval for this was obtained from the Austrian and German Cabinets on 13 and 16 March respectively. The date for informing other Governments was fixed for the 21st.[2] The French, however, had discovered what was planned by the 20th as a result of unofficial leakages, probably originating in Vienna and passed on by Prague. Briand's initial reaction was an immediate attempt to organise a joint *démarche* on the part of France, Italy, Great Britain and Czechoslovakia.[3] Of these states Great Britain alone declined to act in haste: she merely told the German and Austrian Governments that her attitude was one of 'complete reserve'.[4] Vansittart, it is true, added that he felt that 'interested parties should have been consulted sooner', but the reason for this remark was obviously resentment at the manner in which the project had been launched and

[1] Von Bülow to von Hoesch and von Neurath, 17 Mar 1931, G.F.M.R. 4620/E 199091–94, quoted in Stambrook, loc. cit. p. 42.

[2] It is true that as early as 13 March Rumbold, the British ambassador in Berlin, was given the information by von Bülow that 'a sort of customs union' had been discussed between Curtius and Schober. Rumbold's despatch to Henderson covering this interview dated the same day (*B.D.*, 2/I, no. 358) did not reach London until the 18th where, in Bennett's words 'it seems to have attracted no particular notice': *Germany and the Diplomacy of the Financial Crisis*, p. 56 n. For confirmation of this assertion see the absence of comment on the original despatch in F.O., 371/15157. D. L. Busk and George Mounsey of the Central Department at the Foreign Office simply appended their initials. Their lack of interest, however, is not particularly surprising, since Rumbold had been given no reason to suppose that the discussions in Vienna had been about a complete Customs Union nor that they had been brought to any decisive conclusion. On this point, see Ernst Geigenmüller, 'Botschafter von Hoesch und der deutsch–österreichische Zollunionsplan von 1931', *Historische Zeitschrift*, cxcv (1962) 584 n.

[3] *B.D.*, 2/II, no. 1 (de Fleuriau to Henderson, 20 Mar 1931).

[4] *B.D.*, 2/II, no. 3 (Henderson to Rumbold, 25 Mar 1931). On the same day as this telegram was despatched, MacDonald told his Cabinet colleagues that 'he thought it important that His Majesty's Government in the United Kingdom should form their own policy on the proposal and not necessarily follow a French lead': Cabinet Minutes, Cab. 23/66, 19(31)1, 25 Mar 1931.

not, as one writer has suggested, because 'Labour was strictly opposed to secret diplomacy'.[1]

The explosive situation created by the Austro-German announcement was one in which Henderson's mediatory gifts were to be shown to good advantage. Though unmistakably angry at Germany's impetuosity and irresponsibility, he appreciated the need to approach the resulting problem in a constructive spirit. Determined to act in a mediatory capacity and to minimise possible loss of face on both sides, he decided to avoid giving his personal view on the legal aspect of the case, no doubt to the disappointment of optimists in both the Wilhelmstrasse and the Quai d'Orsay. On more than one occasion he prefaced his remarks with the platitude that 'two opinions' could be held on the subject; and when his silence was being interpreted by the Germans as secret approval for their position, he skilfully restored the balance by saying that 'Germany must not assume that we are satisfied that there is no objection to the proposed union on the legal side'.[2] What concerned him most, he claimed, was the psychological effect of the project on disarmament and pacification – and about this he was willing to scold the Germans in no uncertain terms.[3] But the announcement having been made, rebukes were clearly not enough; a positive solution had to be sought. As he told his Cabinet colleagues:

> means must, in my opinion, be found for removing this proposal from the domain of international politics. But this ought to be effected, not by the imposition of a direct veto, but by some gentler method which will save the faces of those directly concerned and not perpetuate the bitterness already engendered.[4]

[1] *B.D.*, 2/II, no. 3 (Henderson to Rumbold, 25 Mar 1931); and Gehl, *Austria, Germany, and the Anschluss*, p. 13. There is abundant evidence that the Labour Government accepted the need for secrecy in diplomatic negotiations and that the erstwhile Union of Democratic Control doctrines on this point were in practice ignored.

[2] *B.D.*, 2/II, no. 29 (Henderson to Rumbold, 1 May 1931). The advice actually given to Henderson by the British Law Officers on the legal aspect was that a Customs Union 'probably would be a breach by Austria of her undertaking . . . of 1922': C.P., no. 86(31) by Henderson, 8 Apr 1931, Cab. 24/220. The Foreign Secretary persuaded the Cabinet that this verdict should not be revealed: Cabinet Minutes, Cab. 23/66, 22(31)7, 15 Apr 1931. No leakage appears to have occurred.

[3] See, for example, *B.D.*, 2/II, no. 5 (Henderson in Tyrrell to Rumbold and Phipps, 25 Mar 1931).

[4] C.P., no. 115(31), 5 May 1931, Cab. 24/221. Henderson also indicated in

Henderson's practical aim, then, was to persuade the Germans voluntarily to surrender the scheme with good grace, but in order to make this possible he had to dissuade the French from making unacceptable demands too soon. Hence the principal objective, from the British point of view, was to win time in order to allow wiser counsels to prevail in Berlin. The Foreign Secretary therefore called upon both the Austrians and the Germans to promise that they would not present the world with an early *fait accompli*; but, on the other hand, he declined to support French demands for a complete suspension of negotiations between Vienna and Berlin, since that would have represented an intolerable humiliation for Brüning.

Henderson's first positive move came on 25 March when, in the course of a visit to Paris, he instructed British envoys in Germany and Austria to suggest that the matter should be placed on the agenda of the next meeting of the League Council, scheduled for May.[1] Germany's response, unlike that of the equivocal Austrians, was an immediate and firm rejection of the proposed course.[2] Henderson retreated to a reserve position, pointing out that he had had in mind only that the League Council should seek a legal judgement from the Permanent Court of International Justice and not that the League Council itself should consider the merits of the matter either in legal terms or in its more political aspect.[3] In the circumstances the Germans decided not to protest against this revised British plan, but Curtius pointed out that 'the German Government must reserve complete liberty of action with regard to any

---

this memorandum that he would like a free hand in trying 'to replace the dangerous Austro-German customs union by some progressive scheme for the economic union of Europe'. The Cabinet, however, instructed him to adopt 'a non-committal attitude' towards any radical schemes involving changes in existing British tariff policies: Cabinet Minutes, Cab. 23/67, 27(31)2, 6 May 1931.

[1] *B.D.*, 2/II, no. 5 (Henderson in Tyrrell to Rumbold and Phipps, 25 Mar 1931). The Foreign Secretary took the extraordinary course of sending this telegram to Berlin and Vienna direct from Paris. The Foreign Office in London was merely sent a copy! It is interesting to note that Briand expressed himself as grateful for Henderson's initiative: *B.D.*, 2/II, no. 13 (Henderson to Rumbold, 9 Apr 1931).

[2] *B.D.*, 2/II, nos 7 and 9 (Rumbold to Tyrrell, 25 Mar 1931; Phipps to Tyrrell, 25 Mar 1931).

[3] *B.D.*, 2/II, no. 11 (Henderson in Tyrrell to Rumbold, 26 Mar 1931).

procedure which may be suggested to the Council'.[1] The French, too, made it plain to the British that there were limits of concession beyond which they would not go. Alexis Léger, Briand's *chef de cabinet*, told a British diplomat:

> privately it was essential to make the German Government understand the position and the inevitable result of persistence in the policy on which it had embarked. To sum up, persistence in that policy, in view of the manner in which it had been initiated and whether or not its first manifestation was in conformity with the letter of the treaties, implied an end to movement to the Federation of Europe, a counter alliance against Germany in Central Europe under the guardianship and leadership of France and the end of disarmament.[2]

In this tense atmosphere a further difficulty arose, namely whether negotiations between Berlin and Vienna should cease until a legal verdict had been received. The French wanted to organise a formal demand to this effect involving France, Great Britain, Czechoslovakia and Italy. But Henderson, as has been indicated, believed that a promise not to present the world with a *fait accompli* would be sufficient. Such an undertaking had indeed already been given by the Austrians at the outset of the crisis, and they eagerly repeated it whenever requested.[3] Thus the German attitude on this point was in a sense merely academic. Henderson, however, perhaps with a view to containing French demands for more drastic representations, told the House of Commons:

> I earnestly hope that it may be found, when the time comes, that negotiations between the Austrian and German Governments will not have been so advanced as to prejudice the friendly atmosphere in which matters are normally dealt with by the Council.[4]

This gesture enabled Henderson to reject French suggestions for a bolder *démarche* on the grounds that he 'had said as much as was judicious for the moment'.[5]

Henderson's overture in his Parliamentary speech produced no visible modification in the line of the German leaders, who continued to avoid

[1] *B.D.*, 2/II, no. 17 (Rumbold to Henderson, 27 Mar 1931).

[2] Memorandum by R. F. Wigram, 27 Mar 1931 enclosed in Tyrrell to Henderson, 27 Mar 1931, Henderson Papers, F.O. 800/283.

[3] *B.D.*, 2/II, nos 9, 21, 23 (Phipps to Tyrrell, 25 Mar 1931; Phipps to Henderson, 30 and 31 Mar 1931).   [4] *H.C. Deb.*, ccl, col. 720, 30 Mar 1931.

[5] *B.D.*, 2/II, no. 20 (Henderson to Graham, 30 Mar 1931).

giving an explicit guarantee in principle against a *fait accompli* but took refuge in the face-saving statement that for purely technical reasons the talks between Vienna and Berlin would not be concluded for 'three months at least'.[1] The Austrians, by contrast, were clearly anxious to fall in with the wishes of the British and even, to some extent, with those of the French. For example, Rumbold had an interesting talk with the Austrian Minister in Berlin, Dr Frank, who stated that Henderson 'had handled the question very well'.[2] Then, in mid-April, the Austrians, apparently eager to make a voluntary concession to Paris, forced the Germans to agree to a complete suspension of the Customs Union negotiations until the League Council had met in late May.[3]

It began to look as if Henderson's efforts had averted an immediate showdown and were now succeeding in relaxing tension. But the impression was illusory, for just as the Sarajevo assassination took some time to produce its most serious results, so in 1931 a similar delay occurred. In fact the most alarming possibilities of the original act of irresponsibility were not properly appreciated until the second week in May, when the Creditanstalt-Bank in Vienna announced on the 11th that it was on the point of failure and Briand was defeated in the French Presidential election on the 13th. The former was much the more important event, though the latter did much to poison relations between Berlin and Paris with results impossible to calculate. Whether the Creditanstalt crisis was the result of *deliberate* political pressure from Paris or simply a spontaneous lack of confidence on the part of foreign creditors is a matter for doubt, but in any case the Customs Union affair had obviously served as the catalyst.[4] Once the Creditanstalt's difficulties became known, the world depression inevitably deepened. In particular, there was a sharp drop in world commodity prices and foreign investors began to withdraw their holdings not only from

[1] *B.D.*, 2/11, no. 12 (Rumbold to Tyrrell, 26 Mar 1931).
[2] *B.D.*, 2/11, no. 22 (Rumbold to Henderson, 30 Mar 1931). Rumbold added that he thought there was 'an increasing realisation that your proposal [Henderson's] has acted as a sort of lightning-conductor to possible French action of a severer character': ibid.
[3] *B.D.*, 2/11, no. 28, n. 1. The telegram referred to (Rumbold to Henderson, telegram no. 34, 17 Apr 1931) has not been preserved. See F.O., 371/15160.
[4] On the possibility of French political and financial machinations *directly* causing the Creditanstalt crisis, see Bennett, *Germany and the Diplomacy of the Financial Crisis*, pp. 101–2, and Gehl, *Austria, Germany, and the Anschluss*, p. 27. Neither writer found the evidence conclusive one way or the other.

Austria but from Germany and Hungary as well.[1] 11 May therefore marked the beginning of the 1931 financial crisis and to some extent determined subsequent events in that it provided an environment in which Germany's desperate leaders succumbed to the temptation to pursue their revisionist objectives on reparations.

The Viennese financial situation was temporarily saved by the Austrian Government undertaking emergency measures and itself accepting responsibility for a large part of the Creditanstalt's deficit. But this action was clearly not enough to restore confidence, and accordingly the Austrian Government had to make urgent appeals for loans in London, Geneva, Basle and Paris.[2] This was the situation when on 18 May the League Council commenced its deliberations on the Customs Union issue. The result was that Austria's financial difficulties tended to overshadow the proceedings. The French, whether or not they had deliberately engineered the Creditanstalt affair, were now in a position to exploit their strong financial position for political purposes. Austrian appeals for a French loan all too clearly depended for their success on a renunciation of the Customs Union; and even French financial 'neutrality' required concessions on timing.

It was widely expected that Briand would present Schober with humiliating demands on the League Council, but in the event Henderson again contrived to act as 'a lightning-conductor'. Briand was persuaded to allow the British Foreign Secretary to put the following request to Schober: 'I hope our Austrian colleague will agree that until the Council has taken a decision on the basis of the advisory opinion of the Court, no further progress should be made towards the establishment of the proposed regime.' Schober acquiesced, 'particularly in the sense that nothing will be done to produce a *fait accompli*'. Henderson thereupon repeated his appeal and Schober unreservedly indicated his concurrence.[3] The moderation of the former's wording saved Schober from complete humiliation while giving to Briand the essential guarantee

---

[1] For the immediate impact of the Creditanstalt affair, see William Starr Myers and Walter H. Newton, *The Hoover Administration: A Documented Narrative* (New York, 1936) pp. 81–2.

[2] On the internal aspects of the Austrian crisis, see Charles A. Gulick, *Austria from Habsburg to Hitler*, 2 vols (Berkeley and Los Angeles, 1948) II 930–2, and Hanns Leo Mikoletzky, *Österreichische Zeitgeschichte vom Ende der Monarchie bis zum Abschluss des Staatvertrages, 1955* (Vienna and Munich, 1962) pp. 183–5.

[3] League of Nations, *Official Journal*, XII, no. 7, pp. 1068–71.

against an early *fait accompli*.[1] How this compromise was facilitated by Henderson is revealed in the Foreign Secretary's own account of a preliminary meeting:

> The meeting was throughout of the most friendly character and in the result I think I succeeded in achieving a sufficient measure of agreement between Briand and Curtius to avoid what I was particularly anxious to avoid, anything in the nature of an unprofitable and unpleasant wrangle in public. It may amuse you to know that Briand arrived for this little conference a few minutes before Curtius and Grandi and murmured more than once that I was his friend and a real friend.
>
> Now unless all indications are misleading I think this difficult discussion will proceed in the sort of atmosphere I should wish for it and that as a result time will be given for the tempers which have been aroused by the precipitate action of Berlin and Vienna to cool. There is another factor which is in our favour. The Austrians have apparently no stomach for further fight. It was reported to me that my interview with Schober . . . produced such effect that he had immediately informed his German associates that he could not proceed further with them. He is said to have adhered to this attitude despite German persuasion continued late into the night. So far as Schober's assurances to me were concerned he made it quite clear that he regarded himself as entirely in my hands.[2]

But even Henderson was unable to prevent an ominous clash between Curtius and Briand on whether an adverse legal verdict from The Hague would be acceptable to France. The French Foreign Minister, still smarting from his defeat in the Presidential elections, insisted that his country was determined to resist the Customs Union whether or not the Permanent Court of International Justice found it incompatible with Austria's treaty obligations; he intended to raise the question at the next Council meeting if necessary from a purely political point of view. Curtius predictably indicated that Germany did not intend to submit to such an examination of the project.[3] The Council took the matter no

---

[1] Bennett, *Germany and the Diplomacy of the Financial Crisis*, pp. 110–11, unlike the present writer, interpreted Henderson's request as an unambiguous demand for a cessation in negotiations between Berlin and Vienna and hence as a humiliation for Schober. Gehl, *Austria, Germany, and the Anschluss*, did not find the incident important enough even to merit a reference.

[2] Henderson to Tyrrell, 16 May 1931, Henderson Papers, F.O. 800/283.

[3] Bennett, *Germany and the Diplomacy of the Financial Crisis*, p. 111.

G

further at its May session and, as it turned out, it did not have to do so at any subsequent meeting because of the premature capitulation of Austria under French financial pressure. A public showdown between Germany and France at Geneva was therefore somewhat fortuitously avoided.

The severe financial crisis, originating in Vienna, was meanwhile having its effect on Germany, where continuous withdrawal of short-term foreign loans took place. Instead of seeking to dispel the excitement, the Brüning administration, whether intentionally or not, only exacerbated the situation by seeking again to raise the issue of reparations revision. In particular, on the eve of a visit by Brüning and Curtius to Great Britain, the Berlin Government prepared an emergency decree accompanied by a warning that 'the limit of sacrifice had been reached' and a call for relief from 'intolerable reparation obligations'.[1] The visit of the German statesmen to Great Britain had been intended originally as a means of strengthening the reputation of the Brüning administration. In so far as any specific subject was expected to be considered, it was not the financial crisis and reparations but rather disarmament; in the event, however, the intensifying crisis in Central Europe meant that most of the discussions turned on the former.

The principal meetings between the German and British leaders took place during the weekend of 6–7 June at Chequers, the Prime Minister's country home. Brüning and Curtius found that most of the British representatives, and especially Montagu Norman of the Bank of England, were, without being optimistic that they could be carried through at an early date, sympathetic to radical revisionist measures on reparations. Henderson, however, showed steady resistance to German incaution. Clearly perturbed by Brüning's opinion that, so far as conditional payments were concerned, 'the limit would be reached at latest in November next', Henderson averred that 'these difficulties could not be settled by one or two countries alone, they were world wide'.[2]

The only effect of Germany's repeated alarmist pronouncements was in fact to inspire still further financial withdrawals from Central Europe; and in particular, the crisis in Vienna became extremely acute. In these

[1] Lindsay to Henderson, telegram no. 314, 6 June 1931, F.O., 371/15219.

[2] For the Chequers meeting, see *B.D.*, 2/II, no. 51 (enclosure in Henderson to Arthur Yencken (Berlin), 13 June 1931). See also the judicious account in Bennett, *Germany and the Diplomacy of the Financial Crisis*, pp. 122–31.

circumstances the French issued what amounted to an ultimatum to the Austrian Government on 16 June, offering a loan in return for the acceptance of the following conditions:

1. The Austrian Government would consent to submit Austria's economic and financial condition to an examination by the League of Nations. It would agree to accept in advance whatever measures were proposed to her by the League Council.
2. This undertaking would imply a formal renunciation of the intention to enter any economic or political arrangement which would modify the international status of Austria. The Austrian Government would authorise the French Government to publish this condition at any time if it thinks necessary.[1]

Paradoxically, the very harshness of these terms enabled Austria to escape from dependence on France, for once the terms of the French Note were known in London, Norman decided to come to the rescue. In spite of the difficulties facing his own country, the Chairman of the Bank of England was determined to thwart what appeared to him to be intolerable blackmail on the part of Paris and he accordingly offered a loan of £4,300,000 to the Austrian Government. The initiative in the matter was taken by the Bank of England, though possibly with the consent of the Foreign Office.[2]

Although enabled to resist the French ultimatum and spared total humiliation, Schober appreciated that the determined opposition to the Customs Union in Paris was too strong for Austria to withstand for any length of time. In fact, as early as 17 June he told the British minister in Vienna, Sir Eric Phipps, that in his opinion 'although of course he could not say so officially . . . there could no longer be any question of putting the Customs Union plan into execution, even should the decision of the Hague Court be favourable'.[3] The Germans, by contrast, showed no sign of capitulation and the issue was to be of some importance as a bargaining counter in relations between Berlin and Paris during the

[1] Kurt Rieth (Vienna) to Ministry, 17 June 1931, G.F.M.R. 6075 H/E 449893, quoted in Gehl, *Austria, Germany, and the Anschluss*, p. 29.

[2] Dalton later claimed that the Foreign Secretary was not consulted and that Norman's conduct was 'a move in the "independent foreign policy", anti-French and pro-German of the Bank of England': *Call Back Yesterday*, p. 254. This account may have been an exaggeration. See, for example, *F.R.*, 1931, I 23, 24–6 (Atherton to Stimson, 17 and 18 June 1931).

[3] *B.D.*, 2/II, no. 59 (Phipps to Henderson, 17 June 1931).

deepening financial crisis of July and August. However, given the Austrian attitude, it was inevitably only a matter of time before the project was abandoned.

The formal end of the affair was delayed until after the fall of the Labour Government, for it was not until 3 September that the Austrians and the Germans renounced their plan at a meeting of the Commission of Inquiry for European Union. This date was chosen in order to avoid an open clash with France on the League Council then in session. All the pressure for capitulation came from Vienna, and hence it would have been quite possible for Germany to have left Austria to surrender alone; but Curtius insisted on showing solidarity with Schober. Two days later the Permanent Court of International Justice announced its verdict on the now irrelevant question of the legality of a Customs Union: by eight votes to seven the international judges found that the project was in fact a violation of the Geneva Protocol.[1] The tragedy of the outcome from the point of view of the friends of international reconciliation was that the Austrians (and hence the Germans) had been forced to back down in the face of naked political pressure from France rather than in deference to the rule of law.

---

[1] For a consideration of the purely legal aspects, see Franz Váli, *Die Deutsch-Österreichische Zollunionsprojekt vor dem Ständigen Internationalen Gerichtshof* (Vienna, 1932), and Mary Margaret Ball, *Post-War German-Austrian Relations: The Anschluss Movement, 1918–1936* (Stanford, Cal., 1937) pp. 157–85.

CHAPTER ELEVEN *The International Financial Crisis from Hoover's Moratorium Proposal to the Fall of the Labour Government,* 1931

THE Wall Street Crash of October 1929 marked the beginning of the so-called Great Depression which endured in its more severe form until Roosevelt's 'New Deal' and Schacht's 'Economic Miracle' brought alleviation to the United States and Germany. Yet although the Great Depression may be said to have lasted for perhaps four years, it was only in the summer of 1931 that the situation appeared to get entirely out of control. The intense crisis of that period should not, therefore, be seen solely in terms of the sickness of 'capitalism', but rather as springing from some other causes of a perhaps less 'inevitable' character.[1] In fact the principal reason for the intensification of the crisis lay in the irresponsibility of German statesmen who for domestic reasons needed spectacular successes in the revision of the Versailles Treaty. Yet German irresponsibility alone, while the primary factor, was not the whole explanation for the near-calamity of 1931. Difficulties were also caused by French use of financial pressure for political purposes, not only against Germany but also against Austria and Great Britain. Nor were the British and the Americans entirely free from blame, since in both London and Washington powerful elements had concluded that drastic revision was indeed the only answer. The public expression of these views served only to encourage in Berlin precisely those policies which were preventing a stabilisation of the situation.

Germany's plight grew steadily worse throughout June, although

[1] For a differing interpretation, see Elting E. Morison, *Turmoil and Tradition: A Study of the Life and Times of Henry L. Stimson* (Boston, 1960) pp. 278–83. Great importance is attached to 'the hidden currents flowing beneath the surface of political history'.

after the Bank of England's loan to Austria on the 16th some restoration of confidence ought to have occurred.[1] That it did not do so may be attributed to continuing alarmist talk about a moratorium in Berlin. Meanwhile in Washington Hoover had persuaded himself that some new dramatic gesture was necessary in order to provide a psychological fillip for international finance, and accordingly on 19 June he told the principal powers of his famous plan for a one-year moratorium on inter-governmental debts, including reparations and war debts.[2] Because of domestic circumstances Hoover was unable to take adequate advance soundings among the European powers, and this fact, it is sometimes argued, may have created French resentment and thereby jeopardised the prospects of the plan.[3] The French, however, had more substantial reasons for resenting the proposal and it seems unlikely that prior consultation would have made much difference to the attitude in Paris. Moreover, it may be said that Hoover's plan was in any case inadequate, because it failed to tackle the essentially destabilising factor, which was German self-pity and not inter-governmental debts.

The British response was one of warm support. This was especially true of the Treasury, which saw Hoover's move as a first step towards the acceptance of the long-standing British theses that war debts and reparations were inextricably linked and that it was the existence of these inter-governmental debts which prevented a return to pre-war free trade and relative prosperity.[4] The French attitude to the moratorium proposal was of a very different order. With the Young Plan

[1] For details of the deteriorating situation in Germany at this period, see Karl Erich Born, *Die deutsche Bankenkrise 1931: Finanzen und Politik* (Munich, 1967) esp. pp. 64–78.

[2] On the background to Hoover's plan, see Bennett, *Germany and the Diplomacy of the Financial Crisis*, pp. 132–42, 159–62; Henry L. Stimson and McGeorge Bundy, *On Active Service in Peace and War* (New York, 1948; London, 1949) pp. 57–8; and Louis P. Lochner, *Herbert Hoover and Germany* (New York, 1960) chap. 6.

[3] See, for example, Bennett, *Germany and the Diplomacy of the Financial Crisis*, p. 170. Great Britain was the only power to receive any kind of prior warning. See *F.R.*, 1931, I 16–18 (Atherton to Stimson, 15 June 1931). The American ambassador in Paris, Walter Edge, sought unsuccessfully to persuade the French that they were the first to be notified: Tyrrell to Henderson, telegram no. 137, 28 June 1931, F.O., 408/57.

[4] For the immediate British reaction, see *B.D.*, 2/II, no. 69 (Henderson to Lindsay, 22 June 1931). See also MacDonald in *H.C. Deb.*, ccliv, col. 36, 22 June 1931.

barely a year old, it seemed to the French intolerable that the Germans should be allowed to cease unconditional reparation payments if only because of the precedent thereby created with regard to the sanctity of other treaties. In the fortnight of intense negotiations following Hoover's announcement, the French sought to obtain from Berlin political concessions in return for financial assistance and, above all, to retain at least the appearance of legality and respect for treaty obligations. At the same time, the French had to avoid a breach with Washington, since the Germans might in any case have defaulted on the unconditional payments, leaving France with continuing war debt obligations to the United States. The French eventually persuaded the reluctant Americans to make concessions to meet their point of view, namely that Germany was to continue the unconditional reparation payments (which would then be re-loaned to her) and that she would also be required to maintain payments in kind.[1] The French had less success in their efforts to persuade Berlin to abandon the Customs Union and the pocket battleship programme. Brüning's only public concession was an undertaking on 2 July not to increase Germany's military expenditure during the Hoover year. He was also prepared to give a private undertaking to postpone the laying down of the third pocket battleship.[2]

The British Treasury reacted strongly to this Franco-American agreement and, influenced by Snowden's Francophobic and somewhat jingoistic outlook, vainly demanded on 7 July an immediate full-scale international conference in order to try to secure a return to the original conditions suggested by Hoover.[3] The narrow nationalism of the British attitude was now even more apparent than it had been at The Hague in 1929, since such a conference convened without adequate preparation could only have undermined whatever renewed confidence Hoover's

[1] Details of the negotiations are in various telegrams in F.O., 408/57 and 58. For the text of the Franco-American agreement reached on 6 July, see B.D., 2/II, no. 148 (Tyrrell to Henderson, 7 July 1931).

[2] For details, see Bennett, Germany and the Diplomacy of the Financial Crisis, pp. 190–8. Henderson's attitude was one of general support for the French, although on the surface his messages to Berlin were no more than appeals for acts of unilateral generosity. See B.D., 2/II, nos 93, 104, 111 and 113 (Henderson to Newton, 29 June, 1, 2 and 3 July 1931). Rumbold was on leave at the time and hence a heavy responsibility fell upon Basil Newton, who, according to Dalton, seemed 'frightened of his instructions': Dalton Diary, entry for 1 July 1931.

[3] B.D., 2/II, no. 149 (Henderson to Tyrrell, 7 July 1931).

plan had provided.[1] But though the French and the Americans succeeded for a time in resisting this British suggestion, they were soon
forced to recognise that the fortnight's delay in reaching agreement
among themselves had had in any case a fatal effect on general confidence in the adequacy of the Hoover plan.

After ten days' respite consequent upon Hoover's initial announcement, the Germans from the beginning of July were faced with a renewed and steadily intensifying financial crisis both at home and abroad,
on which the Franco-American agreement of 7 July had no perceptible
effect. In this grave situation German conduct was as irresponsible as
before. Without adequate preparation Hans Luther, President of the
Reichsbank, set out on a tour of European capitals seeking further loans,
but all to no avail.[2] Encouraged by hints of support given to Luther by
Norman, the German Government next decided to issue a circular
telegram on 11 July appealing for help, thereby increasing rather than
decreasing the panic.[3] As a result, the week beginning 13 July was one
of extraordinary desperation for the German leaders. No financial support was forthcoming from abroad, while at home the major banks faced
collapse. The Darmstädter and Nationalbank failed completely on
13 July, while all other banks were closed by the Government for two
days on the 14th and 15th.[4]

It was at this point the British statesmen began to play a really
significant role in the crisis. In return for their hospitality to the German
Ministers at Chequers, MacDonald and Henderson had been invited
to visit Berlin on the weekend of 18–19 July. Alarmed by the developments in Germany, Henderson seems to have had the idea of attempting

[1] If the idea of an immediate conference to pacify the British Treasury was
resisted by the other powers, this did not mean that a conference was to be
ruled out for the more important purpose of saving Germany from total collapse,
which as July proceeded seemed to be unavoidable without outside assistance.
That the other powers were not indifferent to Germany's fate was proved at the
gathering of statesmen in Paris and London between 18 and 23 July.

[2] For details, see Bennett, *Germany and the Diplomacy of the Financial Crisis*,
pp. 223–31, and Hans Luther, *Vor dem Abgrund, 1930–1933: Reichsbankpräsident in Krisenzeiten* (Berlin, 1964) pp. 184–8.

[3] The substance of the German appeal appears in *B.D.*, 2/II, no. 185 (enclosure
in Henderson to Newton, 13 July 1931).

[4] For details of this and other emergency measures taken in Berlin, see
Bennett, *Germany and the Diplomacy of the Financial Crisis*, p. 237, and Born,
Die deutsche Bankenkrise, pp. 108–9.

to negotiate a settlement between the Germans and the French, and accordingly he decided to hold conversations in Paris en route to Berlin, where he expected to be joined by the Prime Minister. Arriving in the French capital on 14 July, ostensibly to discuss disarmament, he can have had no inkling of the involved diplomacy in which he was to be required to engage during the next few days, nor of the resistance with which he was to meet from his colleagues in London. Believing that a successful international conference required careful preparations, he started out with the idea of using his visit to Berlin to obtain from the Germans the promise of political concessions to the French in return for further financial aid from the Western powers.

On the morning of 15 July, however, Henderson was urged by MacDonald in a telephone conversation to cancel the projected visit to Berlin. Instead, the Prime Minister wanted to hold a full-scale international conference in London at the earliest possible date.[1] Henderson somewhat half-heartedly put this suggestion to the principal French Ministers after luncheon on the same day. Briand retorted that 'suddenly to call together a conference without a programme, without a definite object, is to court failure'. He went on to point out that, since Henderson and Stimson were both in Paris, 'this is a kind of conference and we can try to reach certain common decisions'.[2] Pierre Laval, the French Prime Minister, added that they must obtain from Germany 'substantial guarantees if we commit ourselves to helping her'. In this connection he mentioned a renunciation of the Customs Union and the postponement of the construction of a further pocket battleship.

Henderson now reverted to his personal policy and made no strong fight for MacDonald's suggestion that an immediate conference should be held in London. Nor did he protest at Briand's proposal that decisions should be reached in 'a kind of conference' in Paris. Instead he told the French: 'If Mr MacDonald and I go to Berlin we could sound the German Government. The best course would be that subsequently the Germans should come to explain for themselves in Paris at the

[1] Notes of a conversation between Henderson and various French statesmen, 15 July 1931, in Tyrrell to Vansittart, telegram no. 770, 16 July 1931, F.O., 408/58.

[2] Ibid. Stimson was fortuitously in Paris on vacation. For an extremely bitter attack on Stimson's Francophil conduct during his so-called vacation in Europe, see chap. 3 (entitled 'Wrong-Horse Harry') in R. N. Current, *Secretary Stimson: A Study in Statecraft* (New Brunswick, N.J., 1954).

earliest opportunity.' He also delighted the French by his attitude towards Laval's suggested conditions to be required of Germany. The official record contains the following remarkable passage:

> *Mr Henderson*: Let us go further. We could end by a political moratorium of five and even ten years. We must put an end to all these discussions.
>
> *M. Laval*: Certainly, we might arrange for a political moratorium which would last as long as we are helping Germany – that is, for the period of the loan.
>
> *Mr Henderson*: I agree with you. There is nothing between us.[1]

Henderson next sent MacDonald an extremely misleading telephonic telegram. In this message he concealed his own responsibility for the suggestion that the British visit to Berlin should continue; he did not reveal that the French, with his cordial encouragement, were insisting on political concessions from Germany in return for a loan; and, above all, he did not explain that he and the Prime Minister would be expected to sound out the German Government regarding such concessions and that the Germans would then have to attend 'a kind of conference' in Paris. The disingenuous core of his message merely stated that 'M. Laval expressed himself strongly in favour of our adhering to our intention of visiting Berlin, as it would give us an opportunity of forming our own conclusions as regards the real situation of the German Government'. Henderson's telegram continued: 'In view of this emphatic opinion of the French Ministers, I think you will agree that we should not allow our visit to Berlin to be interfered with.'[2]

MacDonald, however, did not fall in with Henderson's largely unexplained plans. Instead, on the same evening, 15 July, he sent a telegram to the Foreign Secretary informing him that he considered 'immediate action should be taken', presumably in summoning a general conference in the near future in London.[3] This development was in-

[1] Notes of a conversation between Henderson and various French statesmen, 15 July 1931, in Tyrrell to Vansittart, telegram no. 770, 16 July 1931, F.O., 408/58. This record did not reach London until 17 July. It was surprisingly not published in *B.D.*, 2/II.

[2] *B.D.*, 2/II, no. 194 (Henderson to MacDonald in Tyrrell to Vansittart, 15 July 1931).

[3] *B.D.*, 2/II, no. 193 (memorandum by Henderson on discussions in Paris, 20 July 1931). The present writer has been unable to trace the actual telegram in F.O., 371; and the records of the Paris Embassy (F.O., 146) are not available

dicative of panic in London, especially on the part of Norman, resulting from extensive withdrawals of sterling from London on the same day. As well as having a tendency to lose his nerve, the Governor of the Bank of England was a thoroughgoing revisionist and, together with Snowden, could be expected to use any conference held in London to advocate policies entirely unacceptable to the Quai d'Orsay. Of him Vansittart minuted on 15 July after a conversation with Aimé de Fleuriau, the French ambassador:

> He [de Fleuriau] . . . went on to speak with some sharpness of the Governor of the Bank of England. He said that it was common talk in Basle that the Governor had said that he did not wish for further credits for Germany, and that it was much better that there should be complete bankruptcy on the part of Germany as this would raise the whole question of reparations and revision of the Treaty of Versailles, including the Polish Corridor.
>
> It is clear . . . that the Governor has in fact been making indiscreet allusions to a revision of the Treaty of Versailles. I fastened, however, only on the first part of the French Ambassador's statement and said it must be obviously false . . . and that he must necessarily be the last person in the world to desire a disaster in which so many British interests would be involved. . . .
>
> I think it will indeed be necessary to advise the Governor to keep off these difficult and explosive subjects which can only be handled by those who are familiar with their full implications and complications.[1]

Henderson in Paris was now placed in an unenviable position. He was required to do his best to bring the French to a London conference; at the same time he saw that the Treasury's revisionist intentions for such

---

beyond 1915. Its probable gist is guessed at with much shrewdness in Bennett, *Germany and the Diplomacy of the Financial Crisis*, pp. 253–4. Bennett's speculation that it may have been deliberately excluded from *B.D.*, 2/II, does not, however, appear to be justified.

[1] Vansittart minute for MacDonald, 15 July 1931, Premier, 1/195. There is no evidence that MacDonald responded to Vansittart's suggestion. Austen Chamberlain was later to say of Norman with much justice that 'when he talks of catastrophe he does much to produce it': Austen Chamberlain to his wife, 30 July 1931, Austen Chamberlain Papers. For studies of this curious figure, see Andrew Boyle, *Montagu Norman: A Biography* (London, 1967), and Sir Henry Clay, *Lord Norman* (London, 1957). A controversial character-sketch appears in Williams, *A Pattern of Rulers*, pp. 195–221.

a conference would, if known in Paris, cause the French 'to have a fit'.[1] In addition, he did not wish to abandon his own private plan, which was to offer French, British and American support to the Germans in return for political concessions. In these difficult circumstances, however, he found a brilliant resource: he would go in person to Berlin in order to bring the Germans to Paris at the earliest possible moment in the hope that a preliminary settlement could be reached in advance of a full-scale London conference. He accordingly spoke to the French Prime Minister on the evening of 15 July. He later wrote this account of what occurred:

> I induced M. Laval to agree, subject to the approval of the French Council of Ministers, to attend a conference in London on Tuesday (the 21st July) on the condition that the German Ministers would first visit Paris with a view to discussion with the French Ministers. M. Laval made it clear that, without such preliminary discussion in Paris, he had no hope of being able to induce his colleagues to agree to participate in a conference in London. I told M. Laval that, while it might be necessary in the new circumstances for the Prime Minister to postpone his visit to Berlin, I would go there on the following afternoon if only for the purpose of inducing the German Ministers not to delay their departure for Paris.[2]

It is fair to assume, however, that Henderson's real purpose in wishing to go to Berlin was not merely to hasten their departure for Paris but also to persuade them of the need to declare a moratorium on revisionist demands. It would also no doubt have suited him well to have gone to Berlin without MacDonald, who would almost certainly not have been told of the nature of Henderson's mission. The result might then have been that the Germans would have been deceived into surrendering to an apparently united Anglo-French front before the London Conference had even met.

Unfortunately for Henderson, his extremely shrewd plan was once again frustrated by MacDonald. In the early hours of 16 July the Foreign Secretary received a telegram stating that the British Government had issued invitations to a full-scale conference in London on 20 July; in the meanwhile, the telegram continued, 'Prime Minister and Mr Henderson will go to Berlin as arranged on Friday [17 July], returning in time for

---

[1] *F.R.*, 1931, I 257–60 (memorandum of a conversation between Stimson and Henderson, 15 July 1931).

[2] *B.D.*, 2/II, no. 193 (memorandum by Henderson, 20 July 1931).

Conference of Ministers on Monday, when it is hoped Dr Brüning will accompany them'.[1] Henderson later told Dalton that he regarded MacDonald's plan for preventing the Germans going to Paris in order 'to keep them out of the hands of the French' as 'a mad idea', since the French would not in that case have consented to go to London.[2] But Henderson found yet another resource: he would match MacDonald's *fait accompli* with one of his own. He accordingly changed his mind about going to Berlin and decided instead to invite the German Ministers to Paris at the earliest possible moment. He conveyed this message to Berlin by the simple, if unusual, expedient of summoning the German ambassador in Paris, Leopold von Hoesch, to the British Embassy during the early hours of 16 March.

In making this move Henderson acted without the prior agreement of either the French Government or his colleagues in London. Laval, however, made no difficulty about receiving the Germans, though he cannot have been pleased to learn that Henderson had cancelled his promised exploratory mission.[3] MacDonald, by contrast, was extremely angry at his Foreign Secretary's precipitate stroke made in a foreign capital. As Dalton in London recorded in his diary: 'the visit to Berlin is cancelled – and this is announced by Uncle in a telegram without consultation with J. R. M., whose vanity is terribly wounded'.[4] On the

[1] *B.D.*, 2/II, no. 198 (Vansittart to His Majesty's Representatives at Washington, Paris, Brussels, Rome, Tokyo and Berlin, 16 July 1931, 1.15 a.m.). The decision to issue the invitations for 20 July was taken by MacDonald without consultation with either Henderson or the Cabinet.

[2] Dalton, *Call Back Yesterday*, p. 257.

[3] To the French, Henderson offered only this rather feeble explanation for his change of plan: 'The Prime Minister had at first been doubtful about giving up the visit to Berlin, but Mr Henderson had represented to Mr MacDonald that, according to information given to the German ambassador in Paris, Dr Brüning would leave for Paris immediately. This made the Berlin visit impossible': Tyrrell to Vansittart, telegram no. 771, 16 July 1931, F.O., 408/58. The statement that, according to von Hoesch, Brüning would leave for Paris immediately appears to have been false. According to Henderson's own subsequent account, the German ambassador in Paris told him on the morning of 16 July that the German statesmen 'could not leave Berlin before Friday evening (the 17th)': *B.D.*, 2/II, no. 193 (memorandum by Henderson, 20 July 1931). Hence German plans did *not* prevent Henderson following his intention of travelling to Berlin on the afternoon of 16 July. The real reason for his change of mind, which he could scarcely reveal to the French, was of course that he had had to give priority to scotching the 'mad idea' of his own Prime Minister.

[4] Dalton, *Call Back Yesterday*, p. 255. Henderson's subsequent account to

morning of 16 July MacDonald accordingly sought to sabotage Henderson's plan. He instructed Rumbold by telephone 'to tell the Chancellor [Brüning] that, in his opinion, the Germans would be unable to accomplish anything useful if they went to Paris before first seeing our Ministers'. 'I took this to mean', wrote Rumbold, 'that the Prime Minister at that time still hoped that he would come out here the following day.' Later in the morning, however, Henderson emerged victorious when MacDonald informed the ambassador that 'he had received a news telegram from the "Berliner Tageblatt" to the effect that the visit of the English Ministers had been cancelled' and this had finally convinced him 'that his and Henderson's visit had better be postponed'.[1]

Henderson's next move was to ask that Leith-Ross of the Treasury should be sent to Paris to give him expert advice in the forthcoming 'conversations'. But it was now MacDonald's turn to strike a blow in his desperate struggle to thwart the French and his own Foreign Secretary. According to the latter's account:

> That afternoon [16 July] I received the Prime Minister's telegram in response to a suggestion I had made that Sir F. Leith-Ross might come to Paris, urging me to resist any tendency in the direction of the development of the Conference in Paris, and deprecating a visit by Sir F. Leith-Ross to Paris lest it should confirm or strengthen that tendency.
>
> I replied that I had throughout resisted any idea of the transfer of

---

Dalton was slightly different: 'He *had* told the P.M. of the impossibility of the visit to Berlin, before it had been finally cancelled. He had had to get the P.M. out of bed to tell him this; perhaps this was why the P.M. seemed to have forgotten it, he had seemed half asleep at the telephone': ibid., p. 257. This account, even if accurate, does not show that MacDonald agreed to the impossibility of the visit or that he authorised its cancellation. There is also evidence that Henderson consistently gave MacDonald a misleading picture of his conversations with von Hoesch. See Bennett, *Germany and the Diplomacy of the Financial Crisis*, p. 255.

[1] Rumbold to Sir Clive Wigram, 22 July 1931, R.A. GV, M 2329/5. Rumbold added: 'I was in a somewhat embarrassing position myself as I had been receiving instructions from the Prime Minister without a word from my own chief. When, therefore, I rang the latter up and was told I was speaking to the First Secretary at the Embassy, I was somewhat testy and let the latter, as I supposed, have it in the neck for not keeping me informed. I told him that I did not know where I was, but, in the course of the conversation, I perceived that I was talking to Henderson himself. He was much amused and told the Embassy, who repeated it to me, that I had been fully justified in saying what I had': ibid.

the Cofnerence from London to Paris; but that the chances of the French Ministers attending the Conference in London would be seriously prejudiced if any attempt were made to interfere with the arrangement under which the French and German Ministers would first meet in Paris in order to secure agreement in principle, and would then take part in a general conversation at which Mr Stimson and myself would be present.[1]

MacDonald, however, persisted in his determination not to allow Leith-Ross to visit Paris. In addition he sent a telegram informing the Foreign Secretary that the Bank of England could not participate in a loan to Germany 'in view of heavy commitments already undertaken for Central Europe'.[2]

This message was of so firm a character that it appears to have convinced Henderson of the need to pursue his objectives with a greater degree of caution than hitherto. This became apparent when on the next day, 17 July, Laval told Henderson and Stimson that his Ministerial Council had agreed to participate in a scheme for giving financial aid to Germany and that there was to be a Franco-German conference in Paris on 18 July followed on the next day by a general conference 'between all parties'. The British Foreign Secretary now told the French that 'he could not agree to a second conference in Paris in which certain of the Powers invited to the London Conference would not participate'. He added: 'If the French Government wanted a conversation between German and French Ministers, it was free to hold such a conversation, but he must make it plain that in the absence of the Prime Minister and the representative of the British Treasury he could not commit himself to anything in principle and go to London merely to confirm an agreement.' A similar statement was then made by Stimson, who was facing hostility from Hoover curiously similar to that being offered to Henderson by MacDonald. In these circumstances Laval retreated: 'If the

[1] B.D., 2/ii, no. 193 (memorandum by Henderson, 20 July 1931). See also ibid., no. 199 (Henderson to MacDonald in Tyrrell to Vansittart, 16 July 1931).

[2] B.D., 2/ii, no. 208 (MacDonald to Henderson in Vansittart to Tyrrell, 16 July 1931). Norman was playing a particularly significant role at this point. As well as influencing the British Government, he sought to play a part in shaping German policy also. To this end he telephoned to Luther in Berlin to inform him that the cancellation of the ministerial visit had caused 'a certain dissonance' in London and that relations between MacDonald and Henderson were 'undoubtedly not of the best'. He also reaffirmed his personal support for the abolition of reparations: Pünder, Politik in der Reichskanzlei, pp. 167-8.

British Government would facilitate his task he would accept a conversation at Paris, to be followed by a conference at London. But if the conversation with the Germans did not succeed, he would not go to London.'[1]

The shift in Henderson's position was in fact more apparent than real. Despite his declaration that he could not commit himself on any point of principle while in Paris, he nevertheless continued to hope that a Franco-German understanding could be arrived at before the opening of the London Conference. He accordingly sent to MacDonald a somewhat contradictory telegram in which, after stressing that the conversations to be held in Paris on 19 July 'could in no way anticipate' the London Conference, he referred to the possibility of 'pressure being brought to influence the German Ministers by those participating in conversations . . . especially Mr Stimson and myself'.[2] At the same time, Tyrrell, who was working in close collaboration with the Foreign Secretary, sent a telephonic telegram to London in which he made clear the kind of deal the French still had in mind:

> I understand that grave doubts are expressed as to whether the Germans will give political and financial guarantees which are considered indispensable for French participation in any loan. Apparently even in the Cabinet at last night's meeting M. Laval encountered strong opposition from certain Ministers . . . who claimed that guarantees proposed were inadequate. . . . All my information is that M. Laval himself strongly favours a moderate attitude, but general feeling is that pressure will have to be brought to bear both by ourselves and Americans before Germany will come into line.[3]

These messages from Henderson and Tyrrell did not produce the desired effect in London. Instead, according to Henderson, the Prime Minister authorised him to attend the Paris conversations on 19 July 'on the conditions which had been laid down'.[4] This, judging by his subsequent conduct, meant that Henderson was forbidden to put pressure on the Germans to reach a preliminary agreement with the French. On

[1] Notes of a meeting at Paris in Tyrrell to Vansittart, telegram no. 780, 17 July 1931, F.O., 408/58.

[2] *B.D.*, 2/II, no. 212 (Henderson to MacDonald in Tyrrell to Vansittart, 17 July 1931).

[3] Tyrrell to Vansittart, telegram no. 175, 17 July 1931, F.O., 408/58.

[4] *B.D.*, 2/II, no. 193 (memorandum by Henderson, 20 July 1931).

the same day the Foreign Secretary also received this unwelcome message from Snowden:

In the view of all our financial authorities the present crisis in Germany is due to lack of confidence, both abroad and at home, as to the possibility of Germany being able to maintain her economic and financial stability so long as her reparation liabilities are insisted upon. This being the case, no schemes for granting financial assistance to Germany, whether in the form of short or long-term loans could be effective, as they would at the best merely relieve the situation temporarily and leave the fundamental defects unsolved, with the result that a further crisis would inevitably break out sooner or later. For more than five years Germany has been borrowing abroad in order to pay reparations, and I understand that there is no prospect of getting any further credits from the market here or in America unless some long-term settlement of debts and reparations on a rational economic basis can be reached. The same objection would apply to any proposal for Government Guaranteed Loan. Apart from other difficulties, it would be quite impossible to get public opinion to accept such a proposal if the money was to be devoted in any form to paying reparations, which would go mainly to France.[1]

These unequivocal words, following those of MacDonald on the previous day, can have left Henderson in no doubt that a collective loan to Germany was now out of the question. It is indeed surprising that he should ever have thought otherwise. Possibly MacDonald's refusal earlier in 1931 to support his request for the formation of an economic section in the Foreign Office goes some way towards explaining his ignorance of Great Britain's financial position. In addition, there is some evidence that Norman refused to keep Henderson fully informed because he did not trust the latter's discretion. For example, after the fall of the Labour Government, according to Dalton, Mary Hamilton told him that Malcolm MacDonald had

put about the tale that, during the financial crisis, Uncle telephoned to Briand all the financial secrets Norman told the Inner Cabinet. So that Norman refused to say anything confidential in Uncle's presence.[2]

[1] *B.D.*, 2/11, no. 216 (Snowden to Henderson in Vansittart to Tyrrell, 17 July 1931).

[2] Dalton Diary, entry for 5 Nov 1931. Dalton added: 'In fact Uncle never telephoned to Briand, they having no common language. But the story shows how his close friendship with Briand aroused jealousy and ill-natured comment.' A hearsay account of this character may, of course, have been exaggerated or

Whatever Henderson's initial misapprehensions, however, he was well aware of the impossibility of a collective loan by the time the German statesmen arrived in Paris on 18 July. He was, therefore, once again required to modify his plans. He now became genuinely anxious to get the French to come to London in the hope that a full-scale international conference would produce some alternative plan for bringing relief to Germany. But so as not to discourage them, he decided to conceal from the French the impossibility of Great Britain contributing to a new loan. At the same time he sought to deliver a severe check to the drastic revisionists in the British Treasury by ensuring that at the London Conference only the immediate crisis in Germany would be under consideration. In this connection he had the full support of Stimson, who told MacDonald in a telephone conversation that neither France nor the United States would attend the London Conference unless it was understood that discussions would be confined to the immediate problems and that wider questions of treaty revision would be regarded as out of order.[1] The gratifying outcome for Henderson was that he was authorised to make an announcement accepting this condition to the Paris meeting on 19 July.[2]

This concession, though important, did not in itself guarantee that the French would be willing to travel to London. On the contrary, they initially stated that they would only leave Paris after reaching a preliminary agreement with the Germans; and this naturally proved impossible to achieve without the support of Henderson and Stimson.[3] In the event, however, Laval capitulated to the collective pressure of Henderson, Stimson and the Germans. The Paris meetings thus ended in deadlock and the leading world statesmen set out for London.

This outcome must have left Henderson with mixed feelings. On the

---

distorted at some point. Malcolm MacDonald in a letter to the present writer, dated 18 July 1969, commented: 'I have no recollection of the rumour that Henderson telephoned to Briand on the lines suggested, and in any case I certainly would not have spread any such rumour.'

[1] *F.R.*, 1931, I 271–2 (memorandum of a telephone conversation between Stimson and MacDonald, 17 July 1931).

[2] *B.D.*, 2/II, no. 219 (notes of a conversation held on 19 July 1931).

[3] The attitude of the Germans in these circumstances was well described by Austen Chamberlain: 'Everyone is to do something for them unconditionally; after that they will be ready to consider a bargain by which they might give something in return for more.' Austen to Ida Chamberlain, 18 July 1931, Austen Chamberlain Papers.

credit side, as he told Dalton, he had succeeded in his undertaking 'to bring the Germans to Paris and the French to London'; and he had been able to thwart in advance the British revisionists' designs for the London Conference. On the other hand, he had failed to promote a Franco-German agreement and had been forced to recognise that the attitude of Snowden and the difficulties of the Bank of England ruled out a collective loan to Germany. Above all, his activities in Paris had brought his relations with MacDonald almost to breaking point. According to Dalton, Henderson complained on 20 July that 'whenever he went abroad he met with the same experience, lack of confidence, suspicion and jealousy on the part of his leading colleagues'.[1] MacDonald for his part would no doubt have taken the view that Henderson's secretive and high-handed conduct had entirely justified his lack of confidence in the Foreign Secretary.

On the afternoon of 20 July MacDonald opened the hastily convened London Conference, at which seven states were represented, namedly Great Britain, France, the United States, Japan, Italy, Belgium and Germany. It was apparent from the outset that if agreed formulae were to be obtained, these could not be of a very far-reaching character. Since both Great Britain and the United States were by now firmly determined to advance no further loans to Berlin, it quickly became clear that the French (even with Henderson's tacit support) could not expect to obtain political concessions from the Germans. A still more hopeless quest was that of Snowden and Norman for a thoroughgoing revision of Versailles.

There was in fact only one new important proposal on which the powers were able to agree – that recommending a standstill on non-governmental international credits to Germany. Such an extension of Hoover's stabilisation scheme was first suggested appropriately enough by the President himself in a telegram intended for Stimson.[2] Fearing French resentment, the American Secretary of State allowed the plan to emerge gradually with much of the responsibility appearing to belong

[1] Dalton, *Call Back Yesterday*, pp. 256–7. Dalton also recorded that on Henderson's return to London on the previous evening, his conversation with MacDonald and Snowden had been 'a bit spiky'. Rumours of the strained relationship between MacDonald and Henderson reached the Press at this time. See, for example, *The Observer*, 26 July 1931.

[2] *F.R.*, 1931, I 280–2 (Castle to Atherton, 19 June 1931).

to the British and some even to the French representatives.[1] However unflattering this may have been to Hoover, the 'evolutionary' method of presenting the scheme did much to prevent a repetition of the long French delay in acceptance which had vitiated any beneficial effects the President's previous proposal might have had. As it was, when the Seven-Power Conference dispersed on 23 July, full French support for the new plan had been secured and perhaps as a result it met with more success in stemming the run on Berlin than had been generally expected.

The most dramatic moments of the London deliberations came, however, when Snowden, clearly speaking in an individual capacity, attempted to block the partial measures under consideration and instead to place much wider questions upon the agenda. At one point he stated with characteristic bluntness:

> The Governments represented here have, as I said, been concentrating upon some measure which will give immediate relief to Germany, without undertaking to deal with what are the fundamental causes of the trouble from which Germany is suffering at the present time. . . . I should be very sorry indeed if this Conference, met to deal with the practical bankruptcy of German finance, exposed itself to the world as being bankrupt in statesmanship. We cannot shirk hard facts indefinitely. We may, like an ostrich, bury our heads in the sand . . . but the blast will continue to blow and we shall have to face it sooner or later. I do not think that these proposals, even if they were practicable, and I do not believe for one moment that they are practicable, but even if they were practicable they do not touch the fundamental cause and they can do nothing at all to help the permanent rehabilitation of German economy and German finance, and therefore for these reasons I am afraid I cannot give my support to them.[2]

The French Ministers, remembering the Hague negotiations, may have expected that this outburst would be followed by biting invective, sarcasm and personal abuse. The Chancellor, however, remained relatively

---

[1] For details, see *B.D.*, 2/11, appendix I (stenographic notes of the London Conference), especially pp. 444–5, 447–8, 452–3. For two conflicting assessments of Stimson's conduct, see Current, *Secretary Stimson*, p. 62, and Morison, *Turmoil and Tradition*, pp. 297–300. The latter gives a good account of the way in which Hoover by indiscreet statements in Washington came near to undoing Stimson's work in soothing the French.

[2] *B.D.*, 2/11, appendix I, pp. 460–1. On the previous day, as Stimson pointed out, Snowden had taken a different line on the value of immediate measures of a short-term character: ibid., pp. 461–2.

restrained, perhaps because Laval was more guarded in his remarks than Chéron had been. At all events, Passfield was able to write to tell his wife: 'I gather that Philip spoke out plainly this morning in defence of the British Exchequer; but Hankey said that the Conference had been exceptionally amicable *in tone* and merely business-like [*sic* in?] bargaining.'[1]

There were of course essential differences between Snowden's position at the Seven-Power Conference and that which he had held at The Hague: first, he was not the leader of the British delegation, and secondly he had no Cabinet mandate to press for revisionism to the exclusion of partial measures. In checking the Chancellor at the London Conference, the role of MacDonald was particularly significant. After Snowden had put the case for sweeping revision at the Finance Ministers' Committee, MacDonald in his capacity as chairman said: 'I think we shall have to take the world as we find it and go on the principle that sufficient unto the day is the evil thereof and what we have to face now is the immediate evil which we have to take to bed with us to-night and see if we can get over that.'[2] These remarks served to reassure the French and American delegates, who had been justly incensed by Snowden's attempt to disregard the pledge given by Henderson in Paris.

If MacDonald failed to support his Chancellor, he was equally unwilling to back up his Foreign Secretary in pressing for political concessions from Berlin – a diametrically opposite policy to that of the Treasury. Henderson, with his superior diplomatic talent, was wiser than Snowden in that he did not expose himself to humiliation in a plenary session of the conference. Nevertheless, he had a private meeting with Curtius whom he angrily accused of adopting a position amounting 'to nothing else than an attitude of fiddling while Rome was burning'.[3] But without the support of the British Prime Minister or the Cabinet and without even the inducement of a possible loan, Henderson's appeals for a German declaration of a prolonged moratorium on the advancement of revisionist claims inevitably fell upon deaf ears. In these circumstances, the Foreign Secretary, with his customary realism, was not slow

[1] Passfield to Beatrice Webb, 22 July 1931, Passfield Papers.
[2] Stenographic notes of the First Meeting of the Committee of Finance Ministers, 21 July 1931, I.C., Cab. 29/136.
[3] B.D., 2/II, no. 221 (notes of a conversation between Henderson and Curtius, 21 July 1931).

to appreciate that if he was to remain on tolerable terms with Berlin he must not persist too strongly. Accordingly, when he visited the German capital with the Prime Minister on 27–28 July, he avoided further controversy on the subject of political concessions.[1]

Arnold Toynbee disparagingly described the standstill proposal resulting from the London Conference as 'the mouse to which this travail of the mountains gave birth'.[2] But since Germany can be seen in retrospect to have turned the financial corner by the end of July, this verdict seems to have been unduly harsh. Probably a sounder judgement was that of Tyrrell, who in the course of a personal letter to Henderson wrote: '. . . I cannot refrain from congratulating you on the results of the Conference of London. In my wildest dreams I never expected more in the circumstances and atmosphere created by the Press of Europe which attended the meeting of this Conference.'[3] The standstill agreement, however, was not the only factor leading to the improvement; another certainly was the fact that the German leaders, possibly as a result of Henderson's appeals, had ceased to present the world with revisionist demands and had made no self-defeating unilateral gestures for some considerable time. True, Brüning and Curtius had not renounced *the right* to make revisionist demands; but the fact that they had nevertheless ceased *in practice* to make them was of great significance. Of less importance in halting the panic was the report of the Basle Committee of international bankers, which met as a result of the recommendation of the London Conference to consider the implementation of the proposed six-month 'standstill'. By the time this so-called Layton–Wiggin Report was signed on 18 August, the situation in Germany had become relatively normal again.[4]

[1] For the British leaders' visit to Berlin, see *B.D.*, 2/II, nos 228, 229, 230 and 231 (record of a meeting between MacDonald, Henderson, Brüning and Curtius, 28 July; Rumbold to Vansittart, 28 and 29 July; Henderson to Briand, 30 July 1931). Judging by the record, the visit, a return for the one made by Brüning and Curtius to Chequers, appears to have had little political significance.
[2] Toynbee *et al.*, *Survey of International Affairs, 1931*, p. 90.
[3] Tyrrell to Henderson, 23 July 1931, Henderson Papers, F.O., 800/283. Henderson himself was also optimistic about the prospects in the immediate aftermath of the London Conference. He wrote to Briand on 30 July concerning his visit to Berlin and stated that he had the impression 'that nothing but good had resulted from our recent collaboration and that a new spirit of hopefulness had begun to operate': *B.D.*, 2/II, no. 231 (Henderson to Briand, 30 July 1931).
[4] For a differing interpretation, see Bennett, *Germany and the Diplomacy of*

No account of the foreign policy of the second Labour Government would be complete without some attempt to assess the importance of the international aspects of the British financial crisis which eventually brought into being the controversial coalition administration known as the National Government. It is not always realised that there were really two separate crises, even though they almost merged into one. The first was principally brought about by external factors, while the second was much more the result of domestic sins of commission and omission. It is important to appreciate that it was the latter crisis which proved fatal to the Labour administration as well as to Great Britain as a gold-standard nation.[1]

As has already been recorded, the beginning of alarming withdrawals from London occurred around 15 July and these continued for some time, even after the London Conference had helped to stop the run on Berlin. In fact the freezing of the situation in Germany inevitably led to pressure being put upon London, if only because British credit, private as well as public, was tied up in Central Europe to an unwise degree and could not now be withdrawn even in an emergency. It is also clear that Snowden's vain attempts to alter the terms of the Hoover plan proved to be self-defeating, since the French appear to have retaliated by inspiring withdrawals from London.[2] It cannot be too strongly stressed, however, that the worst of this phase of the British crisis was over by 31 July, when the Bank of England gained gold for the first time since 14 July.[3] There seems in fact no reason to doubt that a return to relative stability would have resulted had it not been for a monumental blunder perpetrated by the British Treasury on that same day, 31 July. The error of judgement was the decision to publish the Report of the May Committee without any accompanying policy proposals. Once the announcement had been made that the Exchequer faced a deficit of some £120 million, the issue then became one of restoring international confidence in the British Government's ability to balance the budget. It is no part of this study to examine the debate which ensued

---

the *Financial Crisis*, pp. 286–7. The report is in *B.D.*, 2/11, appendix II, pp. 485–94.

[1] The distinction between the two crises *is* recognised in Skidelsky, *Politicians and the Slump*, p. 343.

[2] On this, see Bennett, *Germany and the Diplomacy of the Financial Crisis*, p. 281.   [3] Toynbee *et al.*, *Survey of International Affairs 1931*, p. 95.

within the leadership of the Labour movement on the question of how this aim was to be achieved.[1] The point was that once a public announcement of an impending deficit had been made, the debate could not take place except in an atmosphere of national and international panic. This together with the Labour Cabinet's lack of a Parliamentary majority meant that the withdrawal of the Labour Party from office was almost inevitable. It did not necessarily follow from this that the Labour Party was bound to split on leaving office. This development, it may be argued, owed more to the personality and outlook of some of the party's leaders rather than to any great national necessity.

It was once fashionable to make much of the alleged machinations of international bankers in discussions of the events of August 1931, but it has nowhere been satisfactorily established that they behaved unreasonably judged by the normal capitalist standards of the period. They were not apparently greatly prejudiced against the Labour Government because it contained a number of nominal Socialists. They merely doubted, perhaps with good reason, the present and future capacity of the Labour Ministers to balance the British budget.

It therefore seems fair to conclude that the second Labour Government did not lose power because of international complications as in 1924, but because of inadequacies in domestic policy arising out of a mixture of incompetence, an absence of imaginative thinking, a lack of unity and the initial failure of the Labour Party in 1929 to gain a Parliamentary majority.[2] The ironic outcome was that three of those most

---

[1] For details, see Skidelsky, *Politicians and the Slump*, chap. 13, and Bassett, *Nineteen Thirty-One*.

[2] A leading member of the so-called Labour History School has recently advanced an explanation of the failure of the second Labour Government in terms which come near to suggesting that it was the result of a newly discovered iron law of history: 'The British parliamentary two-party system is based on the assumption that both the main contenders accept the framework as it stands. The role of the radical or Labour Party is to tilt the balance, from time to time, in favour of the poor and weak. . . . It is a role which Asquith's Liberal government and Attlee's Labour Government filled extremely well. But this role of distributing some surplus cannot function in a slump or in times of stringency, when there is nothing to distribute and when, on the contrary, cuts have to be made. Moreover, at such a time, the system, which is after all still capitalist, needs 'confidence', that irrational ingredient of every capitalist economy, and Labour is vulnerable to the accusation that it commands less confidence by the businessman than his own businessman's government. At such times, the bountiful governments become incongruous. The indications are that this is as

responsible for the shortcomings of the Labour Government continued in office after its fall, while the country lost the services of a Foreign Secretary whom many regarded as one of the few 'successes' in the outgoing administration.

true in 1968 as it was in 1931': Sidney Pollard, reviewing Skidelsky's *Politicians and the Slump*, in *Bulletin of the Society for the Study of Labour History*, no. 16 (1968) p. 42.

Conclusion

THE British Labour Party claims to be a political organisation possessing a principled and distinctive approach to both domestic and foreign affairs. When the party is called upon to govern, however, the ideological element in its day-to-day conduct is not always much in evidence, least of all in the field of foreign policy. There are, of course, good reasons why external affairs should present particularly severe problems for ideologues. First, there exist commitments entered into by previous administrations which cannot lightly be set aside. Even for Communists the repudiation of all inherited national obligations can be a dangerous and doubtfully expedient course, as the young Soviet Republic discovered. For Democratic Socialists, with their fundamental attachment to gradualist and non-revolutionary methods, such conduct is normally out of the question. Secondly, Labour administrations, like all others, are faced with the elementary truth that much in foreign affairs is beyond the control of any individual Government, however unchallenged its domestic authority may be. Hence many well-meaning resolutions carried at enthusiastic foreign policy sessions of the party's annual conference have little chance of practical implementation. Finally, there is the difficulty of advance planning in the foreign sphere where the situation is generally less static and predictable than at home. In external affairs, therefore, Labour Governments have been able to do no more than proceed on a pragmatic and flexible course, albeit within the framework of a general declaratory policy of a somewhat doctrinaire character.

The outstanding characteristics of the Labour Party's broad declaratory programme, as it has revealed itself since 1924, may here be briefly summarised. First, Labour has proclaimed an ultimate commitment to the ideal of World Government, to be achieved gradually by the propagation of and fidelity to the rule of law in international relations and the simultaneous erosion of unfettered national sovereignty. The party has moreover considered it desirable that progress towards this goal should be sought in a world where diverse social and political systems exist.[1] Secondly, the Labour Party has usually held that states are entitled to use armed force in self-defence but not as a means of altering unilaterally an allegedly unjust *status quo*. It has also generally contended that acts of international aggression are matters of universal concern and should be met if possible by collective resistance. Finally, it has consistently sought to negotiate a general limitation and reduction in national armaments as a means of reducing international tension and the danger of war.

All British Labour Governments have tacitly endorsed this broad international programme, but so far only one – the second, from 1929 to 1931 – has in practice been able to carry sufficient conviction with their rank-and-file supporters to command general popularity. Henderson even received a standing ovation from the 1929 Labour Party Annual Conference, a feat no subsequent Labour Foreign Secretary has come near to emulating. Needless to say, his internationalist aspirations outstripped his achievements, but the latter were evidently sufficiently attractive to satisfy most of his potential Left-wing critics. On the subject of arbitration, for example, he was instrumental in overcoming resistance both at home and in the Dominions to Great Britain's signature of the Optional Clause and her conditional accession to the General Act; and he was clearly less interested than some of his colleagues in advancing reservations in the narrow national interest. His vain attempt to close the famous Covenant gap was motivated by the same internationalist principles, but here a clash with France developed, casting doubts in retrospect on his initial tactical wisdom in raising so peripheral and potentially contentious a matter. With regard to disarmament, the Foreign Secretary's personal policy was also more 'advanced' than that of the majority of the Cabinet, which would not permit him to offer to France adequate security guarantees, which he correctly recognised as being an essential prerequisite to long-term progress. Yet during the second Labour Government's term some advance was made in that the Preparatory Commission, after five years of desultory negotiations, finally completed its work; and in the sphere of naval armaments, the London Treaty of 1930 embodied a three-power

---

[1] The Communists also believe in World Government, but they argue that it cannot and should not be achieved or even sought until after the fall of the capitalist system in all major states. See Elliot R. Goodman, *The Soviet Design for a World State* (New York, 1960).

agreement to limit the auxiliary vessels not covered by the Washington Treaty of 1922. On the other hand, Henderson's failure to persuade France and Italy to adhere to the naval treaty was a serious setback. Finally, on the subject of international collective security, it may be claimed that Henderson was the last Foreign Secretary to carry full conviction as a resolute supporter of the League Covenant. Although, as a result of opposition by MacDonald and other leading figures, Henderson was unable to carry through any extension in British international commitments, he certainly maintained unimpaired such obligations as already existed – and these were by no means negligible.

Although clearly less eager than Henderson to pursue a doctrinaire internationalist policy, the Government as a whole also won much credit from their supporters by seeking to improve the character of relations between Great Britain and several states with which the Baldwin administration had been on exceptionally strained terms. First, and most important, were the endeavours to put an end to Anglo-American tension. MacDonald's visit to the United States in October 1929 was a great psychological success, possibly constituting his most significant positive contribution to the Government's record in foreign policy.[1] Then, in 1930, with the negotiation of the three-power naval agreement, Washington and London drew still closer. By contrast, British relations with the Soviet Union, Egypt and China were only marginally improved, since in no instance was it possible wholly to dispel deep-seated mutual suspicions. In the case of the Soviet Union ambassadors were exchanged for the first time, but in other respects the experience of 'Left speaking to Left' was a singular disappointment. In his dealings with all these countries, Henderson, although clearly not a 'jingoist', showed himself to be an extremely capable, resourceful and even devious defender of the national interest. He thereby inevitably annoyed a few extreme Left-wing critics who could not appreciate that any party governing a sovereign state and subject to periodic free elections cannot rationally in every instance act on counsels of self-sacrificial perfection.

Great Britain during this period was of course deeply involved in the principal European relationship between France and Germany. Although not a rigid supporter of the Versailles settlement, Henderson made it

---

[1] Garvin was even prepared to tell MacDonald that 'no Prime Minister since the separation has done anything like your solid and lasting work for Anglo-American settlement': Garvin to MacDonald, 29 Apr 1930, Rosenberg Papers.

clear that he was opposed to unilateral and illegal revisionist acts by Germany. Until the middle of 1930 his approach was one of seeking to secure changes by mutual agreement, and this found expression in the complete evacuation of occupation forces from the Rhineland and a reduction in Germany's reparation obligations. But when German policy entered a more irresponsible and doubtfully legal phase, Henderson's attitude hardened. Although maintaining a correct and generally conciliatory tone in all his diplomatic dealings, he unequivocally discouraged German unilateral action during both the Customs Union crisis and the intense financial panic of 1931. Henderson's policy in this respect, however, was in practice disregarded by the Treasury, with the result that, not for the first time, Great Britain appeared to speak with more than one voice.

In his attempts to bring harmony and consistency into British foreign policy, Henderson faced the greatest difficulties not, however, from the Treasury but from MacDonald. In fact throughout his period at the Foreign Office, he had to contend with the Prime Minister's unconcealed hostility and lack of confidence extending over a whole range of subjects. From time to time, Henderson responded to vexatious interference with vigorous protests, as, for example, when MacDonald criticised his announcement of British support for the Convention for Financial Assistance in 1929 or when the Prime Minister without prior consultation committed the Government to a prolonged postponement of the exchange of ambassadors with the Soviet Union; and on at least one occasion, after an icy exchange of letters about Egyptian policy, Henderson even threatened to resign. But in general the Foreign Secretary, recognising that his departure from the Cabinet would deal a grave blow to Labour's morale both within and outside Parliament, preferred to defer to MacDonald's wishes on a number of issues such as the appointment of Vansittart as Permanent Under-Secretary, the scheme for the establishment of an economic section in the Foreign Office and the possibility of offering security guarantees to the French. Above all, he accepted MacDonald's decision to keep Anglo-American relations and hence British naval disarmament policy in his own hands.

By the summer of 1931, however, Henderson's patience with MacDonald was near to exhaustion, and he accordingly began to pursue a personal foreign policy with a reckless disregard of the Prime

Minister's views. In particular, Henderson's conduct during his visit to Paris in July 1931 has probably no parallel in the history of British foreign policy. That no immediate showdown between the two leaders occurred was probably occasioned in part by the gravity of the international financial crisis and in part by the strength of Henderson's position among the Labour back-benchers. But there can be little doubt that an eventual rupture on foreign policy had come to seem almost inevitable. What remains unclear is whether the conduct of either Henderson or MacDonald during the debate about the economy cuts was decisively influenced by such an expectation. But it may well have been at least a marginal factor behind Henderson's decision to challenge MacDonald's leadership in the Cabinet and equally a factor pushing the Prime Minister towards abandoning the Labour Party over which his rival had begun to establish an ascendancy.

During the years of the second Labour Government the European situation undoubtedly deteriorated, and hence it is sometimes argued that the decisive stone leading to the avalanche of a world war was dislodged at this period. The death of Stresemann, the Wall Street Crash, the fall of the Müller coalition, the National-Socialist breakthrough at the German elections of 1930, the attempt to forge an Austro-German Customs Union and the international financial crisis of the summer of 1931 were certainly all events of momentous significance. Yet none of these occurrences was in itself a direct cause of war, nor even a decisive factor in destroying the collective security system to which Henderson attached so much importance.

The tragedy of 1939, it may be thought, might still have been averted if wiser counsels had prevailed in London and Paris when the collective system of preserving the rule of law was put to the test, first in 1931–2 concerning Manchuria, and then, more decisively, from 1935 onwards in the fact of two revisionist European powers. It may therefore be concluded that while the condition of Europe was less healthy in August 1931 than in June 1929, no completely fatal calamity had meanwhile occurred. Certainly, when the second Labour Government surrendered the seals there remained substantial grounds for believing that European recovery was possible without another war.

Henderson's reputation was not a subject on which his contemporaries were able to reach unanimity, and there is no reason to suppose that historians will more easily be able to do so. He was certainly not a great master of detail nor a particularly lucid debater; and he was not always able to carry Cabinet support for his policies or to resist unwelcome interference from the Prime Minister and the Treasury. Those who wish to describe him as a great statesman or as the best inter-war British Foreign Secretary are therefore probably compelled to attach great weight to his known fidelity to the principles of the League Covenant and collective security, which, it may be argued, was what his successors, with disastrous consequences for European peace, did not possess. In short, his defenders must say, with Dalton, that 'he fought the good fight and he kept the faith'.[1]

Yet historians, like those of whom they write, are unlikely to agree on the merits of a particular 'faith'. Those whose sympathies are essentially with the First Earl of Birkenhead on the subject of 'Idealism in International Politics' will dismiss Henderson as a well-meaning but basically deluded and perhaps dangerous utopian.[2] Marxist-Leninists, to whom 'Bourgeois Internationalism' is in some ways more detestable than narrow chauvinism, will feel equal hostility. On the other hand, one who shares Henderson's international outlook will probably find himself agreeing with the verdict of Selby as expressed to Cecil:

I always think the chief trouble came after 1931 when one and all of our chief pilots in the field of foreign affairs were discarded, including dear old Uncle Arthur of whom I was very fond and for whom I entertained a deep regard. I thought him a very good Foreign Secretary.[3]

[1] Dalton, *Call Back Yesterday*, p. 258.

[2] Birkenhead's 1923 Rectorial Address at Glasgow University is conveniently republished as an appendix to William Camp, *The Glittering Prizes: A Biographical Study of F. E. Smith, First Earl of Birkenhead* (London, 1960) pp. 207–16. In Birkenhead's view, Britons, instead of pursuing utopian internationalist objectives, should accept that 'the world continues to offer glittering prizes to those who have stout hearts and sharp swords' and should 'maintain in our own hand the adequate means for our own protection; and so equipped to march with heads erect and bright eyes along the road of our Imperial destiny'.

[3] Selby to Cecil, 14 Sep 1944, Cecil Papers, Add. 51090. He also wrote in the same letter: 'By 1931 I had become an ardent advocate of the Protocol.'

Sources and Select Bibliography

1. OFFICIAL DOCUMENTS

(a) Unpublished

The Papers of King George V, Royal Archives, Windsor.
Conclusions of Meetings of the Cabinet, Public Record Office (P.R.O.), London.
Records of Cabinet Ad Hoc Committees, P.R.O.
Cabinet Papers and Memoranda, P.R.O.
Cabinet: Registered Files, P.R.O.
Records of International Conferences, P.R.O.
Foreign Office Confidential Prints and General Correspondence, P.R.O.
Records of the Prime Minister's Office, P.R.O.
German Foreign Ministry Records (photostatic copies held in London at the P.R.O. and the Foreign and Commonwealth Office Library).

(b) Published

E. L. Woodward and Rohan Butler (eds.), *Documents on British Foreign Policy, 1919–1939* (London, 1946 ff.), 2nd series, various volumes.
United States Department of State, *Papers Relating to the Foreign Relations of the United States* (Washington, various years), volumes covering 1929, 1930 and 1931.
League of Nations, *Official Journal*.
British Parliamentary Debates (House of Commons and House of Lords).
British Command Papers.
Labour Party, *Labour and the Nation* (London, 1928).
——, *Labour's Appeal to the Nation* (London, 1929).
——, *Arbitration: Tory Record and Labour Policy* (London, 1929).
Jane Degras (ed.), *Soviet Documents on Foreign Policy*, 3 vols (London, 1951–3).

2. DIARIES AND PRIVATE PAPERS

(a) Unpublished

The Papers of Earl Alexander of Hillsborough (deposited at Churchill College, Cambridge).
The Papers of Viscount Cecil of Chelwood (deposited at the British Museum).
The Papers of Sir Austen Chamberlain (deposited at the University of Birmingham Library). A selection covering the period 1929–31 appears in Sir Charles Petrie, *The Life and Letters of The Right Hon. Sir Austen Chamberlain, K.C., P.C., M.P.*, 2 vols (London, 1939–40).

The Papers and Manuscript Diary of Lord Dalton (deposited at the British Library of Political and Economic Science). Extracts covering 1929–31 have been published in Hugh Dalton, *Call Back Yesterday: Memoirs, 1887–1931* (London, 1953).
The Papers of Arthur Henderson, 1929–1931 (deposited at the Public Record Office, London).
The Papers of Ramsay MacDonald (deposited at the Public Record Office, London).
The Papers of Lord Passfield and the Manuscript Diary of Beatrice Webb (deposited at the British Library of Political and Economic Science). A selection from the Diary covering 1929–31 has been published in Margaret I. Cole (ed.), *Beatrice Webb's Diaries, 1924–1932* (London, 1956).
The Papers of Rose Rosenberg (deposited at the Public Record Office, London).
The Papers of Lord Vansittart (deposited at Churchill College, Cambridge) and the Papers of George Lansbury (deposited at the British Library of Political and Economic Science) were examined but found to contain nothing of value for this study. Despite the introduction of the 'Thirty-Year Rule', the Cabinet Office continues to retain many of the latter's Papers, which were forcibly obtained from Mr Raymond Postgate at the end of the Second World War.

(b) Published

Charles Gates Dawes, *Journal as Ambassador to Great Britain* (New York, 1939).
Hermann Pünder, *Politik in der Reichskanzlei: Aufzeichnungen aus den Jahren 1929–1932* (Stuttgart, 1961).

3. MEMOIRS AND AUTOBIOGRAPHIES

Norman Angell, *After All* (London, 1951).
Viscount Cecil of Chelwood, *A Great Experiment* (London, 1941).
——, *All the Way* (London, 1949).
Julius Curtius, *Sechs Jahre Minister der deutschen Republik* (Heidelberg, 1948).
——, *Bemühung um Österreich: Das Scheitern des Zollunionsplans von 1931* (Heidelberg, 1947).
——, *Der Young-Plan: Entstellung und Wahrheit* (Stuttgart, 1950).
P. J. Grigg, *Prejudice and Judgment* (London, 1948).
Basil H. Liddell Hart, *Memoirs*, 2 vols (London, 1965; in progress).
Herbert Hoover, *Memoirs: The Cabinet and Presidency, 1920–1933* (London, 1952).
Sir Esmé Howard (Lord Howard of Penrith), *Theatre of Life*, 2 vols (London, 1935–6).
Sir Ivone Kirkpatrick, *The Inner Circle: Memoirs* (London, 1959).
Sir Frederick Leith-Ross, *Money Talks: Fifty Years of International Finance* (London, 1968).
Lord Lloyd, *Egypt since Cromer*, 2 vols (London, 1933–4).
Hans Luther, *Vor dem Abgrund, 1930–1933: Reichsbankpräsident in Krisenzeiten* (Berlin, 1964).
Sir Walford Selby, *Diplomatic Twilight, 1930–1940* (London, 1953).
H

Philip, Viscount Snowden, *An Autobiography*, 2 vols (London, 1934).
Henry L. Stimson and McGeorge Bundy, *On Active Service in Peace and War* (New York 1948; London, 1949).
Arthur C. Temperley, *The Whispering Gallery of Europe* (London, 1938).
Lord Vansittart, *The Mist Procession* (London, 1958).

4. BIOGRAPHIES

C. F. Adam, *Life of Lord Lloyd* (London, 1948).
A. Andréadès, *Philip Snowden: The Man and His Financial Policy* (London, 1930).
Gregory Blaxland, *J. H. Thomas: A Life for Unity* (London, 1964).
K. R. Bopp, *Hjalmar Schacht: Central Banker* (Columbia, Mo., 1939).
Sir Henry Clay, *Lord Norman* (London, 1957).
Ian G. Colvin, *Vansittart in Office: An Historical Survey of the Origins of the Second World War based on the Papers of Sir Robert Vansittart* (London, 1965).
Colin Cross, *Philip Snowden* (London, 1966).
Richard N. Current, *Secretary Stimson: A Study in Statecraft* (New Brunswick, N.J., 1954).
Mary Agnes Hamilton, *Arthur Henderson: A Biography* (London, 1938).
Edwin Alfred Jenkins, *From Foundry to Foreign Office: The Romantic Life Story of the Rt. Hon. Arthur Henderson M.P.* (London, 1933).
Elting E. Morison, *Turmoil and Tradition: A Study of the Life and Times of Henry L. Stimson* (Boston, 1960).
Sir Harold Nicolson, *Dwight Morrow* (London, 1935).
——, *King George the Fifth: His Life and Reign* (London, 1952).
E. N. Peterson, *Hjalmar Schacht: For and Against Hitler: A Political-Economic Study of Germany, 1923–1945* (Boston, 1954).
Benjamin Sacks, *J. Ramsay MacDonald in Thought and Action* (Albuquerque, N.Mex., 1952).
No biographies of value have appeared so far on Hoover, Brüning or Curtius. Even the six-volume life of Briand by Georges Suarez is extremely thin for the years covered by this study.

5. SECONDARY STUDIES

(a) Books

Mary Margaret Ball, *Post-War German-Austrian Relations: The Anschluss Movement, 1918–1936* (Stanford, Cal., 1937).
Reginald Bassett, *Nineteen Thirty-One: Political Crisis* (London, 1958).
Edward W. Bennett, *Germany and the Diplomacy of the Financial Crisis, 1931* (Cambridge, Mass., 1962).
Donald G. Bishop, *The Administration of British Foreign Relations* (Syracuse, N.Y., 1961).

Karl Erich Born, *Die deutsche Bankenkrise 1931: Finanzen und Politik* (Munich, 1967).

K. D. Bracher, *Die Auflösung der Weimarer Republik: eine Studie zum Problem des Machtverfalls in der Demokratie*, 2nd ed. (Stuttgart and Düsseldorf, 1957).

Gwendolen M. Carter, *The British Commonwealth and International Security: The Role of the Dominions, 1919–1939* (Toronto, 1947).

R. A. Chaput, *Disarmament in British Foreign Policy* (London, 1935).

Catherine Ann Cline, *Recruits to Labour: The British Labour Party, 1914–1931* (Syracuse, N.Y., 1963).

W. P. and Z. K. Coates, *A History of Anglo-Soviet Relations* (London, 1944).

G. D. H. Cole, *A History of the Labour Party from 1914* (London, 1948).

G. A. Craig, *From Bismarck to Adenauer: Aspects of German Statecraft* (Baltimore, 1958).

Robert E. Dowse, *Left in the Centre: The Independent Labour Party, 1893–1940* (London, 1966).

Erich Eyck, *A History of the Weimar Republic*, 2 vols (Cambridge, Mass., 1962–4).

L. A. Fabunmi, *The Sudan in Anglo-Egyptian Relations: A Case-Study in Power Politics, 1800–1956* (London, 1960).

R. H. Ferrell, *American Diplomacy in the Great Depression: Hoover–Stimson Foreign Policy, 1929–1933* (New Haven, 1957).

Arthur H. Furnia, *The Diplomacy of Appeasement: Anglo-French Relations and the Prelude to World War II, 1931–1938* (Washington, D.C., 1960).

John Kenneth Galbraith, *The Great Crash, 1929* (London, 1955).

Jürgen Gehl, *Austria, Germany, and the Anschluss, 1931–1938* (London, 1963).

Brigitte Granzow, *A Mirror of Nazism: British Opinion and the Emergence of Hitler, 1929–1933* (London, 1964).

Charles A. Gulick, *Austria from Habsburg to Hitler*, 2 vols (Berkeley and Los Angeles, 1948).

Akira Iriye, *After Imperialism: The Search for a New Order in the Far East, 1921–1931* (Cambridge, Mass., 1965).

W. M. Jordan, *Great Britain, France and the German Problem, 1918–1939* (London, 1943).

Louis P. Lochner, *Herbert Hoover and Germany* (New York, 1960).

S. Maccoby, *English Radicalism: The End?* (London, 1961).

Hanns Leo Mikoletzky, *Österreichische Zeitgeschichte vom Ende der Monarchie bis zum Abschluss des Staatvertrages, 1955* (Vienna and Munich, 1962).

Kenneth E. Miller, *Socialism and Foreign Policy: Theory and Practice in Britain to 1931* (The Hague, 1967).

Charles Loch Mowat, *Britain between the Wars, 1918–1940* (London, 1955).

William Starr Myers and Walter H. Newton, *The Hoover Administration: A Documented Narrative* (New York, 1936).

Robert T. Nightingale, *The Personnel of the British Foreign Service and Diplomatic Service* (London, 1930).

Raymond G. O'Connor, *Perilous Equilibrium: The United States and the London Naval Conference of 1930* (Lawrence, Kans., 1962).

Lionel Robbins, *The Great Depression* (London, 1934).

Hans Ronde, *Von Versailles bis Lausanne: Der Verlauf der Reparationsverhandlungen nach dem ersten Weltkrieg* (Stuttgart and Cologne, 1950).
Jean Schwœbel, *L'Angleterre et la sécurité collective* (Paris, 1938).
Robert Skidelsky, *Politicians and the Slump: The Labour Government of 1929–1931* (London, 1967).
A. J. P. Taylor, *English History, 1914–1945* (London, 1965).
Arnold J. Toynbee *et al.*, *Survey of International Affairs, 1929* (London, 1930).
——, *Survey of International Affairs, 1930* (London, 1931).
——, *Survey of International Affairs, 1931* (London, 1932).
William Rayburn Tucker, *The Attitude of the British Labour Party towards European and Collective Security Problems, 1920–1939* (Geneva, 1950).
F. P. Walters, *A History of the League of Nations*, 2 vols (London, 1952).
Gerald E. Wheeler, *Prelude to Pearl Harbor: The United States Navy and the Far East, 1929–1931* (Columbia, Mo., n.d., 1963?).
J. W. Wheeler-Bennett, *Disarmament and Security since Locarno, 1925–1931: Being the Political and Technical Background of the General Disarmament Conference, 1932* (London, 1932).
Francis Williams, *A Pattern of Rulers* (London, 1965).
Elaine Windrich, *British Labour's Foreign Policy* (Stanford, 1952).
Arnold Wolfers, *Britain and France between Two Wars: Conflicting Strategies of Peace since Versailles* (New York, 1940).
Ludwig Zimmermann, *Deutsche Aussenpolitik in der Ära der Weimarer Republik* (Göttingen, 1958).

(b) Articles

Hugh Dalton, 'British Foreign Policy, 1929–1931', *Political Quarterly*, II (1931) 485–505.
Robert E. Dowse, 'Left-Wing Opposition during the First Two Labour Governments', *Parliamentary Affairs*, XIV (1960–1) 80–93, 229–43.
Franklin L. Ford, 'Three Observers in Berlin: Rumbold, Dodd and François-Poncet', in Gordon A. Craig and Felix Gilbert, *The Diplomats, 1919–1939* (Princeton, N.J., 1953) 437–76.
Ernst Geigenmüller, 'Botschafter von Hoesch und der deutsch-österreichische Zollunionsplan von 1931', *Historische Zeitschrift*, CXCV (1962) 581–95.
Wolfgang J. Helbich, 'Between Stresemann and Hitler: The Foreign Policy of the Brüning Government', *World Politics*, XII (1959–60) 24–44.
H. Stuart Hughes, 'The Early Diplomacy of Italian Fascism, 1922–1932', in Craig and Gilbert, pp. 210–33.
Donald N. Lammers, 'The Second Labour Government and the Restoration of Relations with Soviet Russia (1929)', *Bulletin of the Institute of Historical Research*, XXXVII (1964) 60–72.
Thomas W. Lamont, 'The Final Reparations Settlement', *Foreign Affairs* (New York), VIII (1929–30) 336–63.
H. Lauterpacht, 'The British Reservations to the Optional Clause', *Economica*, X (1930) 137–72.
Conyers Read, 'More Light on the London Naval Treaty of 1930', *Proceedings of the American Philosophical Society*, XCIII (1949) 290–308.

F. G. Stambrook, 'The German-Austrian Customs Union Project of 1931: A Study of German Methods and Motives', *Journal of Central European Affairs*, XXI (1961–2) 15–44.

M. S. Venkataramani, 'Ramsay MacDonald and Britain's Domestic Politics and Foreign Relations, 1919–1931: A Study based on MacDonald's Letters to an American Friend', *Political Studies*, VIII (1960) 231–49.

D. C. Watt, 'American Strategic Interests and Anxieties in the West Indies: An Historical Examination', *Journal of the Royal United Service Institution*, CVIII (1963) 224–32.

Henry R. Winkler, 'Arthur Henderson', in Craig and Gilbert, 311–43.

——, 'The Emergence of a Labor Foreign Policy in Great Britain, 1918–1929', *Journal of Modern History*, XXVIII (1956) 247–58.

(c) *Unpublished Dissertations*

Eleanor Farrar, 'The British Labour Party and International Organisation: A Study of the Party's Policy towards the League of Nations, the United Nations and Western Union' (London University Ph.D. thesis, 1952).

Peter Richards, 'British Policy in China, with Special Reference to the Problem of Extraterritoriality, 1929–1931' (London University M.Sc.(Econ.) thesis, 1967).

E. A. Rowe, 'The British General Election of 1929' (Oxford University B.Litt. thesis, 1960, deposited at the Bodleian Library).

George W. Shepherd, 'The Theory and Practice of Internationalism in the British Labour Party with Special Reference to the Inter-War Period' (London University Ph.D. thesis, 1952).

P. M. Sheppard, 'Anglo-American Relations during the Administration of Herbert Hoover, with particular reference to Europe' (London University M.A. thesis, 1955).

6. NEWSPAPERS AND PERIODICALS

Daily Herald.
Nation.
New Leader.
New Statesman.
The Observer.
The Times.

Index